SOCIAL STRUCTURES AND SYSTEMS:

A Sociological Overview

SOCIAL
STRUCTURES
AND

WILLIAM M. DOBRINER

Hofstra University

SYSTEMS:

A Sociological Overview

GOODYEAR PUBLISHING COMPANY, INC.   **Pacific Palisades, California**

SOCIAL STRUCTURES AND SYSTEMS:
A Sociological Overview
WILLIAM M. DOBRINER

© 1969 BY GOODYEAR PUBLISHING COMPANY

Pacific Palisades, California

Library of Congress Catalog Card Number: 69-17983

Current Printing (last digit):
10 9 8 7 6 5 4 3 2 1

Printed in the United States of America .

To Eileen

PREFACE

At one time in the development of sociology it might have been possible to write an introductory text which was an adequate general summary of the field and which, indeed, satisfied most classroom teachers. If there ever was such a time, this is no longer the case today for at least two reasons: In the first place, there has been tremendous growth in the field both in the theoretic-conceptual and in the factual-empirical areas. The explosion of sociological knowledge in the past two decades is such that no introductory text, without becoming a burdensome encyclopedia, can adequately "introduce" everything. Secondly, textbooks are designed to service a student body. However, the character of student bodies and institutions of higher learning are now highly diverse and highly differentiated. The general "college" of a generation ago has now evolved into a whole complex of academic types—the great state universities and their affiliated satellites, the church-related colleges and universities, the old and selective "private" institutions, and the newer, relatively nonselective private universities and colleges, along with a host of two-year publicly financed community colleges and specialized semitechnical institutes. Certainly no one "text" can satisfactorily introduce any field of knowledge to such a diversified body of academic institutions and their quite different student bodies.

In comparison to many introductory texts this book is brief. It does not attempt to cover the entire spectrum of current sociological interests. The usual chapters on personality and social structure, the social processes and interaction, demography, the distinctive institutions, deviant behavior and social disorganization, and social control and social change have been omitted. What the book does do is to present the student with a concise and systematic statement of the principal conceptual units from which the unique sociological perspective can be seen and understood. The emphasis here has been on not only the basic conceptual units through which sociology derives its characteristic intellectual form but, equally important, the fundamental linkages and connections between the units. The emphasis is on the growth of the germinal ideas from the "simplest" and most elementary sociological conceptions through to the most complex, with each new level of analysis logically proceeding from the one before. Not only is this book a largely formal analysis of the critical nexus of substantive ideas in sociology but the ultimate and final relational systems (community and society) are seen as the logical end-products of a cumulative conceptual development.

Largely because the emphasis here has been on conceptual inter-relationships, I have avoided the usual supportive and illustrative empirical materials. There are few charts, graphs, illustrations, and pictures. It is not that I discount the value of empirical materials and their strong reality sense, but my primary concern has been on the basic ideas through which sociology takes its intellectual form and, indeed, through which most empirical observations are made. While the primary concerns here have been conceptual and theoretic, in three chapters I have illustrated some of the central ideas by referring to contemporary race relations in the United States. The hope here has been not only to clarify some of the basic ideas in sociology, but to also show how these ideas can shed some light on what is generally regarded as the most pressing social problem in the country today.

Although I have not attempted to footnote heavily or document this book, each chapter does contain a list of recommended reading which the inquiring student may wish to pursue further.

In spite of the brevity of formal acknowledgments, my indebtedness to the sociological literature and my colleagues is enormous and I do wish to mention a few of the intellectual sources that I have drawn heavily on. I have used Kingsley Davis' text *Human Society* for years, and in my opinion it is the finest introduction ever written. In many ways the perspectives of that book are reflected here. In addition, Robert Bierstedt's *The Social Order*, which I have used in class with much profit and learning, also served as a model. Since the idea of social system is a critical turning point in the discussion, this germinal conception in sociology is essentially the product of Talcott Parsons' *The Social System*, and I have selectively incorporated his views along with his conception of the pattern variables. From my former teacher at Columbia, Robert Merton, and his book *Social Theory and Social Structure*, I have introduced the concepts of function and dysfunction, latent and manifest function.

The professional sociologists who read this book, particularly from Chapter III on, will soon detect a theoretic bias: that is, the "point of view" from which the substantive materials are organized is the *functional* perspective. Some may immediately raise objections because they are not persuaded of the functional argument, or some may feel that an introductory approach should be more eclectic and less ideological. Permit me to say that I am not personally persuaded of the functional argument myself in many respects, but I have found that introductory students are fascinated with the implications of this particular perspective. Furthermore, the issue that the functionalists raise —the idea of social system as an emergent reality of interdependent parts—has great meaning and interest to beginning students. In essence, the functional concern *with system as reality* focuses most critically on the Durkheim imperative of society as force *sui generis*. It is this question and this issue that bring the full magnitude of the sociological question to the introductory student. The classroom instructor, of course, can take whatever approach he chooses in lecture—either supportive or critical. For that matter, the relative absence of contemporary research materials in the book may invite the instructor to emphasize this aspect of sociology in class, leaving the burden of the theoretic-conceptual aspects to the book itself.

Finally, I would like to thank those who acted immediately to help me with this effort. My deep appreciation goes to Hofstra University for the research leave in the 1967–68 academic year. Then, too, there are those marvelous people in the office of the Department of Sociology who did the major typing. I am most appreciative of the efforts and energies of our three student assistants Diane Boustedt, Joan Devins, and Richard Nicholls. In addition, I would like to thank our departmental secretaries, Miriam York and Isabelle Johnson, for managing to keep the department in order while assisting with the manuscript. Thanks should go to Hy Enzer, a good friend and colleague, who took over the department's administrative chores during my leave. Then, I should like to acknowledge the forebearance of my wife, Eileen, who like all academic wives from the beginning, struggled with the manuscript largely because she was the most convenient and accessible person that could be burdened with it.

Lastly, although a magnificent intellectual tradition has been abstracted into this volume, the appearance and use of these ideas is purely my responsibility. Like most other scholars who have struggled with some of the basic ideas of their discipline, I can only hope that I have done a minimal violence to it all.

William M. Dobriner

CONTENTS

THE
SOCIOLOGICAL
PERSPECTIVE

Sociology is one of the oldest and yet newest of the social sciences. To be more accurate, we should say that the subject matter of sociology extends down deep in time but the history of the discipline barely scrapes the surface of human intellectual accomplishment. In a sense, men have always been amateur sociologists in that they have found it necessary, indeed imperative, to "explain" the nature of the social world around them—family, tribe, community, nation, state, society. But although the need to make the existing social order rational and intelligible has been felt since the earliest times, it has been only in the past 150 years that the science of sociology has addressed itself to the questions of social reality. Indeed, if we are very careful about the term science, then we might not go back much farther than the turn of the century.

Although, in a sense, this entire book constitutes a "definition" of sociology, even at this very preliminary stage of our introduction some general definitions of terms may prove useful. Note at this juncture that the "sociological question" centers on the phenomenon of *association* between persons. Sociology is the *science* which undertakes the study of *relationships* between individuals. The emphasis is not on the person, or the individual, but upon a form of reality which emerges when two, several, or five hundred million persons are bound together in a *system of relationships*. And mark the term "system," because it is essential to the sociological undertaking that the forms of interaction which emerge through a human plurality be recurrent, orderly, systemic, and consequently understandable through scientific analysis. It is, therefore, in the bonds, the linkages, the patterns of interaction, and the ensuing social structures that arise from the association of human beings that the ultimate sociological question may be found.

Of all the social sciences, sociology probably encounters the most difficulty in gaining acceptance with the lay public, students, and intellectuals in general. Its subject matter is probably the most abstract— after all, what is a "society" or "institution" or "reference group"? Not only is the general level of conceptual abstraction sometimes difficult (some call it "fuzziness" or "jargon") but for many the primary philosophical grounds on which sociology is established are suspect. We will have more to say about social causation in the next chapter; however, the idea that a unique set of causal principles operates through a collectivity is somehow repugnant to our basic belief in individualism. After all, people are real and groups are nothing more than aggregates of people. Sociology, some argue, is simply another form of psychology— the science of individual behavior.

Then, too, many feel that we really know all we need to about the fundamental character of the human condition. Our lives abound with the measureless ideologies, the social homilies and eternal verses sung about the final and definitive features of social man: "After all it's human nature to be aggressive. . . . People always take the course of least resistance. . . . Look, boys will be boys. . . . The most powerful human instinct is survival . . . or mother love . . . or the money drive. . . . Competition is the basic force of human society . . . no, it's cooperation. . . . You can never do away with war, it's human nature to fight. . . ." And so it goes. Why do we need sociology when we know it all already?

And yet while popular ideologies and the old, comfortable myths of "human nature" and society supply ready answers to complex social issues and problems, the problems themselves grow greater and more severe. In the United States, for example, our cities are periodically wracked by civil disorder and racial violence. Yet many of the white racial attitudes persist. The "Negro Problem" is "explained" in terms of nineteenth-century prejudice, or the city riots are viewed as the work of a handful of "radicals" or "Communist conspirators." It is difficult for many white Americans to see the urban riots as a protest against discrimination. Some argue that the answer to civil disorder is more police and bigger jails. The punitive approach seeks to suppress rather than to understand. Such a "solution" is like stuffing a bigger and stronger cork into the spout of the boiling kettle rather than turning off the flame.

There are, of course, sociological facts, concepts, and theories which are extremely useful when brought to bear on current social affairs. And in spite of the intellectual lag between social scientists and the broad public and popular sentiment, sociology is used, increasingly, to help solve current national matters. For example, the *Report of the National Advisory Commission on Civil Disorders* (1968), headed by Governor Otto Kerner of Illinois, made considerable use of sociologists in attempting to understand and explain the city riots. The study by sociologist James Coleman for the Department of Health, Education and Welfare, *Equality of Educational Opportunity* (1966), cast much scientific light on the problems of racial integration in the public schools. "The Moynihan Report," formally entitled *The Negro Family: The Case for National Action* (1965), published by the U.S. Department of Labor, has aroused much public concern. These three studies illustrate the current trend by government to enlist the aid of sociologists and sociological research in understanding and solving current problems. But despite the emergence of sociology as a powerful intellectual resource at the national level, the old myths and inertia remain. Public sentiment and the popular ideologies of a prescientific age continue to block and frustrate a scientific examination of human society and the primary social forces that shape our lives.

In addition to having many widely held notions regarding human nature and the primary social conditions, we are usually able to "explain" almost anything that happens in social life. Sometimes the "explanations" are fairly obvious and a sociologist really isn't necessary. In the final analysis, some might argue, sociology is simply a circuitous description of the obvious. Consider the following widely held opinions regarding the urban riots of the past few years:

1. The riots were instigated and led by outside agitators.

2. The overwhelming majority of the black population in the ghettos opposed the riots.

3. The rioters were largely newcomers to the city and ghetto.

4. The rioters were largely unemployed.

5. The rioters were not representative of the ghetto population but were principally drifters and local riffraff.

Here are five statements regarding the city riots: how are they to be justified? In terms of the first statement, it is clear, at least to many white Americans, that the rioting was the work of a handful of militant black radicals with Communist leanings who took advantage of the ghetto population on hot summer nights to create riots. It was an organized conspiracy from the outside. In terms of the second statement, may we not conclude that the great majority of city Negroes are law-abiding, responsible citizens who deplored the riots created by a handful of militants and subversives? From item 3 we may argue that the rioters were largely newcomers to the urban neighborhood and had much less to lose by the violence and burning than would be the case for ghetto residents who had lived in the neighborhood a long time. In addition (item 4), the rioters would be more inclined to engage in acts of vandalism, arson, looting, and the like, since most of them are unemployed. Unemployment and poverty, in short, probably were *direct forces* in the rioting. Since the rioters were newcomers, unemployed, and dominated by outside conspirators, it stands to reason that they were not typical or representative of the ghetto population. They were riffraff and drifters.

Now, here we have a set of facts (the five statements) and a set of explanations as to why the facts exist. Most of the reasons to explain the facts are probably logical and reasonable to some people. Do you, the reader, agree with these explanations? Look over the five items again. How would you explain them? Possibly you have a different view as to why these patterns exist. Later on we shall have something more to say about the role of logical and rational inference. There are ways of establishing the order of evidence and rational or logical proof. We have, of course, not been systematic or formal in the "explanations" as to why these particular patterns exist among the ghetto population of today's cities—they seem almost a matter of common sense. Or do they? We could put common sense to a more formal test and subject these explanations to a systematic procedure. It would be particularly unwise to do it here, however, *because the five statements listed above are patently untrue! Indeed, each of the five items listed is the direct opposite of what social researchers found to be the case.* The riots were *not* led by outside agitators, and only a small percentage of the black population defined the riots as a form of criminal behavior. In contrast, a third of the white population studied regarded the acts as essentially criminal, inspired by radicals. Furthermore, the rioters were long-time residents of the ghetto and about three-fourths (of the rioters arrested) had jobs—were *not* unemployed as many had thought. Finally, the researchers found the rioters to be fairly representative of the ghetto population itself and not just riffraff or drifters taking advantage of the situation. Here are the actual research findings sponsored by the National Advisory Commission on Civil Disorders:[1]

[1]*The New York Times*, July 28, 1968, Section 1, p. 48.

1. *There is no evidence that the riots were the work of a small minority of conspirators. About 18 percent of the ghetto population in the six cities studied participated in the riots.*

2. *While participation in the riots was held to a "significant minority" of the ghetto population, there is growing evidence that a majority of the black population feel the riots will generally improve the conditions of life for Negroes in the United States and more are inclined to engage in future riots. While most Negroes oppose the violence, the majority feel the riots are justified.*

3. *Most of the rioters were native born to the area in which the riots took place.*

4. *The great majority of rioters were employed. Approximately three-fourths of those arrested had jobs. Unemployment is probably a factor in the riots, but it fails to explain the participation of the majority of employed persons in the disorders.*

5. *According to the data on the 1967 riots, those who participated in the riots were "fairly representative" of the ghetto population and were neither local riffraff out for a lark or drifters with nothing to lose. Most Negroes see the urban disorders as essentially spontaneous protests against the conditions of their lives.*

We intend in a later section to discuss at some length the meaning and significance of the urban riots. At this juncture of our discussion, however, we are basically interested in stressing two points. First, human beings are ingenious in *explaining* anything and everything. We can explain untruths as well as truths. The explanation for a "truth" may in itself be "untrue." As to the argument, therefore, that we already know all we need to know about the essential nature of social man, we submit that we are just beginning to scratch the surface of all social reality. Second, we need many more "facts"—that is, verified observations —before complex explanations can be attempted. Sociology, therefore, seeks to understand the primary nature of social reality. It employs the methods of science in this undertaking largely in three ways: (1) It develops *methods* whereby verified observations (facts) can be made of social reality; (2) it organizes these observations into its own unique language (concepts); and finally (3) it attempts to seek out and identify those principles that unite and bind the conceptual units into larger and more inclusive systems of relationships. Much more will be said about the interplay of these three levels in this and the following chapter. It would be well here, however, to inquire more fully into the term "science" itself, because this is where the sociological story begins.

SCIENCE

Science is a term that we live with all the time. Probably you have had a good deal of experience with it in high school and perhaps college. Remember those lectures in biology in high school and the labs and microscopes and "experiments"? But your experience probably had to do with the physical or biological sciences. In sociology, we are dealing with an aspect of science generally located among the social sciences, which also include political science, economics, anthropology, and sometimes history and psychology. The physical sciences are both older and more precise and exact in their methods; the social sciences, which have been considered full-fledged intellectual disciplines for little more than a hundred years, are usually less exact, formal, and precise.

A good deal of time and ink have been expended on the nature of science, and we shall not labor the issue at length here. Science is essentially a method developed during the past 300 years to enable us to understand the world about us and the reality of events which exist outside our senses. It is a way of behaving—in this sense science may be thought of as a verb—whereby *methods* and behavior are devised through which the scientist makes statements yielding a "high degree of probability" concerning that particular dimension of reality defined by the science. Astronomers develop methods to study the stars as their particular "reality," physicists study the basic "physical" makeup of "matter," and economists study "the distributive system." Now, there are in science, as opposed to other ways in which "truth" is pursued, some rather critical requirements. The methods of science rely heavily on (1) the use of logic or the general principle of rationality and (2) the techniques and procedures of systematic observation, known as the empirical method. In the emergence of science as an accepted and recognized institution in human society, the principle of scientific rationality first flourished among the Greek philosophers, whereas the empirical, experimental, observational principle developed later, probably not until Galileo.

Aristotle probably did most among the ancient Greeks to formalize the principle of rationality into what is generally referred to as the "Socratic" method. Essentially this method leads to the formulation of propositions into consistent and logically interrelated components. The classic syllogism, consisting of a three-termed argument of a major premise, a minor premise, and a conclusion, is a case in point. A statement such as "all men are mortal," the major premise, is followed by the minor premise "Socrates is a man"; the inevitable and logical conclusion that "Socrates is mortal" necessarily follows. Although contemporary logicians have raised criticisms of the Socratic syllogism, it is only important for us to note that *the Greeks developed a system of formal proof and reason*, and through carefully defined rational principles they proceeded logically to define relationships between the conceptual entities they were dealing with. While Aristotle through the syllogism was establishing the foundations of logical proof, Euclid proceeded to found a plane geometry rationally and deductively in terms of a system of mathematical proofs. The development of rational proof, therefore, was one of the essential steps in the evolution of science. The second major step was the perfection of a system of controlled observation and the eventual interplay between logic and observation.

Science does not merely deal with abstract relationships; it ultimately comes to bear on something which can be observed or perhaps we should say, which can be empirically verified. If there are ultimately no empirical referents to reality, then from a scientific viewpoint the entity is spurious, unreal. Galileo (1564–1642) is often regarded as the first modern scientist because he not only kept his speculation within a system of rationality and logic but also furthered and developed the empirical method. He was perhaps the first to illustrate dramatically the twin-edged requirements of scientific method—rationality and empiricism —in what we sometimes call today the "logico-experimental" (rational-empirical) method. He experimented with inclined planes; he studied the composition of forces and the pressure of liquids; ultimately he sought to summarize his findings in the statement of physical laws.

To summarize what we have said about science, consider the following: Science is a *method* to create knowledge about the world around us. That world—that reality—may be the universe whose physical boundaries never end (astronomy) or it may be a world so incredibly small (atomic and subatomic physics) that our layman's imagination cannot comprehend it. The method involves (1) a system of rationality or logic, which is essentially the rule of reasonable inference regarding the relationship between concepts, and (2) a requirement that the concepts subjected to the rules of logical induction or deduction be derived from precise and formal observation. That is, are the concepts which have been developed through logical analysis really representative of something in the empirical world?

In order to fulfill this latter requirement of scientific method, scientists for the past two hundred years (certainly since Newton) have devoted great attention to the procedures of observation. The questions

here basically are "What is it?" and "How can you measure it?" In order
to answer these questions, each science develops instruments to facilitate
the precise and controlled observation of those elements of reality that
particularly concern it. The astronomer uses his telescope to chart the
rhythms of the stars, the physicist may employ the nuclear pile or the
laser beam in a carefully executed experiment, and the sociologist may
use a questionnaire to observe that aspect of social reality that concerns
him. Telescope, microscope, or questionnaire are simply the tools, the
technological instruments which aid in observation, an extension of the
senses. Accordingly, it is through controlled observation whose valid and
reliable data are subjected to the rule of logic and rational proof that the
scientific method unfolds.

THE SOCIAL SCIENCES

In the history of science, the physical and biological sciences formally
emerged first and the social sciences, particularly economics, sociology,
political science, anthropology, and psychology, came later. Dates are
always suspect, but certainly the appearance of these disciplines as academic departments in the universities, either in Europe or America, did
not come until the latter half of the nineteenth century. The first two
departments of sociology in the United States (at the University of
Chicago and Columbia University) were not established until the last
decade of the nineteenth century.

Why the sciences emerged as they did, with astronomy and
physics as the oldest and sociology and anthropology among the young-
est, is an interesting question, which we cannot deal with here. It is
important and necessary to note, however, that the sciences—indeed, the
entire spectrum of disciplines that we regard as science—did not arrive
fully mature and developed. Each in its own way struggled for recognition and acceptance.

The social sciences are "social" in that they all deal in some
manner or other with man and with some major dimension or factor
which men have collectively produced through association with each
other. "Social" in this sense means association. But the spectrum of
significant human activity is too great and complex to be the subject of
any one discipline and, as the social sciences evolved, each took for itself
as a special province of study one of the great and recurrent questions
or issues of the human condition. If we are to understand the unique
question that sociology seeks to study, it might be well to dwell briefly

on some of the basic questions which underlie the other social sciences. The "core" social sciences are economics, political science, anthropology, and sociology. History and psychology are peripheral social sciences which for particular reasons are not quite full members of the social scientific household. Let us consider the cases of history and psychology.

Psychology

There can be no question that psychology employs scientific method in its search to articulate regularities within its general frame of reference. It is this frame of reference, however, which poses the question as to whether psychology may be completely within the social science province.

Psychology is essentially the study of the individual—the human being, his behavior, and particularly the behavior that flows from *personality*. "Personality" is the key term in the psychological *raison d'etre*. And it is in the forces which produce personality that the *social* scientific question arises. Generally speaking, those factors which shape human personality derive from two broad streams of influence, (1) the biological or genetic and (2) the sociological or cultural. Now, from all that we can gather it is from the interplay of these two that the adult human personality develops. The ancient "heredity versus environment" argument springs from these two sets of personality determinants. We will not take sides on this question; we simply point out that biology plays a significant role in personality, and therefore psychology, in its attempt to fully explicate and understand human personality, must take biology into account. The issue of "intelligence" is a case in point. Intelligence is a basic component of personality, and psychologists have given a good deal of attention both to what it "really is" and to how to measure it. Whatever intelligence ultimately is found to be, certainly physical (biological-chemical) factors will be involved. Probably we are not too far away from the time when the biochemistry of intelligence will be so well understood that individual deficiencies at this level of intelligence will be artificially compensated for by drugs or chemicals.

But intelligence is also social—that is, the raw biological potential is acted upon by socio-cultural conditions. A potential "genius" may wither away in a stunting social environment while an "average" intellect (biochemical) may thrive in a productive environment which allows the potential to develop without hindrance. The point here is that psychology in its search to fathom the complexities of human personality proceeds along two paths of inquiry. One leads down the path of biology and may eventually take the psychologist into chemistry and physics. The other leads into the realm of association where the psychologist seeks to learn how personality is affected and indeed created by those social forces which emerge only through interaction and collective experience. It is important to stress finally that psychology is completely committed to scientific method; our reservations arise simply because its subject matter divides between two great determinants of human behavior.

History

Whereas psychology emerged at approximately the same time as the social sciences and pursues scientific method in its search to unravel the mysteries of personality, history is much older and is not quite sure whether it wants to be a science. We will not attempt to trace the emergence of history in the intellectual development of western Europe. Certainly formal historical thinking is found among the Greeks, particularly in the works of Herodotus and Thucydides. A concern with the written and significant past was well established before the relatively sudden and dramatic confluence of the social sciences in the nineteenth century.

The key to the issue of whether history is a social science is not in the duality of its determining forces but in the questions of causation and laws of general occurrence. Simply put, does history repeat itself? Is there law in the historical process? This issue has split the fraternity of historical scholars. There are those who see the past as a series of idiosyncratic, causally unrelated events. From this point of view, a Lincoln is assassinated only once. There is only one War of 1812, one American Revolution, one French Revolution, one George Washington, one Cleopatra. Indeed, from this perspective, what are essentially small and often unpredictable events can dramatically change the course of history. What would have happened had John Wilkes Booth's pistol jammed in his attempt to assassinate Lincoln? Indeed, what would have happened in recent history had Lee Oswald's bullet missed its target in his assassination of President Kennedy?

Such a view of history sends the scholar into the past in search of the reality of events, often in great detail. There are historians, for example, who are specialists in the first day of the Battle of Gettysburg. Their scholarship is centered on twenty-four hours of one battle. But there is no attempt, or at least not much of an attempt, on this level of historical scholarship to create a "theory of history" or to attempt to unite and relate even smaller historical events into a system of relationships between the variables. This kind of history is concerned with detail and accuracy regarding the written human past, and it has great importance even on its own terms. But it is not science because it does not attempt to generalize or to organize (even purely rationally as with the Greeks) a set of interrelated propositions which reoccur through time.

Although the history of the nonrepetitive past is still being written, there are those historians who hope to generalize and who seek for some theoretic principle. As historians, they share a primary concern with the past, but they look at it with social scientific eyes. However, "the human past" is a vague term that may involve economic events, political events, social events, psychological events, cultural events, or some combination of perspectives. As a consequence, the *scientific* historian who studies the past in order to find some pattern, some form of recurrence, usually adopts a "frame of reference" or a set of concepts characteristic of one or perhaps several of the social sciences. Thus, he may study the political past and employ concepts derived from political science. Or he may be interested in some facet of economic history and employ in a sophisticated way the current methodology and theory of economics. The point here is that the past has to be approached from a frame of reference, and the basic set of questions regarding man and society has been pretty much focused through the major perspectives of the operable social sciences—economics, political science, sociology.

Thus, there is much to the human past that historians can concern themselves with—the nonrepetitive, idiosyncratic, nonpredictable sequence of events which have shaped the flow of history, or the formal, functional, causally interdependent variables which through time reoccur and may serve as the basis for a general science of social change. There are, indeed, contemporary historians who have looked into the past and have produced theoretic (generalized) statements or theories regarding classes of events. Crane Brinton's theory of revolutions (*The Anatomy of Revolution*) is a case in point. Brinton was not interested in the particular series of events which led to the American or French or Russian revolutions. He was not concerned with a "traditional" history, but rather with a recurring set of events which in different countries at different times produced revolutions. A primitive analogy with geology might prove helpful here. The Rocky Mountains have a history; they appear only once in space and time (like the French Revolution). So did the Appalachian range, or the Atlas Mountains in Africa, the Andes in South America, and the Alps in Europe. Each is different; each appeared at a different point in time. But the geologist sees certain constant features in the *formation of mountains*. From the geologist's point of view (a scientific point of view) there are certain conditions, certain patterns, certain recurrences through time in which mountains must be thrust up, and he summarizes these in the form of principles, patterns, or possibly "laws" of mountain formation.

We can conclude that history is a social science if historians seek for laws of general occurrence in the human past. It is a science if historians extract valid and reliable data from the past and generalize carefully about the relationships that obtain between their concepts—relationships that stand in some sort of cause-effect pattern. On the other hand, the study of history, as practiced by some historians, is not a science if the question of causality is avoided, if recurring and patterned relationships are not sought, and if the primary question is simply the recording of temporal, nonrepetitive events, such as the first day of the Battle of Gettysburg.

Economics

Although psychology is a marginal social science because it has a foot in biology, and history is a marginal social science because historians are not sure of the operation of recurrent cause-effect relationships, both economics and political science are firmly anchored to the social-scientific point of view. They are both *social* in that the primary objects of their study result only from the collective association of human beings. Whatever political science and economics are ultimately concerned with, it takes at least a group of people to produce it. Secondly, they are social *sciences,* in that they are both committed to the scientific method as the only method which will yield valid and reliable information regarding their ultimate units of study. That is to say, in terms of their development and relative growth toward the scientific ideal, both strive for carefully defined concepts. They seek to generalize patterns of recurrence, and each has developed, in its own fashion, controlled systems of observation.

Of the two, economics is probably farther along the scientific path than political science, which in some universities is called "Government" or "Public Law." Essentially, economics is the study of the distributive system in human society (the exchange of goods and services). Its modern intellectual origins are usually traced to the eighteenth-century "Classical School" in England, with the publication of Adam Smith's *The Wealth of Nations* in 1776 as a major contribution. The Classical School, which was further developed by David Ricardo, Thomas Malthus, James Mill, and John Stuart Mill, sought a system of rationally conceived economic laws. Their concern centered on the interplay of logically deduced relationships among price, supply and demand, input-output ratios, the flow of money, and the like. The system of economic laws they sought to articulate was essentially a product of qualitative conceptual analysis. However, the full development of the *science* of economics did not occur until the nineteenth century, when the discipline became less deductive and more empirical and methodologically conscious. The "historical" economists from Germany and Austria and the "marginal-utility" school of Austria and England were particularly instrumental in shifting attention to methodological matters, first from a historical and comparative approach and later toward a mathematical-statistical model.

Economics today enjoys an advantage over political science in that many of its primary concepts (supply, demand, income, product, saving, consumption, investment, money, price, cost, wealth, scarcity, resources, land, labor, capital goods, etc.) are easily translated into statistical or mathematical terms and are, for that matter, almost always stated in such terms. In addition, massive data are already on hand for economists to work with through the federal government and the financial and banking industries. As a consequence, the economist has an enormous fund of empirical data with which to work. Many of his primary observations, in short, are already on hand in contrast to the political scientist or sociologist who often has to gather the raw data before his analysis can begin. However, as data gathering and data processing became more commonplace in this age of computers, public opinion polling and a complex national census every ten years, the sociologist finds his sources of quantitative data steadily increasing.

The primary tools of economic analysis lend themselves easily to quantitative study because they are stated in numerical form. As a result, the contemporary economist can take these data and organize them into more meaningful economic terms. For example, one concept that has emerged in recent years is the "Gross National Product." This is a complex statistical measure of the over-all annual flow of goods and services in an economy, and as such it is an extremely useful economic measure—but one made possible only by the use of available data. Briefly, one way to arrive at the Gross National Product (GNP) is by measuring the "flow-of-product" consisting of (1) personal consumption expenditure, (2) government purchases of goods and services, (3) net private domestic investment, and (4) net export of goods and services. The Net National Product (NNP) is the sum of these complex measures, and the GNP includes the additional variable of depreciation. Certainly our brief discussion here is not adequate to even a primitive statistical understanding of the way in which GNP is calculated. What is significant here are the theoretic and methodological implications of GNP—it was made possible by available data and it represents an extremely sophisticated construct developed by economic scholars. There is no such equivalent development in either sociological or political science.

Political Science

Political science, or the study of public law and government, evolved from the same font of discussion and speculation from which sociology and economics came—namely, the social or moral philosophers of the seventeenth and eighteenth centuries. Indeed, a direct line of development ultimately to the "sociological question" can be found in the political philosophy of Hobbes, Locke, Hume, Montesquieu, and Rousseau. However, the questions they were addressing themselves to (less perhaps with Hume or Montesquieu) were the nature of governmental authority and the ultimate character and justification of the state.

Contemporary political science has long departed from questions of the origins of the state, just as sociologists rarely consider the question of the origins of human society or of its distinct institutions. Today, political scientists are less concerned with the normative ideal (the ideal state) and tend to regard as the primary mandate of their discipline the study of the generic forms of power in society. To be sure, this study of the nature and distribution of power most often centers on political power as effected by political parties and also on the structure and function of governing institutions. Finally, and particularly in the United States, political scientists are concerned with the nature of constitutional law and the relationships between the executive, legislative, and judiciary branches of government as articulated uniquely in the American system.

Although contemporary political science is directly descended from the moral philosophers of the eighteenth century, it has in recent years taken on the empirical mantle of American social science. Accordingly there is increasing interest among political scientists, particularly of the "political behavior" persuasion, to observe systematically. Much of this form of political empiricism is centered on voting behavior studies. Through the use of computers, voting records, class, race, and ethnic statistics, etc., modern political scientists have made amazing strides in the analysis of voting patterns. In the last two national presidential elections, the decreasing degree of error in predicting election results has been the most telling indication of both the conceptual and empirical precision that has been applied to this facet of the political scene. In the election of 1968 the pollsters were unable to predict a victor because of the steady trend to Humphrey which began about a month before the election. In the final few days before the election most of the major polling organizations were no longer making predictions because of the closeness of the vote.

In their commitment to empirical studies, questionnaires, samples, and electronic computers, political scientists are hardly distinguishable methodologically from their sociological counterparts, but there is a dimension of contemporary political science which sociologists do not share. Almost from the very inception of modern political theory, from the time of Hobbes until today, there is a normative theme in political science interwoven with the traditional social-scientific imperative to be "objective." Sociologists never professionally discuss the "good" society, but political scientists have traditionally had a concern with *good* government—*effective* government, *fair* government, *democratic* government—take whatever normative term you desire.

It is in this question of an arbitrary value position that political science most dramatically breaks with sociology and, to a lesser extent, with economics. This is the direct legacy of the moral philosophy of the eighteenth century and the search for the *ideal* state. Unquestionably, today, the normative dimension in political science has weakened while the empirical, almost sociological, perspective in political science continues to gain.

THE FRAMING OF THE SOCIOLOGICAL RESPONSE

We have suggested in our preceding discussion that the social sciences with their characteristic conceptual systems and research methodologies evolved from a common intellectual source—the social and moral philosophers of the eighteenth century. At that time there were no sharp conceptual distinctions among economic, political, and social speculation, but over a period of 150 years Western scholarship has crystallized the essential themes of the separate social sciences against a backdrop of incredible social change. It is in terms of this broad historical canvas of shifting political, technological, economic, and social change that we wish to trace the eventual statement of the sociological question.

At the time of the Protestant Reformation in the early sixteenth century, European society had begun to shift from a social system anchored in the rigid principles of extended kinship, traditional and hierarchal religion, a fixed class system linked to ancestry and land, the primacy of the local community, and an exclusive reliance on monarchy. It was in this time that cities began to grow dramatically, and national states rather than feudal fragmentation emerged as the new political-governmental configuration. However, it was the combined impact of two revolutions, the Industrial and the French, that forever ripped Western, and particularly European, society away from the social forms of the past. It was the Industrial Revolution, which began in England and later spread to the Continent, that dramatically changed the social fabric of every nation which accepted the consequences of industrialism, or the "English system." In place of the local community, great industrial cities emerged as the characteristic mode of community life. Urbanism, with its twin features of population density and social heterogeneity, overcame rural homogeneity and sparse community life. Manchester, Liverpool, Birmingham, Sheffield, Leeds—rural towns in 1700—were teeming industrial centers a half-century later.

The consequences of the Industrial Revolution were observed in at least five major areas of social life: (1) the condition of labor, (2) fundamental changes in the use of property, (3) the rise of cities and urbanism, (4) the new technology, and (5) the factory system.[2] As industrialism proceeded, millions were drawn from the farms and small agricultural localities to become members of a new class—the workers, the proletariat, the factory class. As the old feudal aristocracy fell before the accelerating wheels of industrialism, a new "upper" class—the bourgeoisie, the capitalists, the new owners of industry—took their place. Accordingly a transformation of class alignments took place: instead of the antagonism of the serf to the landed aristocracy, there was a growing hostility between the underpaid, crowded, slum-ridden, immobile working class and the newly rich, opulent, powerful class of factory owners, financiers, and businessmen.

As the conditions of labor shifted from farm to factory, the very meaning and significance of property altered in the new industrialism. Land, rural land and large estates, were no longer economically so meaningful, whereas the ownership of capital goods, factories, industrial tools, and industrial property became more significant. This ownership combined to produce the factory system, in which workers were paid for twelve or more hours a day of labor and were then "free" to stumble back across the slag heap to the company town or the urban slum to regain strength for the next day's ordeal. With the new cities came sickness, pestilence, plague, alcoholism, brutality, crime, gross human depri-

2Robert A. Nisbet, *The Sociological Tradition* (New York: Basic Books, Inc., Publishers, 1966) , p. 24.

vation—all intensified through the anonymity, density, impersonality, and bureaucratic insularity of the new social order. It was inevitable that the voice of social reform would be raised and heard.

As the English system spread to Europe and the inevitable structural changes were felt there, major political changes had to occur. The French Revolution is a case in point—whatever the many reasons that historians advance for its cause or causes. It was, as Nisbet points out, a great *ideological* revolution, in which a new set of humanistic values and beliefs became the guiding and, certainly, public themes—liberty, equality, fraternity. The Revolution ideologically embodied the humanistic spirit of a new age—democracy, equalitarianism, secularism, and nationalism—and it shook the normative foundations of the past. It raised questions about church-state relationships, the nature and use of property, tradition versus the new reason: it was certainly, in part, the ideological as well as political response to the consequences of unprecedented and uncontrolled industrialism.

Consider this, then, as the setting in which the social philosophers of the eighteenth and nineteenth centuries struggled to find new meaning in the nature of governmental authority and the economic process. It may have begun with the split in traditional Christianity and the rise of the Protestant sects. Quite possibly the discovery of the New World and increased global exploration which brought back stories of strange and exotic peoples increased the speculation over the conditions and circumstances of social development and change. Furthermore, as national states emerged over the smaller feudal forms and as industrialism quickened the speed of change, the ferment of intellectual speculation steadily mountd. The effects of Protestantism, industrialism, capitalism, the factory system, urbanism, secularism, rationalism, humanitarianism, individualism—all of the social, political, economic, and ideological currents set in motion—were to create a climate for social speculation.

The world was now seen as a volatile, radical process, and the comfortable homilies of the older political and religious orders simply no longer applied. With the physical sciences having won their battle with the Establishment and already showing great accomplishment, why not take the methods of science and train them upon man himself? And so the naturalistic quest to seek out the reality of political and economic forms began. There were, however, scholars who were interested in neither purely political nor economic events: their perspectives centered on society and on change itself, and each in his own way called for a *science of society*, a science whose focus was the total structure of relationships, not merely one component or institution *but the total societal system.*

As early as 1725 Giovanni Battista Vico (1668–1744) published *The New Science,* in which he called for a special science to study the development of human society (not the state). He suggested that "society" developed through a series of stages and that these stages are common to all peoples,. There is, he suggested, "an eternal, ideal history, according to which the history of all nations transpires with definite origins and definite continuity." It was Vico, therefore, who anticipated a special science of social change and continuity and who perhaps was the first to suggest an independent science for that purpose alone.

Later, the Marquis de Condorcet (1743–1794) in his work *A Sketch of the Intellectual Progress of Mankind,* written late in his life (1793), suggested the necessity of a special study of social change. We no longer consider his nine "epochs" of human history to be an accurate reconstruction of social development, but he did support the sociological cause by his argument that human society constitutes an order of reality in which natural causation operates and from which laws of social development can be formulated. From Condorcet, the embryonic sociological imperative passed to Claude Henri de Saint-Simon (1760–1825). His ideas of the necessity of rational and objective scientific inquiry (positivism) and the laws of social change directly influenced his most brilliant student, Auguste Comte (1798–1857), who coined the term "sociology" in the third decade of the nineteenth century.

In a sense, Vico, Condorcet, and Saint-Simon are lineal ancestors of sociology because they argued for an autonomous and independent science of social development, which was certainly not the primary concern of the economic and political philosophers. Their combined intellectual efforts eventually suggested that society itself was a legitimate object of scientific study. Some notion of *society* as a reality exterior to political or economic forms, responding to special laws of its own, had come to be accepted. Furthermore, the impact of British empiricism was now so intellectually compelling, particularly through the natural-science example, that there was growing conviction that whatever society was, whatever the still mystical direction of its change, it was nonetheless subject to empirical study.

Thus was forged the intellectual tradition out of which both August Comte and his English counterpart, Herbert Spencer (1820–1903), formally brought the discipline of sociology into the world scarcely twenty-five years before the American Civil War. It was dedicated to the explication of human society as a generic and ultimate form of association. Not only was it interested in the structure of society but, in response to the questions arising out of the transformation of the West during the preceding two hundred years, it also took for itself the study of the causes and nature of social change. The physical and social reshaping of Western society that resulted from the Industrial Revolution along with the ideological and normative changes resulting from the French Revolution demanded such a science.

Although it is not particularly important to specify the substance of sociology as seen by Comte and Spencer, it is useful to note that both had an interest in the nature of human society and particularly in the evolutionary principles through which it evolved. Each in his own way had an interest in both the *structure* of society and its recurrent, static forms, as well as an awareness of dynamics and process. They were the first distinctively sociological pioneers; yet sociology was merely one of their interests. Essentially they were social philosophers, and they saw sociology as an emergent intellectual final form indicating the growing sophistication of mankind's struggles.

Following Comte and Spencer, the developing sociological tradition found expression among a sequence of social thinkers throughout the second half of the nineteenth century. With each decade, a body of sociological literature accumulated, so that by the end of the century the discipline had established itself both intellectually in the world of scholarship and academically in the new departments being created among the Western European universities—particularly in Germany, France, and England. It was not, however, until the generation of Emile Durkheim (1858–1917), Georg Simmel (1858–1918), and Max Weber (1864–1920) that the cumulative literature had reached a point at which fundamental and substantive contributions could be made. Until the time of these three, sociology was largely a system of speculation by individual scholars whose insights were quite independent of others. There was little *cumulative theory* and hardly any formal empirical research. It was Durkheim, Simmel, and Weber, from about the 1890's, who not only contributed a much more sophisticated view of sociology in terms of conceptual substance, but who also influenced greatly the coming pattern of sociological effort in the twentieth century. Durkheim was particularly responsible for creating an interest in the use of statistical data and quantitative measures.

From Europe, the discipline had traveled to America and found support initially from Yale's William Graham Sumner (1840–1910), who was much influenced by Spencer and who gave sociology the terms mores, folkways, institution, in-group, out-group, ethnocentrism, and a host of others. In addition, Lester Ward (1841–1913) did much to popularize sociology in the United States and wrote the first major American sociological book—*Dynamic Sociology*—in 1883.

From Ward and Sumner, as the first generation of American

sociologists, the discipline continued to grow. Indeed, what had begun as a purely European effort in the 1850's had become known as "the American Science" by the 1920's. At the University of Chicago at this time, under the leadership of Robert Park and his colleagues, sociology broke with speculative, deductive, and rationalistic proofs and entered into the empirical tradition which was to become a characteristic of American sociology from that time on. It was with the empirical study of urban life at Chicago that the research-based, quantitative orientation began.

SOCIOLOGY

Pitirim A. Sorokin once defined sociology as ". . . a generalizing science of sociocultural phenomena viewed in their generic forms, types, and manifold interconnections."[3]

In its elementary question, it is the science of association, of collectivities, of pluralities, of interaction. But Sorokin says "in their generic forms," and this suggests that sociological analysis may be applied to any form of association, be it a two-person group or a great national society of 500 million. There are certain characteristics of two-person relationships that could not hold true for a system of relationships binding 500 million persons. The principles of association, of course, are true for political and economic groups and institutions. Authority and power are not unique to political associations, but are found in other institutions as well—familial, religious, economic, and others. But perhaps the critical point is that neither economic nor political associations and systems can function by themselves: both are dependent upon a larger and more complex system of relationships—a "societal" system, the most inclusive structure of relationships. It is the entity *society* that most captures the sociological imagination—the ultimate structure. Political scientists and economists press forward with their analyses of the polity and the distributive system respectively. The sociologist focuses his concern not only on the mutual interrelationships of political and economic forms but on the question of *total institutional integration*—the way in which a society as a viable system focuses and channelizes the activities of persons through organized relationships. It is in this focusing and shaping in all spheres of institutional activity that the reality of society may be seen.

Underlying the currently broad spectrum of activity are two

[3]Pitirim A. Sorokin, *Society, Culture and Personality* (New York: Harper & Row, Publishers, 1948) , p. 16.

fundamental questions which give sociology its distinctive character: (1) What is the essential character of human society? and (2) What forces make it change over time? The first involves a question of structure and, latently, function, and the second concerns itself with the consequences of the structure-function relationship with time. The first is the enormous issue of the nature of association—how associations grow more complex until the societal form is reached, and how subsystems (groups, gangs, families, institutions, etc.) function from the smallest transitory interaction through to the monumental structure of a great national society.

It is, of course, within the first question that most sociologists currently labor—studies and theoretic speculation dealing with the family, class systems, cities, communities, etc. reflect the fundamental concern with association in all of its generic forms. But association also has a dynamic character; the forms alter over time. Studies in the *dynamics* of population, the *growth* of cities, the *processes* of changing class systems, and the voting *trend* all suggest a continuing interest in the phenomena of change along with the elements of structure.

It should be noted that although the ultimate form of society linked to the variable of time is the final fascinating question, it receives relatively little serious interest today. Sociology, like the other social sciences, has generally lost interest in "total-system theory," largely because we still know so little about the elemental units. It short, before we attempt to capture the very essence of society in some ultimate and final equation, we must know more both empirically and conceptually about some of the simpler forms of association. Sociologists therefore pursue theories and research in areas of the "middle range," that is, those areas in which we have a clear conceptual sense and which are translatable into observable study. A sociologist will study, for example, patterns of ethnic or racial settlement in cities before he attempts a formulation of the characteristics of human society. In the former, he can relate concepts to observations, and these observations can usually be expressed in numerical terms. If he has some measure of control over the events under observation, his research design will generally produce valid and reliable results. In total-system theory the sociologist may speculate "rationally," with or without recourse to observable data. It is probably true today that most sociologists in their research would prefer to work in areas in which they can produce something that is "true, if not particularly significant." The total-system theorists of the nineteenth century were certainly working in areas of great significance if relatively little truth.

Currently, sociologists in the United States organize their theoretic and empirical research interests around four major units of study:

1. *Relational Systems:*   The study of small units of association, social action, social relationships, role, status, primary groups.

2. *Social Institutions:*   The study of the distinctive institutions of society —family, religion, economy, polity, education, etc.

3. *Social Organization:*   The study of how the major units of social structure, the basic institutions, are interrelated in the societal system.

4. *Societal Systems:*   The analysis and comparison of the development, structure, and functions of societal systems.

These larger and rather abstract categories, in turn, are expressed in a variety of sociology courses at the college and university level. Consider the following outline of sociological subject matter:

TABLE I.

A GENERAL OUTLINE OF THE SUBJECT MATTER OF SOCIOLOGY

I   SOCIOLOGICAL ANALYSIS
Human Culture and Society
Sociological Perspective
Scientific Method in Social Science

II   PRIMARY UNITS OF SOCIAL LIFE
Social Acts and Social
  Relationships
The Individual Personality
Groups (including Ethnic and
  Class)
Communities: Urban and Rural
Associations and Organizations
Populations
Society

III   BASIC SOCIAL INSTITUTIONS
The Family and Kinship
Economic
Political and Legal
Religious
Educational and Scientific
Recreational and Welfare
Aesthetic and Expressive

IV   FUNDAMENTAL SOCIAL PROCESSES
Differentiation and Stratification
Cooperation, Accommodation,
  Assimilation
Social Conflict (including
  Revolution and War)
Communication (including
  Opinion Formation,
  Expression, and Change)
Socialization and Indoctrination
Social Evaluation (the Study
  of Values)
Social Control
Social Deviance (Crime,
  Suicide, etc.)
Social Interaction
Social Change

SOURCE: Alex Inkeles, What is Sociology?: An Introduction to the Discipline and Profession, © 1964, Prentice-Hall, Inc., Englewood Cliffs, N.J. Used with permission of the publisher.

We may conclude from this discussion that the sociological perspective, in order of increasing complexity and abstraction, fixes on (1) the study of relationships, which in turn may become institutionalized and formalized into (2) more massive systems of organized relationships, finally encompassing (3) society as the final and inclusive interaction system embodying the former two levels but adding its own distinctive form and reality.

What Sociology Is Not

Occasionally a freshman or sophomore, after a particularly interesting classroom session, or after reading some rare inspirational sociological prose, will come to his instructor and say with a certain amount of awkwardness, "You know, I find sociology very interesting and I would like very much to major in it, but I really don't want to be a social worker." He may lamely add, "What *good* is sociology anyway . . . what can you *do* with it?"

The student who raises the question above shows he still is not clear on some fundamental distinctions as to what sociology is all about. There is no direct relationship at all between social work and sociology. Social work, which is a profession concerned with direct, community-based programs to correct social "ills" or "problems" (poverty, family disorganization, drug addiction, alcoholism, etc.,) has as much in common with psychology as with sociology. The essence of the issue, however, is that sociology is a science whose function is to *produce knowledge* about social life and not to correct social problems. As a knowledge-producing enterprise it is not directly concerned with social therapy or action. Indeed, much damage was done to the discipline in the past when "sociologists" championed all sorts of public issues, and to the general public it appeared that sociology was not a discipline at all but a "cause."

The insistence that sociology is a pure science rather than an applied one rests on the question of values and the normative order. One of the central pillars of scientific method has been its claim to *objectivity* —the study of events as external objects or forces in which the observer is neutral and hence does not contaminate the reality he seeks to understand. Science, of course, has had to struggle for acceptance of its view of the physical universe, or life, or society and has quite often run counter to the conventional, popular, public ideologies. Many an early astronomer went to the stake as his radical notions of the universe outraged public opinion. Recall the controversies over the Darwinian theory of evolution and its teaching in the public schools. The issue still goes on in certain states today.

The question of the conflict between science and values, beliefs, norms, ideologies, customs, etc., is even more sensitive in sociology because these are also the legitimate subjects of sociological research. What men think, the values that sustain them, the customs they practice, are central to the sociological mandate. Yet those values must be studied as *objects,* and the particular values of the sociologist or social scientist cannot, in terms of the rigor of scientific method, interfere with the research process. Should the discipline begin to take sides in matters of public policy, it would probably destroy the hard battle the young science has continually waged to gain acceptance as a responsible and "objective" discipline.

Although sociology as a discipline attempts to stand clear of normative involvement, its very existence demonstrates the force of values and moral judgment in the human condition. All of the "pure" sciences from physics to sociology which attempt to uncover the ultimate regularities of the physical and social worlds owe their very existence to the belief, to the *value,* that they are good and necessary. Men believe in science, and while the "pure" sciences are a search for knowledge on the increasingly complex levels of both empirical and theoretic abstraction which is in itself a justification of science (Men must know!), there is also the hope that the new knowledge may be harnessed for socially approved goals and purposes. Einstein in his theory of energy and matter $(E = mc^2)$ made a statement of physical reality—for the moment it is the final physical equation. But Einstein's purely abstract theoretic work led to engineering efforts in which the goal was to release nuclear energy in a fashion to suit public policy, either in the form of bombs for warmaking, or power stations for electricity. Similarly, if sociologists can learn more about population change, city growth, crime causation, public opinion, or family life, this new knowledge can also be used to further public policy purposes through social engineering.

The uneasiness with which the social sciences engage the questions of normative judgment and public policy is illustrated by a story going back to the administration of President Franklin Roosevelt in the 1930's. Roosevelt was considering whether or not the country should remain on the gold standard. He put the question to an eminent economist, who thought for a moment and then replied, "Mr. President, I can't tell you to take the country off the gold standard or not. That is a decision that you must make. All I can tell is what will happen to the economy if you leave it on or take it off." The economist was essentially telling the President that the policy judgment was his or his administration's to make. The social scientist could give him the facts but the policy decision was not his to make.

Sociology, then, leans much more to the "pure" side of science than to the practical or applied. Because it is a science and not a form of social engineering, its concepts, data, and theories tend to be abstract, categorical, neutral, and value-free. Sociology is not out to remake the social world; its aim is to understand it.

Now what happens to students in class as they hear a lecture in sociology and, indeed, read a textbook in sociology, as you are doing now, is *not* sociology. In class, the art (or lack of art) of the teacher is being demonstrated. The skill, the clarity, the brilliance, the theatricality of the sociology instructor is what students are exposed to in class. They are learning what sociology is all about through communication with a practitioner of the discipline. But the only way you can really learn about science—the ultimate research process in which the empirical data are conceptualized and brought into a theoretic relationship—is by doing it. You can hear about it from a brilliant teacher and read about it in a textbook. You can, of course, and indeed must, *read* scientific research reports because the scientific method is visible there. But science is a way of behaving; and to experience its ultimate fascination (the reality principle) *you have to do it.*

THE SOCIOLOGICAL ARGUMENT:

A Case Illustration from Emile Durkheim

In this introductory chapter we have defined the nature of our subject; we have briefly outlined its historical origins; we have contrasted it with its disciplinary peers. We have held a sort of linguistic mirror up for the student and hoped that he could see the face of sociology peer back at him through the reflection of language. Sociology may thus be a little clearer, and, as we proceed through this book, each chapter may make the discipline more intelligible and meaningful. We can define and clarify concepts, method, and theory in sociology, but perhaps the best way to illustrate the unique perspective of the discipline is to show how a sociologist applied the science to a specific research problem. To this end, we shall briefly summarize Durkheim's classic study of suicide.

Emile Durkheim published *Le Suicide* in 1897, when sociology was still struggling for intellectual legitimacy and academic recognition. Three years earlier he had published *The Rules of Sociological Method,* in which he laid down a primary methodological imperative: namely, that social reality, "social facts" as he called them, can be understood only in terms of other social facts. Essentially, Durkheim was saying that social reality constituted a force independent of psychological reality, i.e., the individual and his personality. The social emerged from collective forces and could be understood only in terms of other collective forces, not of individual psychology.

For Durkheim one possible way to demonstrate the power, the force, and the significance of the social over the psychological would be to bring the full power of sociological analysis to bear on what appeared to be a purely psychological problem: suicide. What is a more intimate, personal, and apparently purely psychological act than the taking of one's own life? Yet Durkheim felt that suicide was a product of the social environment. He argued that the suicide rate was more constant than the death rate and that each society had an "aptitude" for suicide. Although the individual in the final act of taking his own life was certainly caught up in powerful psychological factors, what were the influences of his associative experiences, and what complex of social forces had brought him to the final act of self-destruction?

Characteristically, Durkheim begins with a clarification of terms. He defines the act of suicide as all causes of death "resulting directly or indirectly from a positive or negative act" in which the victim realizes the act will result in his death. The suicidal act must involve the intent to die.

For roughly a third of the book, Durkheim considers the "extra-social" factors usually regarded as causing suicide. He classifies the psychopathic explanations of suicide into four types: (1) the maniacal, (2) the melancholy, (3) the obsessive, and (4) the impulsive. In all psychopathic types. Durkheim argues, the motive for suicide is unclear or imaginary. In most cases of suicide, however, he feels that motive can be established. The question of the melancholy, as opposed to the "dejected," suicide is a case in point. For the melancholy suicide no clear motive can be established, but for the dejected person there is often a cause, such as a loss of job or some major disruption in his life. Furthermore, Durkheim's exhaustive study of suicide statistics, which serve as the basis for his extensive quantitative materials, suggests that groups with high insanity rates sometimes have low suicide rates. He points out that Jews, who have high insanity rates, have low suicide rates. Some countries with high suicide rates are low in their incidences of insanity. Women, who have a higher insanity rate than men, have a lower suicide rate. Finally, he shows that alcoholism, another "psychopathic" condition, appears to be unrelated to suicide.

Durkheim then proceeds to analyze the suicide rate in terms of geographic factors, climate, and other "cosmic" forces. In each case he finds no determining influence. Lastly, he dismisses, through a complex argument, imitation as a critical factor. Thus, from an intensive statistical analysis of suicide records from many European countries, Durkheim concludes that neither psychopathology, race, climate, temperature, nor heredity plays a decisive role in the pattern of suicide seen as a collective phenomenon.

Having dismissed the extra-social factors, Durkheim turns to the social concomitants in suicide—the collective, environmental influences whose origins are in association, in human society itself. He proceeds to study the suicide rate by religion, marital status and family size, occupation, sex, educational level, community type (rural-urban), and many other social factors. His observations reveal that Catholics have a lower predisposition to suicide than Protestants and that generally the Jewish rate is lower than the Catholic. He notes that marriage reduces the tendency to suicide and that even fewer married couples with children take their lives. He finds that the "liberal professions" have a high suicide rate and that education tends to increase the suicidal tendency. In addition, poverty does not seem related to suicide because the middle- and upper-income groups have a higher rate. Urban areas have a higher suicide incidence than do rural villages and farming areas. In short, Durkheim's findings suggest that an illiterate, young, married woman who had five sons, who was living in a small village in southern Italy, where she went to church every day, simply could not (in a statistically significant way) kill herself. On the other hand, a middle-aged, unmarried man with a good education, an adequate income, and a Protestant background living in Paris could kill himself with a good deal of statistical regularity.

Here, then, are the empirical regularities that Durkheim's penetrating statistical analysis led him to. But, after all of the accepted and largely psychological arguments were dismissed, what was the social reality that Durkheim hoped to find beneath the surface of his statistical materials? Was there a sociological principle which linked all of the separate observations into an interrelated whole? What was the thread of sociological continuity that bound the discrete, empirical observations into an interrelated system?

Durkheim suggests that the fundamental sociological principle that keeps the Protestant suicide rate high and the Catholic low is the same force that inhibits suicide for married couples with children. The Protestant, he suggests, is uniquely characterized by the value of "free inquiry" which may, in time, lead the Protestant down the path to skepticism and free thought and away from the church. He is no longer gripped by the moral and theological principle of his faith, as is the more restricted and authority-bound Catholic. The Protestant, in short, is in the *process of becoming individuated* and thus separated from the social, moral, and ethical boundaries of the church. Similarly, marriage binds a man and woman together in a social and biological union from which children normally eventuate. Both husband and wife enter into an obligatory relationship to each other at marriage (the conjugal relationship), and in time the obligatory system extends down to the children as well—the principle of consanguinity. Thus, the nuclear family of parents and children constitutes a solidarity system which links the individuals together and binds them with obligation. Suicide in such a system of mutual dependence becomes relatively more difficult than for the "free" and unbonded individual.

The unifying principle which Durkheim sees as operating through his statistical findings is the all-persuasive force of social solidarity itself. When solidarity is strong and binding (authoritative religion and the consanguineal family), the suicide rate is low. When persons have individuated to the point where they are "free" of social groups and restraints, they suffer from "an excess of individualism" and so with no strong ties to others may take their lives with relative ease. Durkheim identified this suicidal type as the "egoistic" suicide—egoistic because there is nothing else but the solitary and isolated individual. Thus, where solidarity is weak, where social bonds are loose, where integration of the individual into the social structure is relatively atomized, the suicide rate will be high.

Durkheim, with a magnificent sense of the imperatives of scientific form, summarized this principle in his classic formulation of a sociological law:

Suicide varies inversely with the degree of integration of religious society . . . domestic society . . . political society.

He then suggested that, whereas the egoistic suicide results from social structures that encourage individualism and weakened bonds between persons, the opposite (intense integration) may also lead to suicide. If inadequate integration of social structures can cause the egoistic suicide, then an excess of integration of social structures can cause *altruistic* suicide. A condition can exist within a society that encourages individuals to sacrifice their lives for the common good. History, Durkheim points out, is filled with the suicides of men who gave up their lives simply because they recognized their obligations to the collective reality.

We are familiar with the Japanese custom of *hara-kiri*, whereby a man is expected to kill himself if he has somehow failed in an important obligation. There is the oft-cited example of the heroic soldier who throws himself on the unexploded hand grenade in order to save the lives of his comrades. Where men are so integrated into the social structure that they would knowingly give up their lives to preserve it, Durkheim called this form of suicide *altruistic*. Its generating force constitutes the inversion of the principle of egoistic suicide.

Moreover, a third suicidal type was suggested by the data. Durkheim noted that in times of sudden economic depression or rapid political change the suicide rate went up. He called this form of suicide *anomic*. Anomie emerges when the prevailing institutions and regulatory systems of a society suddenly fail to function. Anomie is a condition of normlessness, of alienation, of hopelessness for the individual, who no longer feels bound to the prevailing normative or regulatory systems of society. He feels isolated and apart. Life no longer has meaning because those institutions whose function it is to give normative and ideological support are no longer operative and functioning. The very basic ideologies are in question, and the fundamental institutions of society are in a state of disorganization and change. In such circumstances men take their lives.

The perceptive student may suspect that the forces of egoistic suicide and anomie might be the same thing with slight conceptual and empirical modification. Indeed, Durkheim noted that both anomie and the loss of solidarity and integration can easily combine to become the dual-edged instrumentality to speed suicide. There may be the egoistic-anomic or the anomic-egoistic suicide.

The Durkheim analysis of suicide was a remarkable demonstration of the power of his methodological thesis that the cause of a social fact is another social fact. Taking suicide as a collective phenomenon in terms of its statistical frequency, Durkheim traced out the social origins beneath the surface of statistical data.

However, in his search to explicate and reinforce his idea of the generating power of the social, Durkheim ignored the psychological. It was his intention to do so, but the total circumstances surrounding the suicide of each person cannot end with Durkheim's account. There is a point at which sociology must defer to psychology. Durkheim cannot tell us why some individuals in an environmental setting that encourages suicide (egoism-anomie) do not take their lives and why others in a social setting that discourages suicide do. After all, even in the social setting that has an "aptitude" for suicide, most people continue to live out their normal years. Why do some people endure and others yield?

These are questions generally left to the psychological analysis of each individual. But in the sociological concern with statistical frequency and the regularities of pattern, the Durkheim analysis has great meaning and interest.

Since the introduction of *anomie* into the conceptual apparatus of sociology, the term has continued to generate great interest. It has been put to much use in recent years and has found expression in a large number of studies. Currently, social scientists are caught up in the notion of alienation—the manner in which people lose identity and are somehow separated from the main normative and ideological stream of society. In view of current unrest in the cities, of riot and civil disorder, there appear to be millions of Americans who feel the ravages of anomie —alienation, fragmentation, isolation, normlessness, atomization, and separation. Whereas Durkheim used the term to identify a form of suicide, the concept now applies to population subgroups who through one device or another are kept on the periphery of society, so that the integrative norms are meaningless to them. Anomie, normlessness, and alienation seem to constitute a force that may be functioning in race relations, the "hippy" movement, and many other forms of public disobedience, retreat, and "anti-establishment" activities.

SUGGESTED READINGS

BERGER, PETER L., *Invitation to Sociology*. Garden City: Doubleday & Company, Inc., Anchor Books, 1963.

> *A humanistic and literate presentation of the sociological perspective.*

CONANT, JAMES B., *Modern Science and Modern Man*. New York: Columbia University Press, 1952.

> *An exposition of the development of science in the twentieth century with particular concern for the relationships between science, morality, and conduct.*

DAVIS, KINGSLEY, *Human Society*. New York: The Macmillan Company, 1948–49.

> *Perhaps one of the finest introductory books in sociology ever written.*

LUNDBERG, GEORGE A., *Can Science Save Us?* New York: Longmans, Green & Company. Ltd., 1947.

> *A thoughtful essay examining the question of the relationship of science to social problems and public policy.*

MILLS, C. WRIGHT, *The Sociological Imagination*. New York: Oxford University Press, Inc., 1959.

> *A critical view of some of the shortcomings of sociology by one of its leading practitioners.*

NISBET, ROBERT A., *The Sociological Tradition*. New York: Basic Books, Inc., Publishers, 1966.

> *An excellent summary of not only the basic concepts of sociology, discussed as "unit ideas," but also the historical circumstances out of which sociology emerged.*

PAGE, CHARLES (ed.), *Sociology and Contemporary Education*. New York: Random House, Inc., 1964.

> *A series of essays dealing with sociology and its impact on contemporary educational practice.*

SOROKIN, PITIRIM, *Contemporary Sociological Theories*. New York: Harper & Row, Publishers, 1934.

    A useful, if somewhat dated, summary and review of the emergence of sociology and some of its schools.

STEIN, MAURICE, and ARTHUR VIDICH (eds.), *Sociology on Trial*. Englewood Cliffs: Prentice-Hall, Inc., 1963.

    A provocative anthology which essentially calls for a return of social criticism on the part of contemporary sociology.

ZETTERBERG, HANS L., *Social Theory and Social Practice*. New York: The Bedminster Press, 1962.

    Essentially a summary of the way in which sociological knowledge can be applied by social practitioners.

chapter

THE LOGIC OF
SOCIOLOGICAL
INQUIRY

In the preceding chapter we were concerned primarily with the unique sociological perspective; in this chapter we shall focus our attention on the claim of sociology to be a science and on the manner in which the scientific mandate is effected through sociological research. Our interest is in *methodology* and the strategies of research design. Method is the critical term here rather than the sociological claim to "truth." Down through the ages men have probably stated the same "truth" about some aspects of social reality—sociologists certainly can not claim an exclusivity of knowledge concerning the social state of mankind.

Shakespeare wrote that all the world was a stage and that men were actors who "strut and fret" their brief hour on it and then are gone forever. Centuries later sociologists began to use the term "actor" to describe the socialized component of the human personality. And the intention here was very much the same as Shakespeare's—man is an actor, a player of social roles whose primary script is laid down by the normative tradition of society. In a manner of speaking, Shakespeare articulated a sort of "truth" long before the advent of formal sociology. But the critical difference between the artist and poet, both of whom may have brilliant insights into the social condition, and the sociologist, is the matter of *method*. The sociologist brings formal methodology—verified "facts," if you will—into a system of rational or logical relationships. The artist is essentially intuitive or subjective in his statements of "truth," and his claims or viewpoint must be accepted on that basis. The sociologist, in his search for regularity, pattern, and order in the associative or social condition of men, is bound by the rigors of valid and reliable observation coupled with the rules of logical and rational inference. Both artist and sociologist may speak the same ultimate "truth," but the sociologist arrived there by his method—controlled observation, objectivity, and rationality.

The term "methodology" has two meanings, and we shall employ both in this chapter. In its broadest use, the term refers to both the logic of procedure (concepts, constructs, and rational inference) and the specific observational techniques through which the primary data are gathered. Often in the social sciences the term "methodology" refers exclusively to the latter phase—that is, to the instruments and methods of the observational process. In this sense, sociology courses in research methodology usually take the student through the specific forms of sociological observation and its usual attendant features of questionnaire construction, interview schedules, sample design, projective techniques, content analysis, scaling, and the like. As sociology has matured and as historical-speculative sociology came to an end, the emphasis increasingly has been on the production of valid data.

If American sociology, and indeed American social science, has any distinctive character in the global scientific community, it is this emphasis on empirical accuracy and consequently on the specific and formal methodology whereby such accuracy is assured. European social science has tended to continue in the historical and philosophical traditions established in the eighteenth and nineteenth centuries. Only in recent years has the "American" pattern shifted to Europe—that is, the emphasis on formal observation and the reduction of critical variables to quantitative-statistical manipulation.

Let us return for a moment to the question of science. Bertrand Russell wrote:

> Science . . . is primarily knowledge; by convention it is knowledge of a certain kind, the kind, namely, which seeks general laws connecting a number of particular facts.[1]

Cohen and Nagel said:

> The idea of science is to achieve a systematic interconnection of facts. Isolated propositions do not constitute a science. Such proposi-

[1]Bertrand Russell, *The Scientific Outlook* (London: George Allen and Unwin Ltd., 1931) , p. 10.

tions serve merely as an opportunity to find logical connections between them and other propositions.[2]

Lazarsfeld and Rosenberg stated:

> No science deals with objects of study in their full concreteness. It selects certain of their properties and attempts to establish relations among them. The finding of such laws is the ultimate goal of all scientific inquiries.[3]

It is clear from the foregoing statements that science is not viewed merely as a method to insure the accuracy (validity and reliability) of observations but perhaps more importantly as a way to identify the interrelationships and connections between either empirical or conceptual entities. It is the quest for linkages between events and their reduction into the more abstract but nevertheless fundamental levels of reality that science seeks. The movement, the central thrust, of scientific development is up from the empirical (the observed datum) into the conceptual and finally into the purely theoretic—the ultimate principle of logically interconnected conceptions. The more concepts subsumed into a system of interrelations, the greater the theory. However, we are considerably ahead of the story. Perhaps the best approach at this juncture would be to review some of the basic ideas associated with the logic of sociologic inquiry.

SOCIAL CAUSATION

In the preceding chapter we traced some of the circumstances—social, intellectual and technological—from which formal sociology emerged more than a century ago. And even though the young science has had a spectacular development in the intervening years there are scholars and intellectuals, along with many members of the general public, who have serious doubts whether sociology can "really be a science." Although conceding that sociology has contributed some general insights into the social condition, they argue that the central subject matter of sociology—man and his relationships—is beyond the scope and method of science. Essentially those who oppose or who have a dim view of the scientific possibilities of sociology feel that man and society are simply too complex to yield to scientific method. Man is primarily too complicated and

[2]Morris R. Cohen and Ernest Nagel, *An Introduction to Logic and Scientific Method* (New York: Harcourt, Brace & World, Inc., 1934), p. 394.
[3]Paul F. Lazarsfeld and Morris Rosenberg, *The Language of Social Research* (Glencoe: The Free Press, 1955), p. 15.

unpredictable, and collectivities or pluralities of men simply compound the problem. The universe may be orderly and bound by principles that may eventually yield to scientific analysis—but man individually and collectively is simply outside of such order. The controversy stems partly from the old "free will" issue and partly from the idea that human association is ultimately too complex to yield to scientific method. A third argument is that the principles of causality in collective life are of a fundamentally different order from causality in "natural" or "physical" reality.

The idea of causation itself is endemic to scientific investigation. The assumption in all scientific activity is that the universe—"reality," "nature," etc.—is basically orderly and that identical causes produce identical and recurrent events. To illustrate from a common chemical event, if a piece of zinc (Zn) is dropped into sulfuric acid (H_2SO_4), a reaction occurs. The zinc and sulfuric acid react ($H_2SO_4 + Zn \rightarrow ZnSo_4 + H_2$) in such a fashion that the resulting new products are zinc sulfate and hydrogen. This always happens; if it didn't always happen, the science of chemistry would be in considerable difficulty. Behind all science, then, is the assumption that causal principles underlie the entire structure of nature and that if we can identify the critical variables which enter into a sequence of events the same results will always occur. Less precisely, if you strike a billiard ball from the same angle with the same force it will always move in the same direction. Identical causes produce identical effects.

Scientists of all persuasions assume a universe of ultimate law with a causal principle or principles central to that order. It is the foundation for prediction in science, for if the scientist "understands" the primary events in a causal sequence and the substantive character of their interconnections he can predict future occurrences. He can predict how hydrogen can be released from a chemical reaction or he can predict an eclipse of the moon one hundred years from now because he understands the essential units of the given order of natural events and their relationships to each other in time; and so the causal nexus constantly unfolds.

No one can really prove the essentially orderly and causally interconnected character of physical, chemical, and biological events. From a purely pragmatic point of view, the assumption of causality "works," and the entire scientific complex gives itself over to the study of cause-effect relationships. Simply put, there seems to be design, order, and form to everything—order in electrons, order in molecules, order in the relationships between zinc and sulfuric acid, order in the rhythms of galaxies and stars, order in the development of living things. From the far reaches of intergalactic space, which staggers the mind in its incredible immensity, to the subatomic universe of infinitesimal bits of physical particles there is order, pattern, and causally induced recurrence.

But what about man—is he, too, merely another mechanical cog in the still largely uncharted and mysterious order of the universe? Some have traditionally argued a vehement "No!" Man, they say, is independent of whatever orderly processes there are in nature: he has a free will; he is free to decide and elect his own course of action—*free* to sin, *free* to murder, *free* to write a poem, *free* to aspire to greatness. As in the medieval view, the actions of each man ultimately reduce to an act of *volition*, of free choice—the final act is *undetermined* beyond causality and therefore beyond science. For this reason, some argue, psychology and sociology can never really be sciences—man is essentially unpredictable because he is outside the orderly processes of both galactic and subatomic causality.

It is not our purpose here to argue the free-will versus deterministic views of man. The issue now is largely academic anyhow, because the role of influencing factors in the shaping of decision is now seen even by the volitional school as a powerful force. We know that drugs can change personality, perception, and mood, in spite of "will." We know that the sociocultural environment exerts a tremendous influence on the choices of individuals. We know from research that certain populations have a tendency to suicide, others to crime, and others to "success." We now have quite accurate instruments which predict juvenile delinquency in children before they commit their first crime. We predict the growth of populations and of cities and the results of national elections before the specific individuals "act" to have another child, to move to a city, or to vote for a president. In spite of the role of choice or will, there is a mountain of sociological data indicating the massive and shaping role of the social environment in effecting the decisions of specific, concrete individuals.

The crux of the issue today is that some of the "indeterminists," or those who find the free will of human behavior valid, now realize that the extent of completely indeterminant behavior, if it exists at all, is but a tiny mystical fragment of choice in a sea of causally lawful and integrated events. The shaping, influencing, and ultimately determining factors that converge in the moment of decision are simply too massive to be discounted. The free-will school therefore is content largely to argue the "pure" case, where there may be an element of eternal and unfathomable mystery in the chain of physical, biological, chemical, psychological, and sociological events that go into the act of decision.

For the social scientist, that small and possibly incalculable element of choice—if it is there at all—is simply no longer important because the intent of the social sciences is to uncover those events which *do* exist in the social universe, which *do* enter into some sort of causal pattern, and which *can* be observed and understood.

It doesn't take a sociologist to prove that there is some order in the social or interpersonal affairs of men regardless of whether their wills are ultimately free or not, and it is with the *form* and pattern of association that sociologists are primarily concerned. Indeed, every kind and type of human association rests on the tacit assumption of the participants that it is essentially orderly and largely predictable.

In every society and community, almost in every human group, there is a rhythm built of expectations and prediction. There is a time to begin and a time to stop. Everyone who lives in or near a great city "knows" about the rush hour. There is generally a flow of people toward the center of the city in the morning and in the evening there is a flow out of the city. No one knows who all of these people are personally. No one can identify them by name. But collectively these people contribute to a spectacular (and often burdensome) pattern common of the urban-industrial world. Here is a simple illustration of form in association, but in fact our entire lives rest on the assumption of order, form, pattern, and rhythm in our social affairs. "But we always have chicken for Sunday dinner." "Well, the tourist season is about to begin." "Boy, you better get up early if you want to beat the traffic to the beach on Sunday morning." "Well, you really can't expect your father to help you out of this mess." "It's simply the law of supply and demand."

Every day of our lives we enter social relationships and groups with a clear expectation and anticipation of what will occur. The very existence of human society rests on this principle of the essential order of social relationships. Whether the choices of human beings are to a degree forever beyond science is no longer a serious issue. The social sciences have simply found too much of a determining, influencing force in the social environment for the question to be seriously argued in the philosophic context.

As to the issue of unfathomable complexity in social matters which dooms the possibility of a science of society, may not our feeling of complexity merely be another manifestation of our ignorance? Matters are always complex if we do not understand them. Recall how you struggled with a problem in mathematics and, when you finally understood it, how simple it suddenly became! Often when we look at the spectacular accomplishments of the physical sciences and the relative lack of such accomplishments among the social sciences, we fail to take note of the fact that the sciences have emerged at different points in time. Physics and chemistry are considerably older than psychology and sociology—they are more mature, their research procedures more formal, their concepts clearer, and their theoretic integration far more advanced. Today even the high-school student has an understanding of physical reality that Galileo and Newton did not have, and a concept of biology that was beyond Darwin. It seems simple now, but the knowledge built up by these sciences are the products of hundreds of years of effort.

Fifty thousand years ago men roamed the earth in little bands. They had primitive stone tools and not much else. They were killed by disease, hunger, the vagaries of the elements, and each other. When those ancient men looked at the heavens, the jungles, the desert, the ocean, falling stones, hurricanes, indeed all of the awesome forces of nature, what else could they see but unending complexity? Did those ancient men ever suppose that their descendants could one day *understand* gravitation, energy, and mass to the extent of controlling and using them for human purposes? We cannot answer the question of what they really thought, but we can conjecture that all of the multiform facets of their experience with nature in their precarious existence must have seemed incredibly complex. Yet today, certain aspects of that experience are known, understood, and viewed by the knowledgeable as "really quite simple."

We shall conclude this discussion of social causation by introducing one final question. Is social causation—that is, the cause-effect relationship between social events—of the same order as the cause-effect relationships in physical events?

In part, the problem here is that of reduction: can social reality be reduced to psychological reality, and this in turn to biological, then to chemical, and ultimately to physical reality? Is the human group simply the final unfolding of causal forces rooted in atomic physics? Some philosophers have seriously argued the reductionist case, but we think otherwise; and in this issue perhaps we shall come rather close to the basic question of the possibility of a science of human relationships.

When one atom is linked to another to form a molecule of, for example, cellulose or water or salt, the nature of the relationship is pretty well determined by the laws of atomic and molecular structure. Thus, the laws of physics dealing with matter and energy come into play. From another viewpoint, atoms and molecules combine to produce another order of reality—the chemical, with its particular concern for the classification of "substances," the preparation of one known substance from another, and the elaboration of newer substances, unknown in a state of raw nature. At another level, some substances in their molecular structure have a character quite distinct from others: they are *alive*, they possess *life*. Thus we go from physics (matter and energy) to chemistry (the nature of substances) to biology and life. Does biology eventually reduce to chemistry and this in turn to physics? More importantly, do the social sciences eventually reduce into the realm of biology and thence to physics? Is sociology, the study of men and groups, ultimately susceptible to a physical equation of atoms in motion? Are the laws of sociology eventually reducible to physical laws?

The "laws of nature" usually refer to the fundamental forces which govern the universe apart from social man. Atoms, living cells, and vast stellar systems are held in the grip of atomic, biologic, and cosmic law. The principles of causality and order—the basic assumptions of science—are natural and fundamental elements of all reality. And man as a biological and, indeed, eventually atomic system is a part of this law. But what about two or more men in a human group? Are the laws of nature binding here? Must two or more men in a human group follow out the dictates of a social causality with the same recurrent and seemingly inevitable outcome as atoms and chemicals achieve in response to the laws of physics and chemistry—to the order of nature? This is the heart of the issue of social causation.

The elemental fact is that social *forces*, social *causes*, social *determinants*—whatever they may eventually be—are *not* of the same order of lawful necessity as can be found in a state of pure nature. If the apple breaks away from the stem, it always falls to the ground—or we should say, in the proper language of contemporary science and philosophy, there is a high degree of probability that it will fall to the ground. However, the probability that the apple, as it responds to the laws of motion and gravitation, will fall to the ground rather than fly up into the sky is significantly greater than the probability of men responding in a particular way to some social collective or "law." In both physics and sociology the outcome of cause-effect relationships and the unfolding of "law" is a matter of statistical frequency regarding probability—but the probabilities in physics seem greater than in sociology. This is because atoms, cells, and stars are responding to a cosmic design which we have identified in the primary laws of physics, biology, or astronomy. Men in groups, however, constitute an emergent order of reality that is not reducible to the laws of nature but can be understood only in terms of a new order of phenomena—society or association itself. This is what Durkheim meant many years ago when he argued that society is a reality *sui generis*—a thing apart and of its own kind, whose ultimate structure and meaning can be known only through a study of society itself and not by an attempt to reduce it to psychology and then all the way to physics.

Furthermore, since the social constitutes a reality unique and distinct from that of the other physical and biological sciences (which may indeed reduce to atoms in motion), the causal forces which play upon it may be different as well. There are few alternatives for the atoms that form H_2O, but the alternatives that society faces in matters of basic structure are comparatively great. Whereas, for example, all societies must see to it that population is replaced in an orderly way (the functional imperative), the many forms of family organization (the structural consequence) around the globe attest to the alternatives open to the social order. There appears to be a greater range of structural response in the social condition than in the physical. True, part of that greater range or fluidity in the process might be more apparent than real because of the relatively primitive state of sociological knowledge. More data and more concepts will probably cause chance, caprice, and "anti-law" to fade before the sociologist's discovery of order, form, and recurrence. But since the reality produced by men in association does not seem to emanate from a vast and necessary cosmic design of which atoms and energy might be the final variables, we must conclude, at least for the present, that social causation—like social reality—constitutes a system of phenomena unique to the scientific experience. There is order and recurrence in human association, but the possibility of sociology's producing a statement like $E = mc^2$ seems remote indeed.

Still, in a sense all of this is rather academic. The general movement of sociology and all the social sciences during the past twenty-five years, particularly since the widespread use of computers, has seen a continually improving ability to observe, analyze, and predict. If social causation is ultimately such that complete (100 per cent) certainty will always be lacking, then the sociologist will happily settle for 99.99 per cent probability. And since contemporary physics is now content with probabilities in the place of Newtonian certainty, sociology seems to be in rather good company.

By way of summary, at the beginning of this discussion of social causation we indicated that opposition to the possibility of a science of sociology was centered on three interrelated themes: (1) the free-will issue, (2) the so-called "complexity" of social behavior which made scientific analysis all but impossible, and (3) the difference between naturalistic and social causation. To the free-will argument we have suggested that the massive role of biological, psychological, and sociological influences have reduced the element of so-called free and independent choice—if it can exist at all—to merely one factor of the decision-making process. To the "complexity" argument we have suggested that complexity is often a manifestation of ignorance rather than a characteristic of a phenomenon. Lastly, we have suggested that the unique character of social causation and the multiform quality of social relationships admits a wider range of responses than may be the case for physical events held tightly in the fist of natural and cosmic law. So we argue that science is possible in the study of human association, although the patterns, forms, structures, and processes of the social condition are quite probably of a different order of causality than that which rules the flight of stars, the movement of tides, and the growth of living things.

EMPIRICISM AND THE TREND TO QUANTIFICATION

All sciences are empirical in that they rest on sense data. Science assumes that there is an orderly world beyond the senses and that this world is knowable. And no matter how abstract and seemingly removed a concept may be, if it is to have utility and meaning in the scientific undertaking, it has to be reduced eventually to sensory experience. A concept, in short, must have empirical (observational) references.

One of the great difficulties that sociology and, indeed, all of the social sciences encountered in the nineteenth century was the concentration on "total" conceptual systems—total theories of society and social change. These grand schemes eventually collapsed largely because they were supported by the thinnest of data and someone could always find another bit of empirical knowledge that supported another and often contradictory claim. The major thrust of sociology in the twentieth century, therefore, has been toward the production of "hard" data rather than philosophical system building. The force behind this shift has been the general feeling that sociology needed a hard core of reliable data before systematic conceptualization and theory building could begin. This, in short, is the basis for the empirical tradition.

As sociologists became more sophisticated in observing the social world around them, the number of concepts resulting from this observation steadily increased. As regularities in social events emerged in the growing research orientation, concepts were invented to summarize the new empirical discoveries. Data and conceptualization go hand in hand. And as new concepts became part of the discipline, newer hypotheses suggested even newer research goals—but there was always the nagging problem of taking a relatively complex idea or concept (class, reference group, aspiration level, fascist ideology, racism, authoritarianism, primary group, other-directedness, militarism, status-seeking, etc.) and deciding what particular empirical references to look for. What should you systematically observe, and how do you really know that what you observe are the critical empirical phenomena subsumed by the concept?

This is the problem of the empirical validity of a measuring instrument. Does it measure what we want it to measure? Furthermore, is it *reliable* enough to measure consistently what we want it to measure? These two terms, *validity* and *reliability*, are central to the empirical-conceptual interrelationship. Reliability generally refers to the ability of the empirical instrument to measure consistently, and validity bears on the ability of the instrument to translate into sensory-empirical operations the definitive characteristics of the concept.

To this end, most empirical researches rely heavily on *operational* definitions, which are really conceptions of a conception. The problem at this level is to find empirical referents so that systematic observations can be made. For example, "class," which has many meanings in sociology, is a currently popular area of research. Obviously, "class" alone is much too broad and unspecified a term to be meaningful in the empirical phase. The old admonition to college students—"define your terms"—is relevant here. If class figures importantly in a research study, then it must be defined clearly, but also, if class is to be observed, the empirical referents must be specified. Now "class" may be viewed as a purely economic group; it may possess the additional variable of prestige and honor; or it may indeed be the honorific alone. Then, too, "class" may involve the variable of power and influence. The problems of conceptual clarity are obvious here but, once the term is defined, how is class to be observed?

The way in which sociologists operationalize (empiricize) class may be illustrated in the following: If class is seen as a purely economic phenomenon, occupation and income might be two units of empirical study. Both are relatively available for a given population and are easily translated into quantitative units. For example, the Bureau of the Census employs an occupational classification beginning with professionals and running all the way to unskilled laborers. Income levels can be treated in the same manner. Incomes over $50,000 could be assigned to the "top" or "upper-class" category. Now, of course, no sociologist really believes that these two variables translate into completely valid and reliable measures of social class in America. But for the goals of his study they may be adequate.

If a more sensitive measure of class is needed, the research may call for the addition of educational level, or house type, or neighborhood. If the research requires data on style of life, then family expenditure patterns might be part of the observational phase of the research.

There is another dimension to the research process that we wish to call attention to here. Not only must concepts be carefully operationalized so as to yield observational elements, but these elements should reduce to quantitative and statistical analysis. Note from our foregoing discussion not only that class was conceptualized into two-variable or four-variable operations but also that these could be statistically summarized. Recall, too, how science strives to state relationships between events and entities. These relationships are often summarized in terms of variance or invariance between two or more analytic units. Not only social scientists but all of us in our everyday conversation are concerned with "more than" or "less than." Statistics is simply one way, a very precise way, in which relationships between units can be summarized.

We might also add at this point that sociologists are almost always concerned with units of data—the *cases* which sociologists deal with (human beings in collectivities) often yield to statistical summary. And this is essentially what statistics are—they are the logical procedures through which large aggregates or units can be meaningfully compared. Those comparisons might be simply "measures of central tendency" in which we are interested in the manner in which the data or units "bunch" together. Every high school student begins to have an interest in his "average"—which is simply the central tendency of his cumulative grades. This is the familiar arithmetic mean.

However, statistical analysis goes considerably beyond these elementary calculations, and for the sociologist who often deals with extremely large units or counts, numbering well into the hundreds, thousands, and tens of thousands, this is the only way to summarize observations. Note, too, that statistical analysis is an extremely precise and controlled way to state sociological relationships. We are no longer content to say "by and large" and "in the main" or "usually more" people do this, or "fewer" do that. These are primitive statements of relationships. Even elementary statistical treatment enables us to say that *67 per cent* of a population showed a certain characteristic, or 3 out of 4 people did this, or that. Statistics make it possible to summarize central tendency or dispersion and deviation. Critical relationships, therefore, can be reduced to a precise mathematical measurement and this is the prime motivating force behind the steady trend toward quantification.

The assumption behind it all is that if events are qualitatively different—the colors red, yellow, blue, for example—then a series of quantitative differences can be established for "degree" of redness or blueness. If there are qualitative differences between classes in American society, then quantitative measures can be established to distinguish observed variations between them. Qualitative differences, it is argued, are simply the "visible" differences between events, which are essentially established from the smaller and less visible quantitative changes below the surface of things. Qualitative difference, in short, is the summary statement of what are essentially quantitative differences.

The search to operationalize concepts which have quantitative referents, however, may have serious disadvantages. Although there are many tests for the validity of an empirical instrument, it is possible that the operations are not definitively central to the guiding concept. What is even worse, there is always the possibility that the empiricist will come to regard his operational definition and the data his observations released as somehow being "real." This is called *reification*; it is the error in both theory and research in which the concepts are regarded as being somehow an exact semantic replication of sensory experience. The concept and the empirical world are viewed as being one and the same thing. The error here, of course, is that concepts are really abstractions from the sensory world, a way of intellectually organizing it. Our "idea" of an automobile is not the same thing as a "real" automobile. We shall have more to say about the problem of reification when we discuss concepts in greater detail later in this chapter. Note here, however, that the value of operational definitions rests on the principle of validity. Some operations, although highly visible and researchable, may tempt the researcher to enter the marvelous world of statistical analysis with a load of meaningless raw data. The "operations" may be spurious, the instrument invalid and unreliable, but the statistics can be accurate and impressive.

THE INDUCTIVE METHOD

If method is the broad design of procedure and proof in science, the particular form of that method in the social sciences is inductive. The general pattern of induction is to search for small uniformities through reliable methods, and then to discover what principle or force may underlie the discrete observations. Empirical data are observed data, collected through questionnaires, interviews, census counts, or the like. The primary intention of the inductive method is to take valid empirical facts and then to seek out and identify the principle which may unite the discrete entities. For example, the hazing of college freshmen (an empirical datum), the ritual circumcision of young men during puberty ceremonies, graduation exercises, a presidential inauguration, a marriage ceremony, and a battlefield commission, all discrete and seemingly unrelated events, are each a public ceremony in which the participating individuals are entering into a new phase of their lives. They will now occupy a social position having new and distinctive rights and privileges —a college student, a college graduate, a spouse, a commissioned officer rather than an enlisted man, a "man" or adult rather than a child. Each of these specific ceremonies, and they are almost countless in human society, may be conceptualized into a new order of social reality. We might refer to them as the "rites of passage"—public rituals in which the actor passes from one critical social status into another. This passage is duly recognized by the community through a public event which, in effect, clearly dramatizes to the participant in the ceremony, and to those who witness it, a major social transformation. Thus, from a pattern of smaller observed events the principle of interrelationship is drawn, and the inductive method is obeyed. From small, discrete empirical uniformities the principle of interrelationship is sought.

There are no clear-cut *schools of thought* in sociology as there are in psychology. But there has been a distinction among American sociologists between those whose interests tend to be speculative, philosophical, historical, or even humanistic, and those whose interests are in verified facts, observations, and regularities. This distinction might have been stronger in the 1940's than today, but some sociologists still distinguish between the "counters" and the "speculators." The empiricist does prefer data, facts, and observation, but the issue of the primacy and importance of the empirical over the conceptual and theoretic is a false one. To be sure, the largely inductive method of sociology requires valid and reliable data, and it is from such data that new concepts emerge. *But data are never undefined. Even the "rawest" of observations is conceptualized.*

At this phase of our discussion it would be well to consider the relationship between the empirical and conceptual dimensions of science. The very essence of all human communication is language, and language consists of vocal utterances and noises whose meanings are shared by others. The basis of the sharing is man's unique ability to symbolize—to give and establish arbitrary meaning to external events, such as sights or sounds. When a man says "There is a forest on the other side of the hill," he means there are a large, possibly uncountable or limitless number of trees on the other side of the hill. "Forest" is an abstract term meaning many trees. The entity "many trees" is conceptualized, abstracted into a term of general reference. Language, in short, consists of a host of concepts which are abstracted from sensory reality or are derived from other concepts. "Democracy," "capitalism," "honor," "justice," are complex terms that embody other complex terms.

The difference between the conceptualizations of everyday language and those of science lies in the degree of precision with which they are defined. Whereas our everyday terms are often unspecified and share only a general meaning, scientific method requires scrupulous definition and clarity. Public officials and newspapermen may talk of the American middle class, but the sociologist doing a study in which the concept of the middle class is central to his undertaking will clearly define and specify what he means by middle class and then most particularly how he (empirically) observes the middle class in his research procedures. Now the issue of empiricism versus conceptualization can clearly be seen to be a meaningless one. Even the most elemental empirical datum is conceptualized from the very start. Marital status, income level, age, and educational achievement are conceptual categories which are not uniquely sociological—the Bureau of the Census employs them continually. The point here is that a raw datum is never really undefined at all—*all empirical research begins with a set of concepts,* and new concepts are sought through the imaginative and creative sociological interpretation and analysis of the data.

In the growth of each science, there is a continual interplay between the conceptual and empirical dimensions. As new data are observed they suggest newer concepts, and as new and meaningful concepts are built into the mounting language of the discipline they suggest where new "facts" should be observed. In the research process, the level of conceptual abstraction constantly rises as the science moves away from raw, sensory reality into the abstract and specialized world of advanced conceptualization. That is why the layman cannot read a paper in contemporary physics or chemistry. He doesn't know the language—the conceptual nuances and special meanings shared only by the practitioners of the discipline. These sciences have progressed so far into conceptual abstraction resulting from sophisticated empirical techniques that it takes years of special study to understand them.

It is interesting to note that a standard criticism of sociology, launched chiefly by the humanists, is that it produces excessive jargon. There unquestionably is, among some sociologists, a tendency to use complex terms when a simpler and equally meaningful term would do just as well. But "jargon" often is simply the result of the conceptual-empirical-reconceptualization process.

New terms are invented to summarize and identify the newer forms of reality that research produced. As the process goes on, sociology will be increasingly more difficult for laymen to read and understand. This will be particularly the case as statistical procedures and analyses are incorporated in the interpretation of research findings. It is highly problematic if even a well-educated and intelligent layman could make any sense at all from the papers published in the leading national scholarly journals in physics and chemistry. They could probably derive much more meaning from papers published in the *American Sociological Review*—the primary journal of the American Sociological Association. Twenty years from now the papers published in the *Review* will be far more technical, abstract, and "jargonistic" than they are today, because the processes of scientific maturation will be that much further along.

STAGES IN THE RESEARCH PROCESS

Inasmuch as orderly empirical and rational procedures form the very core of scientific method, the stages through which scientific effort flows are fairly evident. We might suggest, however, that particularly in the social sciences and also to some extent in the physical sciences these stages of development are sometimes rather difficult to follow in the actual research process. That is to say, research illustrated in a textbook is always highly idealized. In actual practice there is a good deal of backtracking, often confusion as to the research goals, and at times serious problems in the collection of data. Major changes in research objectives may be made after the data have been observed. The steps or procedures in research, although distinct enough in the abstract, are sometimes quite blurred in actual practice.

Selection of the Research Problem

In research, one starts with the articulation of a "problem." We do not mean a problem in the value sense, but a research intention. Sometimes the problem is stated in the form of a clear-cut and highly systematic hypothesis. We shall have more to say about hypotheses in a later section, but for the moment we can define any hypothesis as essentially the *assumption* that properties or variables are interrelated in some fashion. For example: "As income increases political conservatism increases." If we clarify our terms and operationalize our empirical referents, this hypothesis is highly researchable. On the other hand, some hypotheses are not systematic at all and hardly deserve to be called by this scientific term. Some researches begin with a purely descriptive intention—that is, simply to learn more about a situation—and the clarification of relationships among events is not the research goal.

The selection of a research problem and its level of empirical and conceptual sophistication derive from the researcher's general acquaintance with current theory and research practice. Usually, the more one knows about his field the easier it is to formulate significant hypotheses. As a rule the research problem originates in unguided and fairly random speculation, but as the scientist scrutinizes the problem he changes focus from the general to the specific. In short, the research goals move from general speculation toward specific hypotheses that are researchable. And this element of "researchability" is a critical factor: that is to say, the guiding principles of the research, the hypotheses, must ultimately be reduced to empirical referents. The research goals must be clear and attainable in terms of the general framework of science.

As it has grown and developed, each science has created its own distinctive and characteristic forms of observation. From telescopes to nuclear piles to attitude scales to public opinion questionnaires, the sciences have created methodological devices to further their empirical investigations of the universe. The specific use of these instruments and devices can be taught to students, but the manner in which exciting and significant hypotheses are formulated cannot be taught so easily. The sources of the creative scientific imagination still apparently lie in the mysteries of the human personality, although it is clear enough that the more one knows of his field, and its current state of theory and knowledge, the easier it will be for him to formulate significant hypotheses.

Several years ago I was visiting some colleagues from a department of sociology that had a particularly strong quantitative and research orientation. This was rather unusual for an essentially undergraduate department, although they were soon to develop programs in the graduate area. Sociology majors in this department were required to take two courses in statistics and a full year of methodology, and soon they would be required to take a course in computers as well. These students were extremely well trained in the empirical phases of research, far better than many graduate students. However, the chairman of this department observed: "Yes, we give our students an unusually heavy exposure to research, and this is not only in the formal methods courses. The importance of data and empirical observation is continually reinforced throughout the substantive course work—the family course, population, social stratification, and the like. But you know, while these kids really know their methods they don't seem to be able to come up with a really exciting research idea."

While this department was busy teaching methods it had not been able to "teach" how to formulate imaginative and sophisticated research problems. Perhaps many departments are too caught up with the technology of research methodology and have failed to spend enough time on the theoretic and conceptual dimensions of the science from which research problems emerge.

To summarize: research begins with a general hunch about assumed relationships between variables. As the potential researcher mulls over the vague idea, he familiarizes himself with the general state of theory and knowledge in his particular area of interest. As the general hunch is reduced into researchable form, the problem goes through increasing definition until specific and formal hypotheses with their operational empirical referents have been formulated.

The Sources of Data

Once a clear and answerable set of research questions has been stated, the next problem is to decide where to find data. Many students make the mistake of thinking that this is the point at which they rush out into the field with a questionnaire or interview schedule. The fact is that much research can be done in the library. At this juncture the standard references in periodic literature are examined (actually this was probably done to some extent in the stage of goal formulation), as well as other sources where data and information might be obtained. The point here is simply that there is no sense in using time, effort, and money to gather data or observations firsthand when somebody else may have done it already. That "somebody" may be the United States government through census reports, or local government records, or possibly business sources, as well as scientific and academic publications. At this stage of research, the library becomes a major tool and the available sources of information are completely searched.

The Observation of the Data

It is the stage in which data are actually being gathered that the layman often exclusively associates with science—he has little appreciation of the great effort that has gone before or will come afterward. The gathering or observation of data is perhaps the most spectacular phase of science (which is often so dull and routine), because scientists are overtly doing such things as looking at stars or microorganisms or people in crowds. At any rate, some sort of systematic observation is being done.

In sociology such observation calls for a variety of techniques, depending on the research aims. It may involve simply taking data from library sources and arranging them through the canons of rational inference in a new way, or it may be the creation of a new statistical table using data from various original sources. In some cases, the data must be observed phenomenologically in the social setting. Here a variety of techniques may come into play, such as "participant observation," in which the social observer actually joins the group that he is observing. Or he may use a questionnaire and gather responses firsthand from informants who were selected by some sampling technique. Unfortunately it is not possible here to enumerate the variety of sociological techniques in which observations are made.

Sociologists are concerned with the generic forms of association and the multiform consequences of association. The subjects studied range from simple two-person groups through complex societies of 500 million, from institutions to ideologies, from deviant behavior to conformity, from social systems changing over time to phenomena in which time is not a variable. From the almost endless variety of subjects studied has come a host of empirical techniques developed to produce valid and reliable observations. An entire course could be devoted to these forms of observation, and many books about them could be read before the student would have an accurate sense of the technical methods used by sociologists to observe social behavior.

Finally, we might add, in some cases during the stage of observation an entirely new "instrument" may have to be created to observe a sociological phenomenon if no such instrument exists. In this fashion an "authoritarian personality" scale is developed, or an "Index of Political Predispositions," or a device to predict potential criminality in children. Thus, new devices to solve the observational problems of a specific study are constantly entering the cumulative body of the empirical tradition. If the device or instrument proves valid and useful, it becomes available to future researchers whose research goals suggest its additional use.

Although new instruments are constantly being developed, they are never introduced into the primary observational situation before testing. Even simple questionnaires or interview schedules are pretested before their general use in order to insure that they are producing valid and reliable responses. Once the researchers, through pilot studies and pretesting, are certain of the soundness of their instruments, the final, field stage of observation is entered upon. It is here that the primary data, as guided by the determining hypotheses, are gathered.

Analysis of the Data

Once the observation stage is over, the data must be analyzed. The given form of the analysis is determined by the guiding hypothesis. In some cases, the research goals might have been almost entirely descriptive—that is to say, the data sought after might have been quite general and sociologically superficial, such as the surface description of a population in terms of age, educational level, socioeconomic status, and the like. Here the analysis might simply be made in percentages and arithmetical means. However, if the hypotheses are of a precise and analytic character rather than simply descriptive or exploratory guides to research, then the researcher is bound to bring the methods of rational inference, logic, and statistical calculations (if these be part of the observation phase) to a systematic analysis of empirical materials as they formally relate to the hypotheses. Again, neither space nor intention allows us to dwell here long, but it is important for the student to note that the degree of formal or abstract analysis will depend on the formality of the hypotheses which originated the research process.

The Formal Conclusion and Summary

Following the analysis of the observations, the scientist will formally write up his study. He clearly states the original intention of the study; he locates it theoretically and conceptually in his discipline and states why he regards the research as a significant contribution to the general state of knowledge in the field. He summarizes his research techniques, his data, the primary methods of analysis, and the critical findings. In his summary everything appears very orderly, and basic stages of the research process as we have outlined it here will be clearly visible. What will not be visible are the hours of agonizing thought given over to the entire enterprise, the long discussions with interested colleagues, the search for funds to underwrite the study, the constant reformulations, the omissions, or errors in judgment and technique, and the long hours spent in pretesting and in the final observational stage. What will be missing from the summary statement will be the time spent in converting the raw data onto machine-punched cards and the tense moments when the computers verify or reject the primary findings in terms of the original hypotheses. Neither will the report dwell at great length on those phases of the study which did not bear fruit in some manner or other, but will largely concentrate on those aspects from which published reports might be developed.

For the one study which does make its way to print and receives a positive response from one's colleagues, there are hundreds which fail somewhere along the way, from those who never get past the "thought" stage to those who succumbed from lack of adequate financing. Behind the tidy tables, the statistical formulas, the theoretic and conceptual nuances, lies a complex form of human activity which in the actual process is a good deal different from the neat and orderly stages of research development that we have indicated here.

ALTERNATIVES IN RESEARCH DESIGN

The design of a specific research project, although it will follow the major stages in development that we outlined in the preceding section, will involve at least twelve major decisions in the actual study. These decisions emerge from the unique research project and must be answered in terms of the guiding hypotheses and general research strategy. Consider Table II (next page), which summarizes the alternatives generally facing a sociologist as he establishes the essential empirical design for his study.

Again, neither space nor intention permit us an intensive discussion of the alternatives in research design, but we will take a brief look at some of the decisions a sociological researcher must make in his basic study plan. In Section I of Table II, the nature of the case refers to the primary unit of analysis, from a single person in some role capacity (mother, leader, noncommissioned officer), which would be the smallest unit of sociological analysis, all the way through to a great, complex society. In Section II, the number of cases simply refers to the quantity of units that will be observed, from a single case (a single person or a single "gang"—the familiar case study) to hundreds of thousands of units from a national population.

The sociotemporal context (III) refers to the context in time and place from which cases would be drawn. The alternatives here range from cases drawn from a single society at a single period (Levittown, New York, U.S.A., 1961) through cases taken from many societies, possibly over extended periods of time. The matter of sampling (IV) is now fairly familiar to college students in this age of the public opinion survey, and the question raised here is what particular sampling formula will be used on the population specified by the research.

The time factor (V) centers on the issue of whether the study will consider the element of dynamics—process and change. Some researchers deal with essentially static or "timeless" relationships; others are concerned with factors of time and dynamics. In some research the sociologist has complete control (VI) over the variables he wishes to observe, such as in a contrived small-group experiment in which a carefully prepared stimulus is introduced. In other studies, as in community research or at the level of national societies, the sociologist has little or no control of the empirical situation.

Depending on the nature of the literature and available data (VII), the social researcher may have to gather his observations first-

TABLE II

SOME ALTERNATIVES OF SOCIOLOGICAL RESEARCH DESIGN

I NATURE OF THE RESEARCH CASE
Individual in role (in a
collectivity)
Dyad or pair of interrelated
group members
Subgroup
Group, society
Some combination of these

II NUMBER OF CASES
Single case
Few selected cases
Many selected cases

III SOCIOTEMPORAL CONTEXT
Cases from a single society at
a single period
Cases from many societies
and/or many periods

IV PRIMARY BASIS FOR SELECTING
CASES (SAMPLING)
Representational
Analytical
Both

V THE TIME FACTOR
Static studies (covering a
single point in time)
Dynamic studies (covering process
or change over time)

VI EXTENT OF RESEARCHER'S
CONTROL OVER THE SYSTEM
UNDER STUDY
No control
Unsystematic control
Systematic control

VII BASIC SOURCES OF DATA
New data, collected by the
researcher for the express
purpose at hand
Available data (as they may be
relevant to the research
problem)

VIII METHOD OF GATHERING DATA
Observation
Questioning
Combined observation and
questioning
Other

IX NUMBER OF PROPERTIES
USED IN RESEARCH
One
A few
Many

X METHOD OF HANDLING
SINGLE PROPERTIES
Unsystematic description
Measurement (of variables)

XI METHOD OF HANDLING
RELATIONSHIPS AMONG
PROPERTIES
Unsystematic description
Systematic analysis

XII TREATMENT OF SYSTEM
PROPERTIES AS
Unitary
Collective

SOURCE: *Sociological Research: A Case Approach*, by Matilda White Riley, p. 18, © 1963, by Harcourt, Brace & World, Inc., and reprinted with their permission.

hand by going out into the field, or, as we have indicated previously, the material may already be available from other sources. The methods of gathering data (VIII) are critically related to the over-all research design and certainly to the decisions already made regarding the alternatives we have just discussed. They may involve observation as a participant observer of a street-corner gang, systematic interviewing, the use of questionnaires, or quite possibly some combination of these. In addition, some "observation" may be made of public documents, census reports, or a systematic content analysis of newspapers may be undertaken.

Properties (IX) centers on the problem of the number of variables that the researcher will observe in his study. In some cases, the study will involve the intensive analysis of a single property such as "relative deprivation," an attitude or feeling some persons may have that they are being deprived or denied something more than others, as might be the case of a student who got a C in a course from an instructor who had a reputation for giving a lot of A's. On the other hand, an entire complex of properties, such as class, status, and power, might be observed in a system of social stratification.

Some exploratory studies are almost entirely descriptive (X) in the handling of variables (properties) and so the research is fairly general, "soft," "discursive," "reportorial," or "superficial." However, some researches, with systematic guiding hypotheses which have been reduced to quantitative referents and have subsequently led to reliable and valid observation, may be given over to analyses that are formally logical and statistical.

The same distinctions can be made in the method employed to handle relationships *among* properties as we have just made in the methods used to analyze *single* properties (XII). The researcher must decide whether the materials he has gathered from the sub-units of a social system can be used to generalize to the condition of the larger system of which the units are a part. The question here is whether he can leave his data and in a sense his conclusions at the level of the unitary system (where his observations were made), or whether he can then use his data to generalize in some fashion about the larger unit. For example, if a researcher has data on family income (the discrete units) for a country, he could through the device of median family income make some generalizations about "national income," thereby elevating his data to include a larger social system.

In this section we have briefly touched upon the many decisions researchers face as they move from the broad stages of the scientific process into the many technical decisions and alternatives demanded by each given study. From this brief introduction, the student cannot assume that he is now ready to engage directly in sociological research. Indeed, he should have reached the very opposite conclusion. It should be apparent by now that sociological research is a complex undertaking.

Not only do the technical strategies of research design constitute a series of difficult decisions but perhaps the theoretic and conceptual issues from which empirical research springs constitute the most demanding phase of scientific research.

LEVELS OF SCIENTIFIC ANALYSIS:

A Paradigm

We have seen that scientific research passes through a series of stages, from the formulation of the research problem through to the final conclusions of the study. In addition, we have noted that there are many alternatives to research design from which the sociologist must choose as he reduces the hypotheses or study goals into researchable form.

In this section we shall consider the broad form of the scientific enterprise itself, and in so doing we shall employ something of a conceptual model, a paradigm of science itself. We do not mean to suggest that this construction of scientific levels corresponds identically with "reality"—if there is such a thing as an objective scientific procedure through which all of the discrete sciences find similar expression. The paradigm is an abstraction, a model, an intellectual approximation; but since it is systematic and formal, we can isolate the definite levels of science and trace out the relationships of each level or component to each other. A paradigm is a systematic attempt to formalize and to abstract relationships between complex entities. It focuses thinking because, although it oversimplifies, it nevertheless sharpens our analytic capability to treat those variables or elements or processes that we wish to understand. In our model of science we shall pay particular attention to the empirical, conceptual, and theoretic levels. Consider Figure 1.

In our paradigm of science, we have identified six interrelated levels. The primary level consists of the scientific base—this subsumes the cumulative empirical-methodological, conceptual, and theoretic tradition of the given science. It is the unique and substantive body of knowledge characteristic of each discipline—from physics to sociology. Even today this body of distinctive knowledge is so vast and complex that no scientist has a complete grasp of it.

It is from the knowledge base of each science that particular hypotheses are generated. Recall that a hypothesis is a guess or a hunch about some aspect of reality or events within the scope of a given science. A scientist immersed in his discipline, knowledgeable about the current state of its theoretic and conceptual development, and skilled in the rigor of research design will decide to put his hunch to the test. From the rationalization of hypotheses (level II) the given study design, as we have seen, will emerge.

Hypotheses may differ a good deal in their level of abstraction and scientific sophistication. Some "hypotheses" might simply be directed to the gathering of simple empirical uniformities, such as the median age of juvenile delinquents at the time of their first arrest.

FIGURE 1

Paradigm of the Characteristic Levels of Scientific Analysis

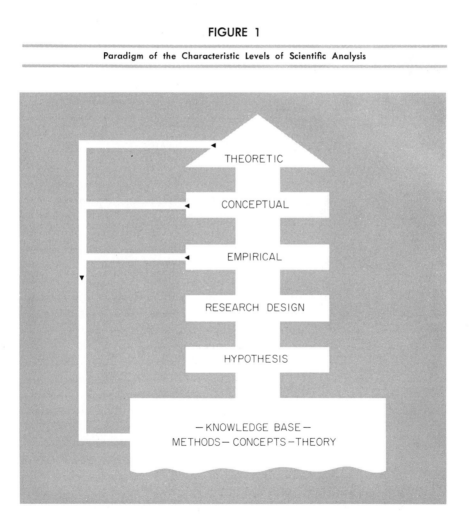

There is very little sociological conceptualization here—although, as we previously noted, all data is conceptualized; it is the extent of the abstraction of the concept that we are concerned with here. At any rate, hypotheses emerge all the way from the observing of empirical regularities through to the formal articulation of abstract concepts. In addition, whereas some hypotheses guide studies of a descriptive or exploratory nature, others seek for patterns of general occurrence and interrelationships among abstract conceptual entities and so pose hypothetical relationships at the level of pure theory. An illustration of hypotheses at this level would be the relative influence of status variables in a static society's system of social stratification as opposed to the status factor in the stratification system of a society undergoing rapid social change. In this case, status, stratification system, and social change become highly abstract but interrelated variables in the hypothesis which calls for an analysis of the relationship between these critical units. Thus, hypotheses range from the empirical to conceptual-constructural and theoretic levels of science. And a given research design (level III) emerges as a concrete adaption to formal requirements set by the hypotheses.

The empirical phase (level IV) consists of the actual study design which was discussed in the two preceding sections. It is the conceptual-constructural (level V) dimension of science that concerns us here. Concepts are the terms of general reference typical of each science. They are the basic language of each science, used to define its primary units of analysis.

Within each science we may distinguish two broad conceptual orders: (1) substantive concepts and (2) methodological or procedural concepts. The former deals with the essential subject matter of the discipline (in sociology, such concepts as "primary group," "institution," "interaction," and "culture"). Methodological concepts deal with the processes of investigation within the science and summarize some essential methodological procedure. Such terms as "reliability," "validity," "random sample," and "content analysis" are illustrative here. For the substantive concepts the primary test is their ability to summarize adequately an aspect of social reality. For the procedural concepts the primary test is their ability to facilitate the scientific process.

Substantive concepts are sometimes divided into "nominal" and "real" categories. A nominal substantive concept makes no inherent claim to final and objective "truth"—it is viewed as an approximation of some element in social reality. A definition of social class merely in terms of income and educational level may be viewed as a nominal construct to further empirical observation, but the researcher is fully aware that there is more to social class than his particular nominal definition. Most sociologists are content to view their conceptions of the social as nominal rather than "real"—the latter implying that the concept is a statement of the essential and "real" characteristics of some entity. Probably in all sciences we strive to produce real definitions but do so through the process of continually reconstructing our nominal definitions toward that ideal.

In terms of the paradigm, Level V consists of the body of concepts to which the research hypotheses are directed. The primary level at this stage begins with the most elemental units of sociological analysis resulting from the interrelationships of human beings. "Role," "status," and the characteristics of primary social relationshpis are examples of initial conceptual forms here. However, as relationships grow complex, they fade from the surface of empirical observation, certainly from the "role," "actor," "social relationship" level, and we encounter a host of nominal concepts whose essential feature is that they are defined by other nominal concepts. Ultimately, these concepts will reduce down the ladder of abstraction into the empirical level. At the upper end are the "constructs," those ideally conceived entities even further along the nominal continuum. Such constructions may be viewed as heuristic devices—diagrams, graphic representations, paradigms, and the like, which represent concepts in an even more abstracted, symbolic manner.

Since all research begins with some conceptual organization—even the raw empirical units are conceptually defined—almost all research leads to some sort of conceptual clarification. That is, it is extremely rare for sociological research simply to plow a mass of unorganized data back into the antecedent knowledge base of the discipline. However, many studies may stop at the conceptual level in that the empirical materials are employed largely toward the development or clarification of a concept. Indeed, sometimes research produces observations or data which are not subsumed by the existent conceptual apparatus, in which case, the researcher would create a new term (concept) based upon the newer empirical materials.

An illustration of this process is Sutherland's concept of "white-collar crime." Most theories of crime causation before Sutherland (*Criminology, 1924,* and *Principles of Criminology,* 1934), concentrating on crimes committed by lower-class criminals, had imputed poverty, slums, discrimination, family instability, etc., as primary causal agents. Crime and lower-class status were constantly intertwined in sociological theories of criminality. Sutherland, however, suggested that crime is much more pervasive than the traditional lower-class forms, which are the most frequently reported in crime statistics. He suggested that there are many offenses committed by "white-collar" persons which do not lead to arrests, prosecutions, or convictions and which, consequently, do not show up in crime statistics. Thus, "white-collar crimes" which may be crimes in the strictly legal sense, often go unnoticed by sociologists who concentrate their studies on the traditional lower-class criminal.

It is important to note, finally, that research stopping at the conceptual stage returns to the discipline's general knowledge base a continually improving and more sophisticated conceptual structure from which new research designs may be created. The process of bringing new data to the conceptual level leads, therefore, to the continual refinement of concepts, the addition of new ones, and the eventual removal of those which no longer have much empirical or theoretic utility to the discipline.

Concepts are the units of analysis regardless of the degree of their abstraction from sensory reality. Theory, on the other hand, or perhaps we should say the theoretic principle, represents the relationship, the variance or invariance, in which conceptual entities stand to each other. Recall that science ultimately asked the question of relationships. The more inclusive the relationship among the most fundamental events of a given order of reality, the more comprehensive is the theoretic statement $(E=mc^2)$.

Thus, theory begins when the scientist focuses on the relationships obtaining between conceptual events. Theory can range from relatively simple generalizations between two concepts, such as the relationship between political conservatism and socioeconomic class, all the way to the primary integrative principles underlying complex social systems. Furthermore, some theoretic relationships are stated through the precise language of statistics (analysis of variance, correlation, etc.).

Some complex constructs, such as Burgess' concentric-ring view of urban ecology, actually enter into the theoretic dimension. Many years ago Ernest W. Burgess (*The City*, 1925) argued that the spatial design of cities consisted of a series of radiating concentric rings. In the center of the city was what he called "The Central Business District"; this was followed by the "Zone in Transition," which was in turn followed by the "Zone of Workingmen's Homes," and so on. He classified these great urban rings as having not only unique kinds of population but unique social functions as well. Furthermore, these rings or zones (for which he had some empirical data) were the products of certain ecological processes, such as the competition for land. Burgess and his colleagues at the University of Chicago developed a complex construct of urban spatial structures and their relationships, which they attempted to explain in terms of certain basic urban social processes. In effect, Burgess not only developed a broad concept of the city but major sub-units as well, and he explained these structures and their relationships to each other in terms of certain fundamental urban social processes—the social processes unique to urban ecology.

Burgess not only produced a major construct of the city but also attempted to demonstrate the existence of causal relationships between the conceptual units. Complex "models" of this type, therefore, are not merely abstract conceptual entities but, when relationships are sought after, can reach the theoretic level. We might also point out that, although Burgess raised his analysis of urban concentric rings to the theoretic level, it was, nonetheless, theory based upon rather fragmentary and unrepresentative empirical data. However, what is important to note here is that complex constructs—abstract entities like the Burgess view of urban ecological form—do undertake to establish *relationships* among the subconcepts of the system and thus reach the theoretic level of science.

Note also from the paradigm that at any of the major levels in the scientific process valuable contributions to the science may flow back into the cumulative base. If hypotheses are oriented strictly to the gathering of relatively simple uniformities at the empirical level, these data will become part of the intellectual heritage of the discipline. At some later date, they may find a useful purpose at the conceptual or theoretic levels in another undertaking. Furthermore, even when a hypothesis is not confirmed, a negative finding may be as useful as a positive one. The discovery of what is not true in a science may be just as valuable as the discovery of what is true.

The paradigm can also be a useful tool in the comparison and analysis of the procedures and methods of specific studies. We may, for example, contrast with the model the essential method that Durkheim employed in his study of suicide. Recall that Durkheim's original intention was to demonstrate that the suicide rate is a "factual order" which expresses a group's "suicidal tendency." In short, Durkheim's underlying hypothesis was that suicide, and particularly a *rate of suicide*, was an expression of some societal and external force. His primary design, therefore, was to locate and demonstrate the reality of that collective imperative, the social factor which was responsible for the suicide pattern.

Next, on the empirical level, his major observations of the "factual order" were the suicide rates and statistics that had been assembled by public agencies and departments, along with data that other social scientists had gathered in their own research dealing with suicide. From among these data Durkheim found that lack of marriage ties, Protestantism, a high level of education, advancing age, middle-income level, and membership in the urban community, the ethnic and racial majority, and the male sex were all positively associated with suicide.

From the empirical materials Durkheim saw the thread of continuity that bound all these concrete bits of fact into a new conceptual reality. He saw the force of *egoism* as essentially the primacy of the self and ego shorn away from meaningful and obligatory group relationships. *Anomie* constituted a state of normlessness and alienation. In *altruism* he found a condition of "over-integration" to the social order—the very opposite of egoism, the lack of integration in the social structure. Thus, the three types of suicide which Durkheim abstracted from the empirical materials represent the formation of new concepts required to summarize and identify the regularities and patterns brought to light in the empirical stage. The conceptual level had been reached.

However, Durkheim was not content merely to identify three major suicidal types that resulted from collective or social causes; he saw all three as a response to society's need for integration and solidarity. Finally, at the theoretic level, Durkheim announced his classic "law," according to which ". . . suicide varies inversely with the degree of integration of the social groups of which the individual forms a part." In this fashion, Durkheim took his analysis to the final impera-

FIGURE 2

Durkheim's Study of Suicide and the Levels of Scientific Analysis

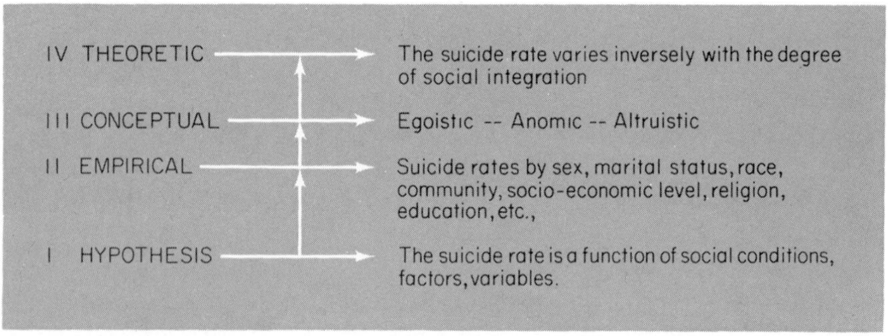

IV THEORETIC	The suicide rate varies inversely with the degree of social integration
III CONCEPTUAL	Egoistic -- Anomic -- Altruistic
II EMPIRICAL	Suicide rates by sex, marital status, race, community, socio-economic level, religion, education, etc.,
I HYPOTHESIS	The suicide rate is a function of social conditions, factors, variables.

tive of scientific method—the theoretic level in which relationships of variance or invariance between the delineated concepts are formally established.

The incredible aspect of all this is the time in which Durkheim did his study—Europe in the last decade of the nineteenth century, when sociology had hardly been intellectually established. Through the use of the paradigm we can see the great insight of this sociologist regarding the forms of scientific method and understand why this book has been read again and again by generations of scholars who followed. It is truly a classic design in which a sociological problem is formulated and analyzed in terms of the requirements of scientific method.

SUGGESTED READINGS

COHEN, MORRIS R., and ERNEST NAGEL, *An Introduction to Logic and Scientific Method*. New York: Harcourt, Brace & World, Inc., 1934.

> *Now regarded as one of the basic standards in the explication of scientific method.*

DURKHEIM, EMILE, *The Rules of Sociological Method*. Chicago: University of Chicago Press, 1938.

> *Durkheim's famous statement of the essential forms for sociological investigation.*

GOODE, WILLIAM J., and PAUL K. HATT, *Methods in Social Research*. New York: McGraw-Hill Book Company, 1952.

> *A readable and well-organized introduction to basic research methods.*

GROSS, LLEWELLYN (ed.), *Sociological Theory: Inquiries and Paradigms*. New York: Harper and Row, Publishers, 1967.

> *A current and largely theoretic collection of papers dealing with the basic modes of inquiry of sociology today.*

HAMMOND, PHILLIP E. (ed.), *Sociologists at Work*. New York: Basic Books Inc., Publishers, 1964.

> *A collection of reports dealing with the development of thirteen research projects and the problems faced by the researchers along the way.*

LAZARSFELD, PAUL F., and MORRIS ROSENBERG (eds.), *The Language of Social Research*. Glencoe: The Free Press, 1955.

> *A sophisticated and useful collection of essays by sociologists with strong research interests; the book is valuable as a source of explication of various empirical research methods and problems.*

LYND, ROBERT, *Knowledge for What?* Princeton: Princeton University Press, 1939.

> *The primary concern is that the knowledge produced by sociological inquiry should be put to use to aid the human condition.*

MACIVER, ROBERT, *Social Causation.* Boston: Ginn and Company, 1942.

> *Now a classic and definitive analysis of the distinctive character of causality in the social condition.*

RILEY, MATILDA WHITE, *Sociological Research: A Case Approach.* New York: Harcourt, Brace & World, Inc., 1963.

> *One of the best of the current introductions to research methods utilizing actual research studies for illustration and methodological analysis.*

THOMLINSON, RALPH, *Sociological Concepts and Research.* New York: Random House, Inc., 1965.

> *A brief and useful book for introductory students focusing on research design and specific empirical methods.*

chapter 3

THE PRIMARY
CONCEPTUAL
UNITS

The preceding two chapters dealt largely with methodological issues in sociology and were not substantive in terms of its content. We may now direct our inquiry to the primary conceptual units of sociology—that is, the basic conceptions from which the discipline takes its primary intellectual character and form. We have already said that sociology concerns itself with the reality that emerges from the interaction of two or more persons. Consequently, we shall focus in this chapter on "micro" social systems—that is, the elementary forms of association which develop around and through a limited number of persons. In this discussion we shall go from "the actor" to small groups. In order to understand how the sociologist conceptualizes even the smallest and simplest of the units of social reality, we must first consider the socialized component of man himself.

THE ACTOR

Social relationships are effected through and between human beings. Men are the raw, nervous stuff through which interaction unfolds. It is a commonplace to note how "complex" men are—from a chemical, biological, or psychological point of view men seem to be infinitely variable. However, as we have seen, it is the mandate of science to seek out order in what appears to be almost eternal and impenetrable mystery.

One of the first and perhaps most difficult lessons that introductory sociology students must struggle with is the sociologist's method of looking at the individual. Whereas psychologists in particular are much concerned with variations in individual behavior, the sociologist regards the individual as a constant, as a given, and the social environment is the variable. In a sense, for the sociologist the individual is the abstraction, and the group the reality. Recall how Durkheim treated suicide as a collective phenomenon whose causes were traced to other collective phenomena. We noted that Durkheim was not interested in individual psychology and unique motivation; he sought to identify those social forces (egoism-anomie) which shaped a society's "aptitude for suicide."

The sociologist sees the individual as essentially an "actor" playing out a role whose primary definitions are located in the normative system. The actor represents that component of the individual which has been "internalized" from continuous and systematic exposure to social expectations. Those expectations cohere and cluster around specific social situations. The actor, therefore, is that dimension of the adult personality which represents the expectations (the social norms) of the collective reality. Needless to say, the actor is merely one facet of the total adult personality, which is, of course, also shaped by, for example, psychological (emotional) and biological (glandular) determinants. The sociologist is aware of these forces, but he chooses to ignore them in favor of sociological factors.

Consider, for example, what a human being would be like if for twenty years since his birth he had been kept from human association. Let us imagine that in some peculiar circumstance (which would be impossible in real life, although there have been some fairly close approximations) a child had been hidden away from other people in a room of some sort and had been fed through one device or other. After twenty years of living in a closed room without human contact, what kind of individual would emerge? Would he be able to walk? Would he respond to external stimuli? Certainly he would be without language, and without language we are incapable of abstract thought. That individual would almost be virtually without a sense of self-identity.

We know who we are because others have told us who we are. "Johnny is a nice little boy." "How smart Mary is, and how well behaved." "We are Catholics, but most of the people here are Protestants." "Remember your Italian background and be proud of it." "I'm sorry, but we don't serve colored here."

It is clear enough from this simple although admittedly artificial illustration that much of human nature, as we define it, is not the mechanical unfolding of powerful internal (biological-psychological) forces but is molded by the expectations of the given human community as to how a person should behave. Those normative *expectations* of the human group, in all of its forms, are not random. They are organized. As the child grows, these expectations are internalized into his maturing psychic structure and become an intrinsic part of his personality. In short, a major dimension of personality derives from social experience. Some of that experience, however, is random, such as having a tyrannical father (which certainly has great psychological meaning to the individual), and some experience is common to all because of the very normative design of the society. Certainly a father who is a "tyrant"— who physically and psychologically abuses a child to the extent that the child develops an abnormal personality—is not generally regarded as a condition of social structure.

The kind of parents we get, and whether they do a "good" job on us or not, is pretty much a matter of chance, although some societies —such as Germany up until fairly recent times—do produce "authoritarian" fathers. In this case a father is expected to rule his family in quite an arbitrary way and often without regard for the feelings, needs, or desires of the other family members. It is pertinent to note here that some personality traits result from "chance" experience in life (the idiosyncratic tyrannical father). On the other hand, that dimension of personality which we have identified as *the actor* results from recurrent exposure and the eventual internalization of the cultural and normative order into the human personality.

Children in all societies are exposed to a basic family form and recurrent parental values which reinforce the internal actor and the sense of self-identity. "That is not the Hopi way." "You never strike another child; you speak to your teacher or to me." "Look, Charlie, if another kid hits you, belt him right back!" The French mother might characteristically say to her child "That is not wise"; the American mother says "Don't do that—it's bad!"; and the German mother says to an errant child "Get in line!" These values which parents all over the world carefully and continually reinforce in their children are not idiosyncratic or personal beliefs but represent culturally approved values characteristic of the society or a major component of it.

The combined institutionalized (formalized patterns, procedures, roles) and normative expectations unique to each society, as internalized by each person, constitute the "actor." The actor in each of us is a player of social roles, the occupant of social statuses, and the internalized conscience which reflects the basic values and norms of the external social system. We are actors because in much of our lives we act out the script established for us by society. And behind the concept of the actor is the implicit assumption of a sociological determinism. Man is the actor. He is worked upon by the external social environment. He is passive. He is a product. He is like a leaf in a stream, whose course is completely determined by the currents—inert, shaped, forced by the external.

But you say, "I am more than a leaf. I think. I react. I am creative. I am unique. I am *myself.*" The sociologist knows all this and probably thinks the same of himself. Certainly we are all aware of the "stream of consciousness" that is unique to our own personalities. But note that the mandate, the charge, of sociological science is to hold individuals constant, to eliminate individual differences entirely, and to study the social environment as it *acts* on individuals.

We are playing the necessary game here of "All things being equal, then. . . ." Most of the sciences do the same thing. The physicist says, "Let us imagine that there is *no such thing as friction*; then. . . ." Or the psychologist says, "Let us imagine that the social environment is *constant* in the study of intelligence and see what we can find out in terms of individual variation." Or Euclid says, "Let us assume that there are two parallel lines that *never* intersect. . . ." Or another mathematician says, "Let us assume that there is a *perfect* triangle . . ." though he knows quite well that a perfect triangle is a *concept* and that all empirical triangles have flaws. So the sociologist says, "Man is an actor; he is the constant stuff, the nervous energy through which culture and society effect their reality. Consider him as a given, and quite inconsequential in the analysis of social reality." It is the game that all the sciences must play, restricting and limiting the focus of their inquiry. If they did not do so, science would be impossible. And yet the sophisticated scientist fully knows that the formal boundaries he erects, which separate his discipline from the others, are really not there at all.

CULTURE

Perhaps one of the most remarkable features of human (in contrast to lower-animal) association is the *normative* character of social life. Although the animal world is filled with highly "social" species (ants, termites, bees, zebras, lions, wolves, horses, etc.) the determining force of their sociality seems to be biology. That is, the "herd" or associative principle seems to lie in their genetic inheritance. If you should take a number of newly hatched ants and termites and transport them halfway around the world, they would eventually produce, as adults, a social system identical with that of their parents, although there would never have been any communication between the two generations. Similarly, the herd animals associate with each other and perhaps share a primitive division of labor. For instance, consider the ecology of the grazing herd where a group of male animals stand guard against potential predators, along the periphery of the herd, while toward the interior the other animals graze peacefully seemingly aware that they are protected. However, communication is limited to primitive meanings and purposes shared on the sublingual level.

Man, on the other hand, is not only "social" but has developed the societal principle to a level that is impossible for any other species. And the generic force or reality or principle that makes man unique we call *culture*. Whereas the social systems sustained by the insect world are shaped exclusively by biologic-genetic principles, the social systems sustained by men are shaped by a system of culture. Only men produce culture and, in turn, culture produces men. That is to say, culture shapes a man in terms of its own design, image, and style. We recognize this when we see a Russian, an Iroquois, a Mexican, an Englishman or even a "mid-Westerner."

Unfortunately, the layman often sees differences in cultural behavior as somehow a manifestation of biological factors. Thus the behavior of an Iroquois will be explained in terms of racial rather than cultural determinants. A particular social act or pattern alleged to characterize Jews, or Italians, or Irish, or Negroes may be described in terms of race and biology. Skin color or race in general is so obvious that few inquire into the less visible forces of society and culture.

The concept of culture is very possibly the broadest and most inclusive idea that one can encounter in the social sciences, and because of this a universally accepted definition is virtually impossible. The term has come to stand for a number of interrelated ideas. Culture is *acquired*. That is to say, whatever it is, you do not arrive in the world with it. You acquire it from others; it is transmitted through social relationships. Furthermore, culture is *cumulative*. It grows through time as each generation adds to the cultural heritage. Perhaps this is a basic key to the understanding of the idea. In its broadest usage, culture is the total design for living sustained by a people. It is the way of life—the organization of ideas and beliefs and of technology and material. Culture unfolds in the characteristic ways in which a people *think*, *associate*, and *produce tools* and *goods*. It grows and accumulates through each generation and it guides the primary forms of social life.

The source of culture appears to lie in a peculiar human ability to symbolize and give abstract meaning. Language is a form of symbolic communication that is found exclusively among men. Simply put, language consists of vocal sounds and noises whose meanings are shared. Again, the symbolic representation is critical. But it goes further than this: the symbolic element seems to be present in all forms of human activity. A color *means* something. In Western society green implies safety and red danger. White stands for purity and black for seriousness. Traditionally the cars driven by clergymen have been black. The *meaning* of colors is cultural and is not implicit in the color itself. Black is a symbol of mourning in the West, but white is the symbol for mourning in the East.

There seems to be no facet of human experience in which symbolic elements do not play a critical part. A style of haircut "means" something—ethnic affiliation, lower- or upper-class membership, rebellion from the establishment. A *manner* of speech suggests something that is not inherent in the words themselves; a gesture implies something; a smile can suggest happiness, a threat, or danger. Flags, automobiles, clothing, addresses, universities and colleges, names, fraternities—indeed all facets of social life and experience—are arrayed along a continuum of symbolic meaning. Tool-making is symbolic and unique to men. It is mankind's peculiar ability to symbolize that generated language in pre-historic times and so thrust man up from his ape ancestors and set him on the road to culture-building.

We have been talking of culture as a generic force in the human condition. The term has also been used to refer to place-time entities—Zuni culture, Hopi culture, Hottentot culture, and the like. In this sense, cultures can be compared and studied in terms of their characteristic ideational, value, and belief systems, their normative systems, and their technological features. Essentially we are differentiating between "culture" as the most inclusive and unique characteristic of mankind and "a" culture, such as *Mohawk or Arunta,* which relates specifically to a unique culture system in time and place. The former refers to the cumulative symbolic, linguistic, ideational, normative, and technological reality which began more than a million years ago. The latter refers to the specific forms in which these primary units appear in various parts of the world, past or present—Iroquois marriage patterns, Bushman arrows, Samoan dancing, American automobiles circa 1930, Eskimo gods, Dobu incantations, and Kwakiutl status competition.

The characteristics which we have identified with culture do not seem to be found, in any appreciable way, among the lower animal orders. Apes apparently have all of the vocal apparatus for speech, but they lack the symbolic element from which speech can be derived. Although there are some primitive forms of *tool use* among the apes, there is nothing like the complex of *tool making* and tool development found among human beings in all specific cultural settings. We are not implying here that cultural reality can be reduced to psychological reality but suggest, rather, that the ability to symbolize is the primary quality or condition of men in making culture a possibility. From that potential an incredible variety of cultural traditions has developed throughout the world.

But why culture? What does it do—is it necessary? The answer would seem to be a strong yes. For without a cultural tradition human life—social life—would be impossible. To get to the crux of the issue, without culture human association could not endure, society would have no form, and human interdependence, which is the key to social reality, would collapse.

Recall that two major components of culture are a system of basic ideas and a system of norms, rules and guides of conduct. Each culture, in the ideational dimension, answers the great questions. What is life . . . time . . . beauty . . . death . . . ? Who are we and what are we doing in this place? What is good? What is justice? Why must I do this? And so the fundamental dialogue goes on, but each culture supplies the answers. Reality is defined and explained and the human actors are comforted.

NORMS

Not only does the culture system surround the society with an atmosphere of ideational and value justification but it is also important in setting up a system of normative guides which facilitates social interaction. The norms filter the major ideational pronouncements into a system of conduct. They define and give form to relationships among the actors.

If men were bees, culture would be unnecessary because the primary relationships in the community would be determined by biology. But men have no powerful instinctive or biogenic forces which insistently shape their social order. It is culture, therefore, that provides the normative stability which permits human beings to carry on their lives. The norms of one society may say, "Men will remove their hats when attending religious services." Another society or even subgroup norm may say, "Men will cover their heads when attending religious services." Social norms define more than just the relatively trivial expectations of everyday social life. These norms—sexual rights, privileges, taboos, the "legitimacy" of the newborn child, the relationship of parent to child, wife to husband, the relationships between the generations—define the critical relationships upon which the perpetuation of society is based. Norms, thus, may vary from one cultural setting to another—but the *function of culture* remains the same. Norms define the character of social relationships, and the source of the definition lies in the ideational and value system of each culture.

Let us consider a social situation with which every student is familiar—the nine o'clock class on the first day of the fall semester. The student checks his program, makes sure of the building and room number. He starts early enough to get to his class on time, in this case 9:10. At 9:07 our student arrives at his classroom, opens the door, and steps inside. He notes that there are about twenty students already there. There is little conversation, and the students are sitting expectantly. A few more students enter and take seats. At 9:12 a middle-aged man appears, but rather than taking a seat with the students he drops a heavily loaded briefcase on the desk in front of the class and turns to the blackboard, on which he writes "John Smith, Sociology I." From his briefcase he takes out a sheaf of mimeographed pages and gives them to the student sitting closest to him. The student takes a course outline and hands the others to his closest neighbor. The outlines are quickly passed among the students.

The professor, meanwhile, has written on the blackboard the titles of five books, which the students copy into their notebooks. He finally says, "You now have copies of the course syllabus, which I will be going over in detail today. Are there any questions so far?" A student raises his hand, and the professor nods his head in the student's direction and says "Yes. . . ."

Thus, the course begins. An incredibly complex form of human activity is about to unfold, and yet it began quickly, simply, and efficiently.

The secret lies in social norms. Both students and professor understood the relationship through their grasp and internalization of the essential norms which gave meaning and definition to the situation. Note that the students took their seats and quietly waited for the professor. He, in turn, did the kind of things professors are *expected* to do—he spoke, he handed out the necessary course materials, he began to discuss the course. He indicated that he would entertain some questions. A student raised his hand in response. The professor recognized him in the accepted way. Meanwhile the class sat quietly, and so whatever professors and their students achieve in this kind of relationship was about to begin again. But it was the norms defining the collegiate classroom situation which made the relationship possible. And the sociological principles that apply to the classroom apply equally to any other social situation in any other cultural setting in this world.

Norms are rules, standards, expectations, or guides which define social situations. They are abstract patterns for specific conduct held in the mind of the actor. He acquired the normative expectation from others (parents, peers, teachers, etc.) but, once internalized, the normative pattern has become a component of the actor and is a viable dimension of the social personality. Norms not only define what a person should do (take off his hat in church) but also limit the content of interaction (it is not polite to tell the lady she has a run in her stocking). Furthermore, once internalized, the norms create in the person a sense of obligation, a feeling that he ought to act in a particular way or fashion.

Norms are essentially imaginary constructs, in the sense that the only objective indication that they exist is seen in the patterned behavior of persons in recurrent situations. That is to say, we can observe the external regularities of conduct and thus infer that social norms are the generating force. Furthermore, since there are significant differences (psychological-biological) among people and they in turn have differing social experiences in normative exposure and internalization, we may conclude that the normative order for any group is not a fixed or rigid thing. In short, each person's sense of the normative expectation is somewhat different from that of other persons.

For most norms there is a tolerable range of deviation, or some degree of personal interpretation. Take our classroom illustration as an example. Generally the norms say that students should be quiet and not engage in conduct that would disturb other students or the professor. Now, although the norms of the classroom define the general conduct of the student in this fashion, it is nevertheless generally accepted that students may whisper to a neighbor for a moment or two. When students become so noisy or their behavior so grossly disturbing that it becomes clear to the professor and other students that they are outside of the legitimate limits of normative expectation, another element of the normative order may intervene. The students who have violated the limits of normative tolerance may be *sanctioned.*

A sanction is simply the penalty exacted for violation of a norm. Since norms vary enormously in their significance and meaning in human society (Thou Shalt Not Kill; No Smoking), the extent and significance of the sanctioning vary equally. For the violation of the normative imperative of not killing people, the sanction exacted of the violator may be his own death, or imprisonment for life. For smoking in a "no smoking" normative situation the sanction may simply be the raising of an eyebrow or a look of displeasure by the sanctioning party. The sanction is some negative act—the withholding of friendship or approval, the loss of prestige, ridicule, fines, imprisonment, excommunication, expulsion, and so on.

Furthermore, whereas sanctions represent the power of negative thinking, normative conformity (the range of tolerable expression) usually rewards the actor positively. He is given social approval, honor, wealth, medals, power, authority, testimonial dinners, honorary degrees, etc., as an indication of general approbation accruing from adherence to the norms. The rewards are given not merely for conformity—the "average" response—but for symbolizing *the normative ideal* rather than merely duplicating or repeating the usual, expected pattern. The normative heroes—Distinguished Professor of the Year, the Congressional Medal of Honor winner, the Phi Beta Kappa member, the Nobel Prize winner, the Mother of the Year—are the embodiments of normative excellence and become models for the average to emulate and aspire to.

Norms that require certain actions are usually identified as *prescriptive* norms, and norms that forbid certain actions are *proscriptive.* Thus, we are *required* to take a driver's examination before we are issued a license. We are *forbidden* to drive without one. We are required to attend classes regularly. We are required to be at work at nine o'clock in the morning. We are required to register at the local Selective Service Board. We are required to attend religious services. We are forbidden to go into that house of religious worship. We are forbidden to enter a certain area of the ship. We are forbidden to exceed 60 miles per hour. We are forbidden to smoke.

Finally, in addition to the prescriptive and proscriptive character of norms, it should be noted that in particularly complex societies norms may vary from group to group, from one geographic region to another, from one business concern to another, from one religion to another, and so on. When norms apply to an entire society, they are generally called *communal norms,* such as the expectation that gentlemen will rise from their chairs when a lady enters the room. Norms which apply to a subgroup are called *associational* norms, such as the expectation that Catholics will regularly confess their sins before their priests and that Jewish men will cover their heads during religious services.

It is impossible to conceive of a social situation in which some form of normative expectation is not operating. Norms are the cohesive principle that unites individuals in social relationships. They insure order, stability, meaning, and form in the content of interaction. Without norms there could be no predictive element in social relationships. Mankind would be reduced to the suspicious and aggressive sniffing, the muted hostility and raised hackles characteristic of the jungle animal. Accordingly, norms define all possible and conceivable social situations within a culture system, and we can often recognize the normative principle behind many terms in everyday language. The following terms are commonplace indicators of normative design—etiquette, fashion, fad, laws, convention, ceremony, custom, ritual, taboo, statute, usage, regulation, law. There are subtle changes in meaning in the use of each of these terms, but we will here emphasize three ways in which norms may be classified: folkways, mores, and enacted laws.

Folkways

The terms *folkways* and *mores* became part of the American sociological tradition with the publication in 1907 of *Folkways,* by William Graham Sumner. Essentially Sumner was calling attention to the "ways of the folk"—the customs and practices found among all peoples that characteristically give order and stability to their social lives. Sumner suggests that the folkways may be likened to an atmosphere of custom into which all men are born and from which, accordingly, their lives are shaped. Like fishes, who are born into the ocean and whose lives adjust unconsciously to the currents, so do men adjust to the sea of custom surrounding them. And after a while, Sumner suggests, no one bothers to think about the folkways, or reflect about them—he simply responds to them.

Folkways are the countless normative imperatives that focus our behavior in our daily activities. They are the customs and standardized expectations that facilitate interaction. They are the durable and expected practices not required by law or any other institutional group. So white-collar workers wear white collar and ties to work and blue-collar workers go tieless. Well-mannered gentlemen open doors for ladies, and students sit politely mute while the professor wades through a dull lecture.

Since the folkways are the normal practices expected in everyday life, the sanctions they carry are relatively painless and inconsequential. An informal expression of normative displeasure from an actor integrated with the norm may be all that is required to move the deviant or slacker back on the path to conformity: "Now, if the gentlemen in the rear row will stop their talking, we shall get on with the explanation of this formula. . . ." "What's the matter, Charlie, don't you have a jacket and tie? Everybody's *dressed* but you." "Where were you brought up—in a barn? This place is a mess." "Didn't you know? Everybody is supposed to bring a bottle. . . ." And in a hippie colony, "Hey man, look at old Sam. He's cut his hair and shaved off his beard. Sam, you goin' square?"

Mores

Whereas folkways are the glue that holds a social structure together and gives definition to the countless and necessary forms of social intercourse, the mores constitute those essential norms that form the very core of the normative order. The term *mores* is derived from the Latin word meaning *customs*, but Sumner implies something more important than customary practice. He writes that a *mos* (singular) was believed to be essential for the welfare of the group. Mores, therefore, comprise those powerful norms that support the very base of a society's social structure. They are those expectations, those patterns, those relationships that *must* be fulfilled and met. They consist of those usages and practices that are regarded as "God-given," so utterly essential to the welfare of the group that their violation brings down on the head of the violator the most powerful sanctions.

When a *mos* is violated, the society's collective reality has been mortally damaged and it must seek to restore the structure of these primary relationships. Whereas the violation of a folkway arouses criticism and concern, the violation of a mos arouses horror and repugnance. The mores demand a powerful sense of moral obligation and they carry, as Sumner says, their own justification. The mores (from the standpoint of the mores) are not to be rationally reflected upon or examined from an objective point. In fact, the mores are not to be consciously thought about at all. They are best left to their virtually unconscious and subliminal unfolding in the actions of the actor.

Although the mores in time may serve as the basis for written law, even when they remain unwritten they govern our lives today in many critical ways. For example, in most of the states, with the exception of the hard-core South, there are no laws, preventing interracial marriage. And even there the laws prohibiting such marriages are currently being tested in the courts for their constitutionality. In New York state, for example, there is no law preventing marriage between the races. But, although the law cannot prevent such marriages, the mores for certain subgroups (and subcultures) can and do. What would be the typical reaction of an upper-middle-class, Anglo-Saxon, suburban family to the sudden announcement from their son that he has married a Negro? Although the intensity of the attitudes and values regarding interracial marriage varies from group to group, it is probably safe to predict that the reaction of many conservative families to this situation would be a combination of sadness, anger, and humiliation, and very possibly the dramatic expulsion of the normative deviant from the family.[1]

The same kind of general, if less dramatic reaction, might occur if the son had announced he was a Communist. Again, there is no law against being a Communist in the United States, but such an affiliation would violate the political mores of many groups. Finally, subgroup mores would be similarly disrupted by the small town, middle-class girl bringing her illegitimate baby to be reared within her immediate family or the son proclaiming atheism within his family of devout Catholics.

Enacted Law

It is often assumed by the culturally naive that nonliterate peoples live in a state of continual internal violence and anarchy. "Civilization" is known, they apparently believe, only among the "advanced" Western nations. Nothing could be further from the truth. Actually nonliterate peoples live in highly normative circumstances and, indeed, probably exist under greater normative control than persons living in the "civilized" West. The inexorable power of the mores and folkways, of convention and ceremony, of taboos and fixed usage, of

[1]This theme was explored a few years ago in the film, "Guess Who's Coming to Dinner?" However, the parents of the white girl in the film were much more liberal and tolerant in this situation than would be the "typical" white, upper-middle-class family.

ritual and the "cake of custom," in nonliterate cultures has no parallel in the democratic, urban, industrial West. Although the folkways still shape the character of our lives in countless ways, the sheer complexity of urban-industrial society is such that social order cannot be left to the informal vagaries of customary law—the normative design of nonliterate cultures.

Customary law and informal social controls are functional to small tribal communities. Word of mouth, the almost total social visibility of each actor in the entire spectrum of community events, and the unyielding weight of public normative consensus are sufficient to maintain the essential forms of social structure. But when cities arose, as they did for the first time in human history around 3500 B.C. in the fertile river valleys of the Tigris and Euphrates in Mesopotamia, customary law yielded to enacted law. From small and homogeneous Neolithic villages, cities became large, dense population centers characterized by a growing heterogeneity and complexity of structure. Increased specializations of skills and division of labor continued to draw migrant peoples from the hinterlands into the cities. It was inevitable that institutions of formal control should arise in which the essential normative needs of the community could be articulated through governance and the polity. In short, enacted laws, a judiciary, a court system, and a system of rationalized authority and power emerged out of the evolving functional requirements of the early cities. Enacted and rationalized law, formal social controls, *supplemented* the mores and folkways. Indeed, the most critical mores, folkways, customs, conventions, and practices served as the basis of the ancient penal and civil codes as they were written into enacted or rationalized law in the early cities. From that point on, of course, enacted law has become a major vehicle for normative integration and control.

The emerging enacted laws and formal social controls (replacing customary law and informal controls) had to be articulated in a vehicle whose essential function to the collectivity was social order, solidarity, and the integration of the total community. That vehicle, or institutional complex, we now identify as the state—the ultimate principle of governmental authority and power. It is the state, the idea of sovereign, independent power that stands behind the formalization of government, which emerges almost simultaneously with the early cities. Indeed, these early cities of ancient times are often identified by the term *polis*—city-state. It is at this juncture of social development that political science, with its concern with the basis and foundations of government, shares a concern with the human past along with history and sociology.

THE SOCIAL RELATIONSHIP

There are two essential elements to any social relationship: (1) two or more actors and (2) normative definition. Recall that by "actor" we are referring to the socialized dimension of the person—that facet of the personality that has been shaped and molded through cultural experience. In order to grasp the primary social reality of the social relationship we should examine it in its most elementary and simplest form.

You have engaged in many social relationships in the past twenty-four hours—at home, at college, or possibly at work. We hope to deal eventually in this book with all of these relationships and social forms, but for the moment try to think of the most primitive, even transitory, relationship in which you engaged in the past twenty-four hours. It must involve yourself and at least one other, and social norms must define, limit, or give definition to the interaction.

Take, for example, the last time you walked through your neighborhood or your college campus. The paths and walkways were filled with students and, as you walked along, possibly to your next class or the library, you saw a familiar face in the crowd. Now, what did you do? As the familiar face got within ten or fifteen feet you said something like "Whaddoyasay?" And the face smiled briefly and said "Howzitgoin'?" And if you didn't have much time, it might have been simply "Hi!" "Hi!"

In the "Hi—Hi phenomenon" we have one of the most common everyday experiences and yet one illustrative of a uniquely human and incredibly meaningful social event. Now generally, at least within Western culture (and this may also be culturally universal, with a few exceptions) it is necessary to recognize and respond, in some way, to people we know. The norms say it is impolite simply to walk stonily past someone without some indication of recognition. The prescriptive norm says: "Acknowledge" the other person. But the circumstance of walking to your next class (or anywhere you have something else to do) indicates that you do not have a great deal of time, or possibly desire, to talk. So society has developed all sorts of short greetings that simply acknowledge recognition and then the two actors are gone.

There is another quality to this relationship—the norms have given it a *high degree of predictability*. In the social relationship, the actors *take each other into account*, and they share a mutual *definition of the situation*. They respond largely to the expectations of the other.

A marvelous normative alchemy has enabled two human beings in a brief encounter to share a mutual definition of the situation and promptly respond to it and to each other's expectations. It all lasted less than a second, but in that simple social act lies the foundation of the more complex society.

We can illustrate this process further by asking what would have happened if either actor had not responded in the way the norms say he should respond. For example, many times during the day people will greet you by saying, "How are you?" This common greeting carries with it the *implicit assumption that you will not say how you are!* When people ask you how you are, particularly in the sense that we have been using it here (not in the way your doctor uses it), you reply by saying something like "Fine" or "Very well, thank you." And that is all there is to it—both actors share the same and necessary definition. What would have happened if you had responded to the greeting by saying, "Oh, not very well, thank you"? The chances are the other actor would have smiled and said "That's good." Quite probably he would not even have heard the unpredicted reply.

The principle underlying the social relationship suggests that all relationships, since they are defined normatively, and since the normative definitions are shared by the actors, yield up a high degree of predictability. Social relationships are "understood" by the actors, who respond to the cultural and normative forces which shape the relationship and give it form. The jungle animal may growl and snarl, but the human being caught up in the symbolic-cultural-social context "understands" and so he smiles as he says "Howareyadoin?"

"Fine" comes the immediate response from the socialized man. And behind the quick smile may be a throbbing headache and real worry over a hundred personal problems.

STATUS AND ROLE

There seem to be normative definitions in all facets and phases of our social lives. Whether we are aware of it or not, the norms subtly guide our conversation and even the content of our thinking. They move our conversation away from certain "sensitive" areas so that the interaction goes smoothly and both actors enjoy a high degree of predictability. If, for example, a person has a particularly large wart on his nose, and that wart seems to push all other matters out of your mind, you certainly *don't* say, "My, that is quite a wart you have there!" The norms, the expectations, *proscribe*, in this case, mention of the subject, and so you may mumble something about the weather. But although an atmosphere of normative expectation weighs down on all actors and although norms give definitions to even inconsequential social situations within a socio-cultural system, they are not random or idiosyncratic. They are organized and logically interconnected. Indeed, norms may coalesce and form a composite and interrelated set of prescriptions, imperatives, and definitions. When a series of norms is built around a recurrent identity in a social system they form a new reality of their own. The concept that refers to a distinctive set of rights, duties, obligations, expectations, usages, etc., we identify as *a social status*.

Status

A status represents the smallest unit of a social structure. It is, in effect, a set of potentials for interaction. The character of the inter-action is established by the distinctive normative imperatives which give the status its unique form. Actors occupy statuses and through this social vehicle enter into relationships and interaction with other actors occupying other statuses. This may seem a very mechanical way of look-ing at social relationships, but unquestionably the most critical rela-tionships that human beings have with other human beings occur only through status positions.

To illustrate the significance of this idea, ask yourself what status positions you occupied in the last twenty-four hours. Previously we examined in the "Hi—Hi" situation, the most minute kind of social relationship. We are now going much further than a fragmentary social experience in which normative definition applies. We are now consider-ing the major positions, the modal social identities you have occupied within a short period of time. A status consists of interrelated prescrip-tive and proscriptive norms which characteristically cluster about a rather major element of social activity. As our question indicates, you occupy many statuses within your lifetime or indeed within a twenty-four hour period of your life. As you move from group to group in the course of a day, you shift from one social activity identity to another, in each case entering into a new position, with new normative defini-tions which guide the character of your relationships with others.

What statuses have you occupied? Well, depending on sex, you have been either a male or female today, either a teen-ager or an adult. This may surprise you somewhat, but even sexual differences (which have an obvious biological dimension) are much more elaborated in human society through the vehicle of status.

You have occupied the position of male-female, but you also have been other "persons." More than likely you have been a "son" or "daughter" in your relationships recently. You may possibly have been an "employee." You may have been a "boy friend" or "girl friend" in a relationship not long ago. And at this very moment you are engaged in a form of status behavior—you are reading a sociology text, in all probability as a consequence of a "prescriptive" norm attached to your status as a "student."

The significance of status positions in human society is that the norms which define the position make it possible for actors to move in and out of groups while the relational system within the group remains relatively stable and orderly. Complex normative imperatives are attached to status positions and subsequently are linked to other statuses within the social system. Through a combination of statuses with their host of normative injunctions, the most complex forms of association endure and function. Consider the great corporations or religious and military organizations in the United States. Individually, they may involve millions of human beings. But since each actor occupies his position within the system—i.e., "sergeant," "Bishop," "Vice President in Charge of Product Development," "communicant," "relay assembly worker," "sales clerk," "brigadier general,"—they "know their place" and can perform within the system. Together, status positions enable complex as well as small, simple groups to exist and function.

In effect, status positions which are articulated within the context of social groups act to focus the normative definitions that we noted in simple, tertiary social relationships. This focusing brings to the interactive and relational level between actors the same quality of prediction, definition, and order that are necessary for an enduring and stable structure of relationships. The actor derives predictability, security, and social identity, which are necessary at the psychological level. The group is also assured that its essential form and structure continue. The critical nexus in which both psychological and sociological needs are fulfilled is thus maintained. That is the ideal situation, but in many situations the actor is psychologically strained because of excessive and even contradictory demands of the social system. Recall Durkheim's concept of *anomie*. This is a condition of normative breakdown, in which the actor is no longer integrated into the structure, the status system no longer holds him, and consequently he suffers the psychological pain of hopelessness, anxiety, and alienation.

Role

If status is a unit of social structure defined by abstract norms, role is the sensory phenomenon which is actually perceived. Role is the dynamic integration of the potentials of a social status by an actor who puts the status into play. A status is a unit of social structure; it is an abstract set of possibilities defined by norms. Status may be viewed as the "positional" unit located within a social system and linked to other actors occupying other statuses. Role, on the other hand, consists of the *process* dimension of status—that is, what the actor *does in his relations* with others within the system. Status represents the normative possibilities; role represents what the actor actually does with these possibilities. Finally, the distinction between status and role focuses on the two basic perspectives involved in any interactive situation. When an actor views himself as an "object" of orientation for himself and other actors (norms, rights, duties, etc.) the *status* dimension prevails. But when the actor orients to others, when he *acts* (and does not serve as object), he is playing a role.

When an actor occupies a position and begins to utilize it, he is playing a role—a role determined by the normative design of the position. Perhaps an analogy would be useful here. An automobile, like a status position, has certain possibilities. Now, note that even in the case of one automobile as a discrete entity, let us say a 1967 Ford LTD, there is a distribution of possibilities. It has a range of speed. It has a characteristic ride. The time it takes to come to a complete stop from a certain speed is statistically different from that of other cars. Like a status, the car has possibilities—it can't float and it can't fly, but over a hard-surfaced highway it will get you where you are going. Ten people (actors) will probably take this identical car and drive it in ten different ways.

A status position may be likened to that car: it has a potential for relationships, and ten different actors may "operate" it in ten different ways. The norms, of course, will determine what the range of "tolerable" limits may be, just as the technology of the car limits what can be done with it. Thus we may liken status to the empty automobile, which can do certain things but not other things, and role is the way an individual actually utilizes the position within the group structure.

Although useful analytic comparisons have been made regarding the distinctions between status and role, from this point on when we use the term *role* we shall be referring to the status-role combination. For our purposes, no further conceptual distinctions need be made. Finally, it should be noted again that status/role is a unit of structure, primitively analogous to the particle in physics and the cell in biology. They (status/role) are attributes of the actor only insofar as they have been internalized from the organized sociocultural system.

THE PATTERN VARIABLES

Actors in complex societies may play out hundreds of roles within a lifetime; nevertheless, there are regularities and patterns in the normative form which give each role its distinctive social character. It is sociologically useful to distinguish at least five variations among role patterns. In essence, there are five fundamental distinctions in all social roles, and within each variation there are two possibilities. We can identify each of these dichotomous possibilities as *the value of a pattern variable*. The pattern variables within social roles that we shall consider are:

1. *Affectivity—Neutrality*

2. *Universalism—Particularism*

3. *Diffuseness—Specificity*

4. *Quality—Performance*

5. *Self-orientation—Collectivity-orientation*

AFFECTIVITY—NEUTRALITY: This dichotomy of patterns deals with the "gratification—discipline" dilemma in human relations. The primary issue is whether a role permits or indeed encourages the expression of *affect*, emotion, or feeling. Certain roles (husband-wife) permit and even encourage the expression of love, anger, fear, etc. in a free and open manner. In short, there is personal gratification and expression permitted within the role. On the other hand, other roles carry with them the injunction of *neutrality*. They require emotional discipline and stress self-control. As the child grows he learns to differentiate between those roles in which personal gratification and affect expression are permitted and those in which they are not. He may, for example, expect his teacher to respond to his needs for love and personal attention and to be acceptant of his demand for affect gratification and response. In time he learns that the teacher expects him to "control himself," that it is unmanly to cry and that he must take his disappointments like a "little soldier."

UNIVERSALISM—PARTICULARISM: In certain roles, relations are guided almost exclusively by formal, impersonal, legalistic, objectified, rationalized, and universal codes and standards. Other relationships are guided predominantly by the particular positions which individuals occupy in a system of relationships. When relationships are shaped predominantly by particular positions, the pattern variable underlying the relationship is *particularistic*. A daughter's relationship to her mother is not shaped by an objectified *universalistic* code of motherhood but by the unique and particularized relationships which build up between two people in an intimate and enduring social relationship. This is not to say that there are not regularized, normative expectations in the relationship between mother and daughter. It is simply that they treat each other as particular and distinct persons and not merely formal role models.

A good deal of the chore of growing up may be seen in the transference of the pattern variables from affect to neutrality and from particularism to universalism. In his early years the child's relationships with siblings and parents are heavily weighted toward affect and particularism. A childhood memory recounted by a student illustrates both. At the age of ten or eleven, Bob was caught up in the creative adventure of writing stories. Once, after spending the better part of an afternoon writing, he took his finished product to his grandmother for her judgment. After she had read the story she said, "Bob, that is one of the best stories I have ever read. You have a great talent for writing."

Bob was so pleased and gratified by his grandmother's judgment of his work (highly particularistic) that he put his arms around the old lady and kissed her in the emotional spontaneity of the joyful moment (affect response). Later, and with great expectations, he took his story to his elementary school teacher. After she had read it carefully she said, "Well, Robert, it is not really too bad, in spite of the poor spelling and awkward sentence structure. You certainly tried, and the plot is rather interesting even if your characters are not clearly drawn. You must really ask Diane Rodgers to show you the story she wrote last week—she and Alice Simpkins are doing very well. Although, I'm afraid, this class isn't as good as my group last year."

The young author was so deflated by the objective and universalistic judgment of his teacher that he was close to tears (affect response) but strove to maintain the emotional neutrality demanded by the situation. In time he came to realize that his grandmother's judgment of his writing was based purely on her particularistic response to him—as her grandson and a member of the family. He was a unique person and she responded to him that way. In time, Bob came to accept the teacher's hard and universalistic judgment of his work—the rules of spelling, grammar, syntax, and simple prose. He accepted the discipline of scholarship, and eventually produced a work that his teacher read to the whole class. In a real sense, that accomplishment and the pride Bob felt for it represented a shift in his childish need for particularism and affect to an intellectual understanding of those roles and relationships governed by universalism and affect neutrality.

DIFFUSENESS—SPECIFICITY: Some roles are formally limited in the degree, type, and kind of interaction they make available to their occupants. Other roles are "diffuse" in that normative regulation and definition leave much of the interaction to the personal interpretation of the actor.

Roles such as sales clerk-customer, doctor-patient, teacher-student, judge-convicted felon are highly *specific* in normative definition. The actors follow out quite formally defined relationships. On the other hand, the roles of friend, son, mother, daughter are relatively diffused, in that many of their obligations, rights, and privileges are never clearly or formally articulated. In a sense, diffuseness as a pattern variable refers to a role that is open-ended—the dimensions of the role are vague and flexible, offering a wide range of individual response and interpretation. On the other hand, a pope, a general, a municipal judge, a vice president in charge of retail sales, all constitute roles of high normative specificity. Generally speaking, specificity of role expectation increases as a consequence of the size and the internal complexity of social organization. As we shall see, as roles are institutionalized, the quality of specificity increases.

ACHIEVEMENT—ASCRIPTION: A role may possess a certain quality if another actor reacts to some objective characteristic of the role, such as age, sex, race, or family membership. That is to say, some roles are assigned (*ascribed*) to an individual as a result of a characteristic that is beyond his control. In this fashion, status/role characteristics may be assigned to a person on the basis of sex (male-female, boy-girl, man-woman) or age (infant, child, youth, teen-ager, young adult, middle-aged man, elderly woman) or race (white, black, yellow, etc.).

Society, in fact, has certain expectations of individuals who occupy positions fixed through ascription. For example, as young adults we are expected to dress and behave in certain ways. Generally an attractive twenty-four-year-old woman (according to the current norms of fad and fashion) will be expected to dress in a certain way. And if fashion dictates that an evening gown for such a young woman be so designed as to properly emphasize the unique qualities of the feminine form, most of us would approve. That is to say, the ideational and nor-

mative systems define the nature of feminine beauty and then proscrip-
tively and prescriptively say how it is to be publicly displayed. Beauty
is appreciated in all societies no matter how differently it may be defined.

Now let us take that same revealing evening gown and have a
woman of seventy-five wear it while cavorting in a night club just like
our beautiful twenty-four-year-old. What would be the reaction of most
people? Probably negative. They would be "disgusted" with the old
woman's behavior. As an "old lady" she is *ascribed* a role. She may be
given respect, honor and attention, but she is no longer young, and she
may no longer claim the role of a young woman.

Whereas some roles may be fixed by ascription—factors and
forces beyond the control of the actor—some roles may be *achieved*
through performance. A particular *characteristic* of the person is no
longer a factor, but his *performance* is. Although as children almost all
of our roles are fixed by ascription and by our objective characteristics
(age, sex, caste), when we pass through adolescence the emphasis on role
attainment shifts to achievement and performance. Your occupational
roles will reflect performance rather than ascription, although certainly
sex will intervene to some extent (there are many female school teachers, very few female research chemists). Who you marry will depend on
what you *do*, what you *achieve*, how you *perform*.

SELF-ORIENTATION—COLLECTIVITY-ORIENTATION: In some roles the
actor is quite free to pursue his own personal ends without a great
deal of regard for the interests and, indeed, feelings of others who are
also bound into the relationship. However, other roles carry the expectation that the actor must subordinate his own interests for the benefit
of the group or relationship. If you are cast in the role of house buyer
and you are being shown a series of houses by a real estate agent, you
generally know that the agent wants to earn a commission by selling
you a house. As a perceptive member of society you realize that the
agent may be putting his own interests (the commission) over your
interests (a satisfactory house) by encouraging you to buy a house that
has many defects. The agent in his role is responding to self-orientation
rather than collectivity-orientation. Thus, you don't really expect salesmen to "tell you the truth," and you are usually on your guard in the
buyer-seller relationship.

There are other relationships, however, in which the actors
subordinate their idiosyncratic needs and ends in order to respond to a
role obligation that is collectivity oriented. The family as a group produces a "we" feeling among the members. They are a collectivity and,
although each member may pursue his own needs and interests, these

are not expected to weaken or destroy the family as a collectivity—as a group. Hence, the family induces collectivity orientation among its members. As an employee, on the other hand, you may constantly weigh your own interests rationally against the interests of the company, and if the company seems to treat you unfairly you may simply resign. It is not nearly so easy to "resign" from the family because interests are not so clear and one must not act selfishly or, indeed, rationally in terms of family relationships. The collectivity sense is strong on this level, whereas in business relationships self-interest is obvious.

Some roles, of course, represent a combination of the pattern variables. If we look into the structure of the family as a social system, we will note that roles generally emphasize the pattern variables of affect, particularism, diffuseness, and collectivity orientation. In business and political institutions beyond the family system, roles are generally characterized by affect neutrality, specificity, universalism, performance, and self-orientation.

THE ACTION ELEMENTS

Up to this point we have discussed certain primary considerations in the analysis of social reality—the actor, culture and the normative order, role/status and how these components flow into elementary social relationships. The sociological perspective, the impact of the external social environment and what that environment consists of, have been the central concern. Perhaps by now you have come to feel that the individual is utterly passive and completely dwarfed by the demanding and uncompromising forces of society and culture. The relationship of the individual to the social structure, however, remains a major question. How do the personal ends that each of us pursue in our private lives relate to the needs and interests peculiar to society itself? In short, while each man directs his behavior toward certain goals (success, happiness, salvation, wealth, love, power, prestige, etc.) how are these individual ends related or tied into the massive social order outside of each "unique" individual?

When an intelligent and perceptive student starts to make his way through an introductory sociology course, somewhere in his intellectual odyssey he may discover the "reality of society"—much in the manner of Emile Durkheim's notion of society as a *sui generis* order of events. The student stops seeing individuals but suddenly has insight into the bonds, the relationships, the systems of interdependence that constitute the reality of sociological study. Individuals disappear, relationships between actors loom into focus, and a major intellectual discovery is the consequence.

Up to this point in our discussion we have not really set out the critical conceptions which illuminate the final reality of society itself. And, unfortunately, that ultimate discovery is still a chapter away. But it might be appropriate to examine a few of the basic questions dealing with the relationship of the solitary human being, even as an actor, within the framework of the social environment.

It perhaps goes without saying that, while human beings are conscious, self-aware, motivated, and goal-striving organisms, social structures and, indeed, social reality are not. That is to say, human society is *not* a system of self-awareness, does not have personal goals, and literally does not collectively think. In the past there was much speculation about the "organic analogy" between human society and living organisms. Although there are some interesting comparisons and similarities, only human beings aspire, hope, think, strive, and direct themselves toward personal goals and ends they hope to achieve. Society, on the other hand, is a reality that emerges only through association among human beings; it is, as we shall subsequently see, the ultimate structure of relationships. That structure, if it is to endure, has needs peculiar to itself. Thus, human beings must somehow manage to gratify their own biological and psychological needs, but if they are to associate permanently with each other, they must also respond to certain requirements of collective life.

We have already taken note of the normative system, which consists essentially of definitions affecting the manner in which interpersonal relationships will occur. But note that society exists only through human beings; its reality consists of the bonds between persons. However, the basic biological and psychological needs of persons cannot be completely frustrated by the collective order. For example, human beings must consume food in order to live. No society can refuse to accommodate this biological requirement. All a sociocultural system can do (through the normative order) is to define what is to be eaten, when, by whom, and how.

Similarly, there are certain psychological needs that must be met. No society can develop a relational system that is so damaging to the personality that the actors within the system are turned into a horde of shaking neurotics who cannot function. The strains and demands of the normative order cannot destroy the personality system of the human being. There must be, therefore, a reciprocal tension between the biological-psychological requirements of the individual and the functional needs of the social system. If the normative system of the society is poorly designed, if it is contradictory and dysfunctional, individuals will break down and will not perform the necessary social functions. On the other hand, if human beings become so completely caught up in the gratification of biological and psychological needs that they neglect to maintain the viable structure of their social relationships (a condition similar to *anomie*), then their social life will decline, fade, go into eclipse, lose vitality, and, indeed, disappear.

The term "social action" is often used to identify the particular patterning of acts from the subjective perception of a solitary actor. That is to say, "the action frame of reference" focuses into the particular social acts of an actor as he goes about his daily life. Social action refers to the behavior of a solitary individual and the manner in which a subjective act becomes linked with other actors similarly engaged in the action reference. Now, each "social act" consists of four discrete units— (1) the *actor*, (2) the *goal* or *end* he strives for, (3) the *means* he employs to achieve his goal, and (4) the *conditions* or obstacles he encounters along the way. *An act* may consist of so simple a thing as picking up a pen in order to write a letter. But although the pen was for a short while the *goal* of an act, it soon became one of the *means* to write the letter. The letter was a goal for a while, but then it became a *means* to communicate. Social acts therefore range along a continuum of ends, becoming means to other ends, which in turn may be means for even more remote and longer-range goals.

Our personal lives are a tissue of means-ends decisions which underlie the context of our social actions. Every actor's behavior constitutes a web of interrelated separate acts, all fused together by the long-range personal goals. Some acts are purely *technical*, in that the end sought is simply a means to another end. In other situations, the actor must choose from between competing ends. That is to say, since the means he has available to gratify his ends are limited, he must choose which end is the most important. For example, a student has so much *time*, and time, in a sense, is part of the means. He may use his time to study for an exam, or he may use his time to be with his girl friend. The student must make an *economic* decision. He must *allocate* his scarce resources (time, energy, money, etc.) to those ends he considers the most important. At this level of the action frame of reference, the decision is no longer technical (which means are the most efficient) but which goal is the most important in the long run.

An entire lifetime can be given over to the question as to what are the primary or ultimate goals that human beings seek. Is the ultimate goal "security" or "libidinous pleasure" or "response, security, and recognition"? Or are the final goals that motivate people really social in their origin? Is it "power" we seek, or "salvation" or "money" or "status"?

Certainly we cannot answer those questions here, and possibly they never will be answered. But in the posing of the question lies an interesting sociological revelation. Some of the personal ends that men seek for themselves may, at the same time, force the actor into roles whose normative definitions ultimately are *functional* to the collective reality. Indeed, an act which may be nonrational on the level of the action frame of reference (the level of the actor) may be *functional* on the level of society. Recall that social action involves four primary units—the actor, the end, the means, the conditions. Because an actor strives to achieve an *end*, in spite of the conditions, through the utilization of the available *means*, there is the element of *rationality* in all human behavior.

In an attempt to achieve ends there is always the possibility an actor will act in a nonrational manner. If, for example, he is unclear as to his goal, he may not be able to adopt efficient means to achieve the goals. He may be unaware of the available means to achieve his goals, or normative definitions may not permit him to utilize the most efficient means to achieve them. For example, if an actor has a need for money, he has several legitimate means available to get it. He may *work* for it. He may *borrow* it. But he may not (normative restrictions) *steal* it. Now, note that it may be *rational* to steal it because this may be the most efficient way for the actor to achieve his end. But the norms deny him the utilization of what may be purely rational personal behavior.

Although the act of theft may be rational for the actor, the norms are designed to maintain a balance of orderly, predictive, and functionally integrative stabilizing relationships *between* actors. A society whose essential economy is predicated universally on theft and violence would be functionally unable to survive over any period of time. It is true that some societies virtually approve theft under certain circumstances and by certain classes of the population, and the norms are designed to accommodate to this. But a society characterized by continual and widespread theft by all persons under all circumstances would be patently impossible. So although theft might be viewed as a rational means for the actor, it would be dysfunctional on the level of society. Thus, from a sociological point of view, nonrational forms of behavior in terms of the individual's action frame of reference may contribute to the functional integration of relationships on the level of the group, community, and society itself.

This is a critical point which many scholars have failed fully to appreciate. Freud, for example, was generally critical of the psychological impact of religion. He felt that belief in God was essentially the pursuit of illusion and unreality. From a psychological point of view, Freud, and indeed many psychologists, wanted man to be objective, rational, and "in touch with reality." The "God illusion" was a form of mass fantasy and collective escape. Furthermore, religious ideology imbued in Western society a particularly strong sense of guilt when the strict moral codes were broken. In this way, Western man's preoccupation with "good versus evil" and his overriding sense of guilt and sin were destructive, Freud argued, to psychological health and a realistic sense of the world. Freud, therefore, was generally critical of the role of religion, not only because it created guilt in men but because the ultimate referents of religion—gods, deities, supernatural forces—were, in his view, simply unreal and false. Men caught up in religious events and behavior were, therefore, behaving in a nonrational way.

We will not pass judgment here on the validity of Freud's view of religion, but even if we accept his assertion of the essential nonrational facets of religion, may not religion and all that it entails be functional to the collective order? That is to say, even if the pursuit of supernatural states be judged as a nonrational act in terms of the actor, his behavior collectively with others in the religious context may be integrative on the societal level. In short, men who act to "save their souls" may be sustaining norms, beliefs, morality, ideas, values which aid in the stabilization and integration of the social order. In this fashion, the pursuit of an ultimate, personal end (salvation), which certainly plays a major role in the lives of literally billions of human beings today, becomes a necessary condition of social life—the stability of the human community.

This, then, is the answer to the question posed earlier. Men select personal ends, ultimate ends which they seek to fulfill in their own private sphere of action. All of our lives are spent in the selection of legitimate means to move us on to the acquisition of ends, some immediate and others more final and ultimate. In these ultimate ends which we seek—*honor* from the community, or *power*, or *wealth* or the salvation of our souls—we almost invariably engage in behavior (the job, prayer, community service, etc.) which is normatively approved through the status/role structure. Therefore, in the pursuit of what appears to be individual ends, we contribute to the major social forms of the community: familial, economic, governmental, and religious associations. Each of the major areas of social activity sustains an "end" which only the actor can internalize and seek after, but in the quest, in the actualization of behavior oriented toward the personal goal (salvation, wealth, power, love, family relationships) human beings in collectivities sustain the functional necessities of society.

Not all acts, however, are to be regarded as ultimately functional—i.e., integrative and stabilizing. Indeed, some scholars have argued that "dysfunctions" (disruptive, anomic conditions, the loss of integration, etc.,) may also occur within the context of seemingly stabilizing social acts. For example, although religious institutions may be seen to be integrative, it has been pointed out that dysfunctions may accrue from such behavior as well. The crippling "guilt" which may damage personality on the psychological level is a case in point. Also, although religion may integrate the members of a particular denomination in complex industrial societies, the existence of many "religions" within the society may result in religious prejudice, parochialism, and hostility at the national level.

THE FORMS OF INTERACTION

Social relationships emerge through the primary associative units (norms, status/role) and are fused to the psychological element of predictability and anticipation. These basic units of relationships, moreover, occur in a broader context of *reciprocity*. That is to say, in mutual contact the participating parties expect that the ends which they individually seek will be furthered through the relationship. This is what reciprocity involves—both parties gain through mutual obligations, mutual and reciprocal statuses, means, and ends.

The term which best identifies the mutual and reciprocal character of social relationships is social interaction. The forms of interaction define the generic and recurrent contexts in which pluralities of actors enter into relationships. We shall discuss three of the major forms: conflict, competition, and cooperation. Through these three the primary forms and meaning of most social relationships can be seen.

Conflict

Because it seems so destructive, it may be surprising that conflict is regarded as a form of interaction, and yet there is ample evidence that conflict is a basic and recurring relationship between individuals and collectivities. Technically, conflict is a relationship in which the shared ends of a group (or the ends of an individual) are in total contradiction with the ends of another group or individual. In a sense the realization of group ends cannot take place as long as the other group exists. For example, on the level of the national society, the collective end of "national security" may be achievable only if another national society is eliminated. That is to say, neither society can have "security" as long as the other society exists as a threat.

War is an example of conflict at the national or tribal level. It is a relationship in which there is a relative absence of normative restraint. The object (the end) is the elimination or destruction of the existing social form of the opposite party. Although there are certain "rules of warfare," the intention of physical violence and the maximization of violence are the primary means to achieve the ends of conflict —destruction of the enemy.

There are other forms of conflict within societies which always make use of physical force. There is not a society in which on certain occasions people do not resort to force and violence. It takes place in the family (wife-beating), the school (fights between children), the factory (fights between workers), and neighborhoods (fights between neighbors). This form of conflict, however, is not the all-out maximization of destruction, as is warfare. The end of the gang fight may be simply to establish status, control, and priority over a "territory." The fight was symbolic in a sense, and the end was not to kill or completely destroy the "enemy."

Competition

Whereas conflict employs force and violence, competition as a generic form of interaction is limited to normatively approved means. Competition constitutes a relationship between parties in which a scarce end can be had by only one. The competitors are struggling to obtain a mutually desired goal, but the struggle is shaped by rules that both agree to observe. For example, two business concerns may be competitors in that they are struggling to dominate the same market, but the rules of economic competition establish the legitimate ways in which the two concerns may compete. They can lower prices, increase their advertising, or offer certain price advantages to the dealers and wholesalers. All of these are "normal" competitive techniques. They cannot, however, use violence on the salesman of the other company or threaten the dealers with bodily harm. Similarly, two boys may desire the same girl, but all is *not* fair in love and war. The boys can "wine and dine" the young lady, they can separately "turn on" all of the charm that they possess, but if one of the competitors should employ violence on the other to obtain his goal, he would have moved from competition to conflict. It is here that the law would intervene, for the normative expectations defining this sort of relationship would have been violated.

Although conflict and its accompanying violence develop within a social system only occasionally, there are many relationships within social groups that are competitive. Wherever there are scarce goals that cannot be shared, the possibility of conflict and competition exists. Furthermore, neither form of interaction is intrinsically harmful or destructive. Conflict, in the form of warfare, may help to integrate a society by uniting the subgroups into a cohesive whole. The free-enterprise system, which is at least classically or ideally competitive, has certainly helped make the United States a great economic power. Whether there are legitimate economic alternatives to private enterprise and the "competitive system" is not the issue here; in view of the high standard of living of American society, there is some justification to the pragmatic judgment that "it works."

The universality of conflict and competition as generic forms of social relationships can be illustrated by the family. Within the family system both forms can easily be seen. Physical violence erupting from a conflict situation occurs over and over again within the family. Siblings struggle for a common goal (a toy), and since neither is willing to share, a form of partial conflict (a fight) ensues. Husband and wife sometimes engage in physical violence; although the norms strongly disapprove of "wife-beating," the frequency with which it appears on court calendars suggests that it is a fairly common practice, particularly in the lower class and among some ethnic groups.

Psychologists have identified a form of struggle for parental affection as "sibling rivalry." There is just so much attention or love that a mother can give her children; in effect, there is not enough "mother to go around"—hence children can be rivals to a goal (mother love) that cannot be *exclusively* secured—hence struggle and competition for affection.

Cooperation

If competition and conflict involve struggle for goals that cannot be shared, cooperation is a form of relationship which the cooperating parties *share* in the goal. The family, as we have just noted, though occasionally lapsing into conflict and quite frequently involving competitive relations among the members, is essentially a cooperating group. That is, the entire system is devoted to goals which all members share. Not only is the father's salary raise a source of personal satisfaction to him (he got it through essentially competitive practices) but now the family may be able to afford a new house. All the members may co-operate economically to build the family's financial resources in order to obtain this goal, in which they will all share.

In most social relationships, between either individuals or groups, the two primary forms of interaction are competition and cooperation. There is always the struggle for scarce goals that cannot be shared. Indeed, some goals have meaning only if they are scarce and hard to come by. Status or social honor can have meaning only if there is not much of it around. To be "esteemed" means that someone else is less esteemed. Prestige is worth while only if somebody or something has less of it. A world of Cadillacs is meaningless in terms of status honor; there must be the Fords and Chevrolets for the Cadillac to base its claims on. In short, some things in life are necessarily scarce and must be competed for.

However, although competition runs through much of our social lives, so does cooperation. Indeed, to live in social groups and society, there must be collective goals that all can share in. Although we compete for grades, money, and girl and boy friends, we cooperate as well. In a classroom, for example, there is competition for grades; not everyone can get an *A*. But in spite of this, students cooperate with each other by remaining relatively quiet during the lecture, by sharing notes with a student who was absent, and by being generally supportive of the norms and statuses that facilitate learning within the classroom. Americans have been called a competitive people, but the very anatomy of our society is held firmly in place through mutual sharing and cooperation.

As we have previously noted, mutual orientations and expectations render predictable the character of the social relationship. Through norms and status/role, the actors have definition of the situation. However, the social relationship and the concept of predictability deal essentially with the psychological preparation of the actor. The forms of interaction (conflict, competition, cooperation) focus upon the broad contexts and generic processes in which most relationships occur between both individuals and collectivities. No matter what the relationship, it will contain elements of cooperation or competition, either singly or in combination.

Throughout this chapter we have been dealing with the elementary conceptual units around which basic social relationships emerge. The individual as an *actor* has internalized the *normative* order (mores, folkways, laws, customs, etc.), which through socialization has become a component of the personality system. A combination of actors, through normative mediation, enters into social relationships. These relationships are characterized by a high degree of predictability for the actors as they orient to the expectations of others. Because each actor occupies a status position and plays out a *role*, the normative expectations are even further formalized into given structural units of the social system. Although each person in his own lifetime seeks to fulfill and gratify a complex of private goals (happiness, salvation, wealth, power, etc.), he normally does so by availing himself of the institutionalized and legitimate means society makes available to him. When the actor plays out one of these roles as a means of achieving something that appears to be an exclusively "private" matter (an end viewed in the language of intended manifest function (see page 126), his behavior and that of other actors within the system may be contributing to the social welfare—economic production, governmental stability, normative integration.

Finally, these relationships occur through certain generic forms of interaction—conflict, competition, and cooperation. These three basic forms constitute the essential social processes through which relationships build and flow among human groups. Although conflict and competition were found in many social situations, cooperative relationships are essential for the survival of any group.

SOCIAL ROLES AND THE MEANS-ENDS FRAMEWORK:

An Illustration in Contemporary Race Relations

We can now examine, in terms of a major national concern, the utility and usefulness of two of the concepts we have just discussed. For the past decade there has been a literal "revolution" in race relations within the United States. Let us therefore consider the Negro in America from the vantage point of (1) status/role and (2) the means-end relationship.

Traditionally the role of the Negro, as a person and as a collectivity, has been fixed by the pattern variable of quality or ascription. The racial quality of the Negro—a physical condition of skin color, hair color and texture, facial characteristics, etc.—has locked him into a very rigid set of role expectations. Until the Civil War his role was that of "slave." He was a piece of property to be bought, used, and sold by the white owner. After the Civil War, the status of slave was legally abolished in the United States and for the next fifty or sixty years a new role emerged in which, again, the racial (ascriptive-quality) dimension was paramount in shaping the Negro's primary life chances.

In time, the Negro was fixed into a caste *stratum* in American society. The chief characteristic of caste is the lack of exit from it. This is to say, the Negro became a member of a caste, determined by race, from which he could not move. The ability of a caste system to lock persons within the structure was facilitated by the physical "visibility" of the Negro—a minority black race in a society dominated by whites.

Now, whereas the Negro was held to the confines of caste, the general American social structure (for whites) was an *open* class system. That is to say, the broad form of the American class system, as idealized by "the American Dream," permitted whites to "move up," to "become somebody," "to get ahead in the world," and to be "successful," whereas the Negro was bound to a life course fixed by the unyielding strictures of caste.

Note too, that although limitation of opportunity was not unique to the Negro—certainly the Irish, the Italians, the Jews, the Poles, and other European minorities were exposed to various forms of prejudice and discrimination—these white minorities had the opportunity to move up in the open class system and to assimilate into American society. The white minority member could lose his accent and his strange customs and eventually internalize American culture to the extent that he could participate, or at least try to, in the normative ideal of upward class mobility. He could at least attempt to actualize the American Dream of rags to riches through "hard work, initiative, and personal responsibility." The Negro, physically visible and bound to the limitations of caste, was held outside the class system and the dream of success.

The tightly knit normative world of the Southern Negro changed somewhat in the North. The northern black could go to the public schools with whites (mostly lower class); he could vote; and he had a wider range of job opportunities—in contrast to the South. The North, in short, gave to the Negro a wider spectrum of alternatives but, even so, the boundaries of the caste system operated in the Northern states almost as much as in the South. It is at this point—the wider range of alternatives yet within a system of caste—that the problem of discontinuities and contradictions of role expectations can be seen. In the North, the Negro was never entirely sure where he stood—at least in certain social situations that we shall illustrate.

In the South, until the Civil Rights movement, the Negro knew where he stood. The structuring of caste relations was so obvious, so overt, so clear, that the Southern Negro rarely had any doubt as to "who he was." His total "place" (status/role) was constantly made explicitly clear. His physical characteristics rendered him visible, and the dominant white culture constantly reinforced his sense of identity and the primacy of caste. If he "got out of line," Southern culture quickly acted to sanction the deviant act by anything from public embarrassment in a minor transaction, ("Come over here, *boy!*") to a lynching for even a suspected transgression of the fundamental mores of race relations. Simply put, the Negro knew who he was: he knew he was something inferior, something lacking essential dignity, something to be used, something to be acted on by others—something less than a man.

In the North, matters were somewhat different. Generally the degrading terms were not used publicly, and there was the atmosphere of at least superficial democracy. Thus, the status/role dilemma for the Negro in the North was (and still is), "How far can I go?" In the South, he never raised the question; he *knew.* But in the North, particularly from the 1930's on, as more blacks worked alongside whites, caste relationships began to weaken as genuine human friendships between the races occurred with increasing frequency. But although the pragmatic and human democracy of the job linked the races momentarily during work, at the end of the day the Negro returned to his shadowy caste world: the Negro ghetto, the Negro church, the Negro grocery—the world of the encapsulated blacks.

It is here that the ambivalence and confusion of the role structure may be clearly seen. An elderly and wise Negro put the issue succinctly when he said, "The difference between the North and South is this. In the South they will hand you some rat poison and tell you to eat it. In the North they will hand you some rat poison and they will tell you it's honey!"

In the South, the Negro understood his role. In the North, the caste structure was obscured beneath the imagery of popular social democracy. The nuances of race relations are thus finer and more subtle and, although Negroes may have full and free social relations in interracial groups on the college campus and on the job, the restraints of caste relationships still function at the level of the neighborhood and the family. In short, the forms of caste have faded from the dramatic, overt, and humiliating reminders typical in the Southern rural town, and in the North there is free and easygoing public intercourse between the races. Northern mores would be grossly offended if a white man publicly abused a completely innocent Negro in, say, a bus simply because of his race.

Thus, the norms which continue to maintain caste relations in the South have relaxed in certain institutional contexts in the North. There are simply more alternatives for the Negro, and less clear, less sharply defined norms to follow. But the weakening of caste and the traditional role of "the Negro" has opened up an entire new series of problems. The sweet air of freedom has raised hopes ("Maybe I could go to college *too*." "Maybe I could get out of this dump and buy a house in the suburbs *too*." "Maybe they would consider me for the job *too*.") but it has also raised powerful anxieties and doubts ("Will I be embarrassed?" "How far can I go with these people—are we really friends?" "When will my blackness stand in the way?" "They may be friendly here on the job, but what would happen if I moved next door?")

The problem for the Negro, particularly in the North, where caste is fast fading, is to claim roles that have been traditionally confined to whites without being sanctioned for it. The total impact of the Civil Rights movement on American society has been to loosen the caste structure so as to move millions of blacks into the open-class system. Whereas a Negro "militant" might say that he wants what *"you have,"* the vast majority of Negroes in American society would probably say, "I want the chance to earn what you earned."

If ambivalences and contradictions of role expectations are a consequence of changing race relations in the United States, the means-end schema illustrates that Negroes in certain respects are quite well integrated ideologically into the value system. Negroes share some of the ultimate ends that whites do. They seek wealth and status just as much as their white counterparts. However, the traditional frustration of the Negro has been the discrimination he faces in finding legitimate means to secure these ends. For the white middle-class American in pursuit of fame and fortune, the legitimate means has usually been a college education and an executive position in an established company. However, the Negro, locked up in the confines of his caste, was never encouraged to get an education, and that which he did get in the Southern Negro school was inferior to that of his white counterpart. Even if he happened to get a good education, he faced an almost impenetrable barrier of discrimination in terms of job opportunities. The only jobs the Negro could get were jobs that whites didn't want, jobs which generally lacked prestige and paid little. The result was that the Negro, while seeking wealth, was systematically denied the legitimate, institutionalized means (the job) with which to acquire it.

As a consequence of denial of the approved ways to acquire money the Negro tried other ways in the pursuit of wealth. If he couldn't earn it, he could steal it. The relatively high rate of Negro crime seems to be at least a partial reflection and consequence of the denial of job opportunities. Indeed, it is interesting to note that blacks have entered in great numbers, the fields in which discriminatory job practices have been removed. Why are there so many Negro professional athletes? The answer, it would seem, is that athletic ability, rather than race, is the prime standard as to who gets a position on the team and who does not.

As we have already seen, the ends which actors pursue (salvation, wealth, power, status, etc.) pervade the social structures which comprise the anatomy of society. In the next chapter, we shall analyze these structures and the ways in which they insure the collective well-being. But it is important to note again the functional congruence between the personal ends and goals of participating actors within the system and the needs of society to survive, function, and continue.

Now, the ends of the actor may be secured through the legitimate and institutionalized means of the social structure. In order to achieve wealth, the *means* are work and the job, in order to save one's soul, the *means* are the good moral life instrumented through the body of the holy church; in order to win the honor and respect of the community, the *means* are to uphold and emulate those social forms the community holds dear.

The traditional plight of the Negro as a caste member is that he has been denied the legitimate means to achieve the same ends that whites pursue. It is probably true that Negroes would like to be rich and esteemed, and in this regard share the same ultimate ends as many whites. But what are the realistic chances? How many Negroes can be a Jackie Robinson, Ralph Bunche, Lena Horne, or Sidney Poitier? It is true that opportunities for Negroes in politics, business, sports, education, etc. have increased enormously within the past decade and will continue to do so as caste restrictions fade and Negroes participate more fully in the class structure with its potential for mobility. But there is today in the black subculture a legacy of 300 years of slave-caste status which almost frustrates the new opportunities, and there is still the grim reality of ghettoes and barriers. In spite of the changes of recent years, the Negro "community" still continues to be a part of and yet also withdrawn from American society.

The primary belief systems of American society, the definitions of racial reality and their attendant norms, have quite plainly told the Negro that he is inferior. The entire normative practice in traditional race relations is epitomized in that elemental belief. What kind of psychological response can a Negro make to this? If he accepts the dominant white belief, then he must say that the Negroes are inferior and that "I am inferior." Perhaps he might say, "Well, Negroes are inferior but I am not—I am a superior Negro." But regardless of what ego-saving device a particular Negro employs to maintain a degree of self-love, he must hate his blackness, for he has been told that it is degrading, inferior, ugly, and primitive, and he has accepted the judgment. However, if he does not accept the normative and ideological definitions of white society, if he believes Negroes are more beautiful than Caucasians, then he must learn to despise the dominant white society for its persecution of the beautiful and superior blacks.

Probably in most Negroes there is some unique psychological alchemy in which both responses are maintained in peculiar tension within the personality. There is probably some racial self-hate ("I would really like to be blond, with blue eyes and a fair complexion") and also racial pride ("Man, did you see Gayle Sayers bust right through those three linemen? Those white boys will never get up!").

Now, if the Negro has been continually reminded of his basic inferiority and lowly status, and if the social system is designed to facilitate opportunity (the legitimate means) for whites and systematically withhold it from Negroes, how, over a long period of time, does the denied group come to respond? Simply put, they ideologically withdraw from the dominant normative order. There is widespread cynicism and disaffection with the norms and aspirations of white middle-class society, for it is unobtainable and unreal. There is simply no psychological or sociological sense in the acceptance of beliefs, values, norms, and practices if they cannot be realistically put into play. An end or personal goal for which there are no means simply engenders frustration and pain. Realistic aspiration should equate with realistic opportunity.

The white middle-class ideal (at least one of the modal prototypes) would certainly be the stable, integrated, relatively affluent suburban family. The father, a college graduate, is a white-collar commuter to the nearby central city. The mother, active in the local bridge club and PTA, devotes her primary interests to her family and home. The two or three children are progressing "nicely" through school and on their way to college—and a "good" college at that. They live in a quite residential street and they embody in their life style all of the good things of American society.

On the other hand, Negro reality suggests a dense urban ghetto, rat-infested substandard slum housing where possibly a third of the families are fatherless. The rates of illegitimacy and crime are spectacularly high, and the number of families living at the poverty level may range from 25 to 50 percent of the ghetto population. Under the brutal and corrosive forces of the ghetto, it is difficult to see how much a population can internalize and sustain the norms and aspirations (means-ends) of the dominant culture—particularly when the means have been denied for generations.

There is a sociological concept which illuminates the social condition of many millions of Negroes in the United States today: it is *anomie.* Normlessness, cynicism, alienation from the dominant white culture seem to characterize a significant segment of the current black population. Now, although *anomie* has its obvious social roots in generations of Negro denial and frustration, there is a question as to its functional role today. Values, beliefs, popular definitions of reality change slowly. The actual circumstances of race relations in the United States are now changing rapidly. Opportunities for Negroes in government, education, and politics have increased greatly in recent years. So it may be that the anomic, alienated Negro youth who today drops out of high school is not realistically tuned to the times. His sense of despair and hopelessness might have been sociologically more realistic for a time now past.

There are now clear indicators of positive change which may, within a generation, sweep the entire Negro population into full membership and participation within the society. The traditional "role" of the Negro within the caste system is fast fading from the social scene, and a new identity within the class system (lower, middle, and even upper) is clearly emerging. There is already a steady stream of Negroes into the middle class. And as caste forms continue to loosen—as new *means* become realistically available—there will be cathexis and congruence among increasing numbers of Negroes with the ultimate "ends" (the functional prerequisites) of the social order.

SUGGESTED READINGS

COOLEY, CHARLES H., *Human Nature and the Social Order*. New York: Charles Scribner's Sons, 1902.

> *Now a sociological classic but still meaningful in terms of Cooley's formulations of the self and the relationship of the individual to the social order.*

COSER, LEWIS A., *The Functions of Social Conflict*. New York: The Free Press, 1956.

> *A critical analysis of the role of conflict in human relationships, suggesting both the negative and positive consequences.*

GERTH, HANS, and C. WRIGHT MILLS, *Character and Social Structure*. New York: Harcourt, Brace & World, 1953.

> *A systematic examination of the basic element of "character structure" as a product of both biological and sociological determinants.*

GOFFMAN, ERVING, *The Presentation of Self in Everyday Life*. Garden City: Doubleday & Company, Inc., Anchor Books, 1959.

> *An enlightening and perceptive discussion of roles and self-identity in the context of daily living.*

LINTON, RALPH, *The Study of Man*. New York: Appleton-Century, 1936.

> *One of the great texts in which the concepts of status and role were first introduced.*

MEAD, MARGARET (ed.), *Cooperation and Competition in Primitive Societies*. New York: McGraw-Hill Book Company, 1936.

> *A collection of papers by anthropologists dealing with cooperation and competition among nonliterate peoples.*

MYRDAL, ALVA, and VIOLA KLEIN, *Women's Two Roles: Home and Work*. New York: Humanities Press Inc., 1956.

A cross-cultural analysis utilizing statistical materials on the conflict between family and work roles among American, French, British, and Swedish women.

SIMMEL, GEORG (trans. by Kurt Wolff and Reinhard Bendix), Conflict and the Web of Group-Affiliations. Glencoe: The Free Press, 1955.
Two of Simmel's major essays on the dynamics of social organization.

SUMNER, WILLIAM GRAHAM, Folkways. Boston: Ginn and Company, 1906.
Sumner's major written work, in which he develops his basic idea of folkways.

WHITE, LESLIE, The Science of Culture. New York: Farrar, Straus and Giroux Inc., 1946.
A stimulating and provocative book whose central theme is the explication of the role of culture in the human condition.

SOCIAL SYSTEMS

In the preceding chapter we examined the micro-conceptual units in sociology. These were the basic concepts—actor, norms, status/role, social relationship—around which the primary or elementary social interaction occurs. But there is obviously much more to the social condition than what might be transitory and fleeting social encounters, in which all of these four elements appear. Indeed, most sociologists use the term "social structure" to indicate an almost generic quality of social order.

The idea of "structure," in the social sense, refers to relationships which are comparatively stable and orderly. A social structure, in short, consists of recurrent, stabilized, orderly relationships. It is a structure of expectations, much in the manner that a bridge is a structure of steel members—each member having a *relationship* to and *bearing* on the others. Similarly a social structure consists of predictable and "bearing" relationships (norms, status, role) which are empirically manifest in the behavior of individuals functioning within the system. It is the fundamental sociological qualities of social structures, viewed as *social systems*, that we shall now consider. In doing so, we move to a higher level of conceptual abstraction in which we hope to clarify finally the distinctive order of reality on which sociology centers. The conception of social system, perhaps more than any other, focuses on the unique quality of that reality.

As we have already noted, the "units" of a social structure consist of:

1. *Pluralities of actors*

2. *Normative definition*

3. *Status/role expectations*

4. *Social relationships-interaction*

Normative definition, of course, stems from broad ideational assumptions and ultimately from the characteristic value and belief systems endemic to the basic culture system. The norms within the social structure will accordingly define the positive and required obligations between roles and also the extent to which permissible deviation from the normative ideal will be tolerated.

The structure of a social system may also be characterized by *subgroups* within the larger unit. If society is the point of reference, it is clear that there are almost countless subgroups within its total structure of relationships. For example, if we consider a fraternity as a concrete group in terms of social structure, we find subgroups within it. There are the "leaders" and "followers"; there may be the smaller cliques of the "Athletes," the "Brains," or the "Sophs" as differentiated from the "older guys" or "Seniors." Within the family the two generations constitute "subgroups" to the total structure—substructures based on ascribed status. Even if we consider a social "dyad," a two-person group such as a boy-and-girl relationship, as a social entity, a social structure, the element of substructure is latent in the two distinct role patterns the two actors play out in the relationship—the norms which define the expectations for the girl and the boy.

The four elements that we have just discussed will be found in all social structures, from the dyad all the way to a complex society of more than 300 million persons. But an additional perspective must be introduced here. Although we have noted the necessary units of structure, we have not raised the question of the *systemic requirements* of social structures. We have dealt with the structural realities, but what of the peculiar *functional needs* of the collective reality? A social structure may be viewed as a functionally interrelated and interdependent system of relationships. But what is the nature of the functional interdependence—what sort of collective imperatives must be met within the system of relationships if the social structure is to endure?

There is in this question a kind of primitive biologic analogy. In terms of the biological or sociological reference we can ask, "What kind of functions must be maintained if life (social structure) is to go on? What are the basic elements of the life (social) process, and how are these prerequisites for life (social structures) answered in the biological (sociological) subsystems within the living creature (social structure) or group?

THE FUNCTIONAL IMPERATIVES

If they are to survive and endure, social systems must solve four functional imperatives. These have been identified as (1) *goal attainment,* (2) *adaptation* (3) *integration,* and (4) *pattern maintenance and tension management.* Within the characteristic normative expectations, the status/role units, and the social relationships of all enduring collectivities these four imperatives are solved.

Goal Attainment

All social systems have a reason to exist. This is, the actors within the system—in terms of both their private (action-motivational) system and the announced, public, visible, intended purposes of the group—share a basic understanding and general agreement as to what the group or relationship is about. The purpose of General Motors is to make a profit by making automobiles. So the actors within the structure bend their concerted efforts toward this collective goal, although each in his own may seek his unique personal end—money, work, status, activity, etc. Similarly, a college is a social structure whose ultimate goals are the creation and dissemination of knowledge. The actors within the collegiate structure concentrate their activities to this ultimate end.

There is, therefore, within the structure of social systems the means-ends framework in which the actors occupy status positions and relate to each other through the normative forms in order to move toward the realization of the collective purpose. Thus an element of rationality is characteristic in the system's ordering of relationships. There are collective ends to be pursued and means devised to move toward these ends. In this fashion, through the ordering of relationships viewed principally through the means-ends scheme, the social system moves toward the goals it has established for itself—or which quite possibly were established for it by another, larger structural unit of reference, such as society itself.

Adaptation

All social systems are located in a social and physical environ-ment, and each system must in some manner or other take that environ-ment into account; it must, in short, adapt to that environment. In this fashion, a substructure of the total structure takes as its primary functional mandate the task of adaptation, in which it acts to manip-ulate the external circumstances in such a way as to facilitate or aid the system's goals.

On the level of the national society, "security" in international affairs is certainly a major structural goal. In order to achieve "secu-rity," a goal for the substructure of government, the functional impera-tive of successful *adaptation* to the international environment is made. Similarly, a college fraternity, which has a host of goals ("brother-hood," "status," "friendship," "dormitory accommodations," etc.) has an adaptive problem in the total college environment. The fraternity must "take into account" the dean, the faculty, its competitive position in regard to the other fraternities, its general prestige in the collegiate community, and the like. Because of its need for successful adaptation to the environment, the fraternity will devote an extraordinary amount of its internal energies to adjusting to this functional imperative. If it did not successfully adapt to changing environmental circumstances, it would simply fail. And on every college campus fraternities that have been unable to adjust to this functional problem eventually disappear from the campus scene.

On the level of national society, part of the adaptive function is undertaken by the economic substructure. Certainly the development of technology, which may be thought of as energy adjustment and con-trol over the physical environment, has largely emerged through eco-nomic institutions—although recently, in connection with atomic energy, the governmental substructure has been involved, too. Note, also, that in complex societies the functional imperatives can be met by combina-tions of substructural involvement. Government, the polity, is unques-tionably involved in matters of adaptation as well, as in the internal functional concerns of integration and goal attainment. Similarly, the same fraternity leadership which is concerned with the fraternity's "image" (adaptation) is also interested in the problems of internal integration, goal achievement, and pattern maintenance.

The functional imperatives of adaptation and goal attainment are both involved in some fashion with the *external* environment. Cer-tainly the adaptive mechanisms are clearly related to forces outside the social system. However, goal attainment also may have meaning to levels and units of social structure outside of the given unit of reference. For example, the "goals" of a given corporation may be the construction of aircraft. This goal, however, may be viewed as *adaptive* to the national society in that aircraft may be a means of controlling or manipulating the environment for society's functional purposes. Viewed in this fashion, the goals of subsystem functions have to be related to units outside of each given group. Note, however, that within each social system, no matter what its level of structural complexity, these two functional imperatives must be solved.

Integration

If goal attainment and adaptation refer in some fashion to linkages and relationships outside of the functioning group, integration deals purely with matters *within* the system. And it is at this point in our discussion that the unique sociological perspective can be seen most clearly.

A comparison with the "social systems" of the insect world might be useful here. A society of ants, termites, bees, wasps, or the like shares the two functional imperatives that we have already considered —goal attainment and adaptation. The total communities of social insects and the subgroups (workers, warriors, drones, queens, in collectivities) obviously share a division of labor in which they strive toward goal attainment. The goals of the insect world would appear to be at least two: (1) to support an "economy" in which goods and services are produced, distributed, and consumed, and (2) to reproduce their kind so as to insure the organic survival of the species. Thus, each insect society seems clearly directed toward the attainment of at least two significant goals and, judging from the number of insects throughout the world, they seem highly successful in meeting their goal obligations.

Secondly, the insect community, as a social system, must *adapt* to the external situation. That external environment may be the physical climate, geography, and other living things, including creatures who constitute the "natural" enemy of the insect world: other insects, birds, animals, and man himself. Thus the necessity of successful adaptation is similarly a feature of insect social systems.

The principle which holds insect society intact is essentially biological. Insects relate socially to each other because of the response and interactive necessities that derive from their bodies, their biology, their instincts, their nervous systems. Their behavior, their social forms, are an expression of pure biologic, organic, residual, internal forces. Their integration and pattern maintenance are achieved, in short, through the genetic process.

Men, on the other hand, are plastic, adaptive, intelligent, and, perhaps most critically, culture-creating and culture-sustaining creatures. The social structures of men are held together not by automatic response but by normative integration and shared symbolic meaning. This places a great burden on human social systems because, since social structures are not biologically sustained, they must continually be reintegrated, resustained, and refurbished by their human agents. In short, the integrative mechanisms require endless and continual attention—for, if the social system should "fail," there would be no "life" for each individual man.

Integration refers primarily to a condition between or among the units (subgroups) within the system. A system is integrated if there is a functional interplay among institutionalized means (status/role), the personal ends of the actor (happiness, security, wealth, status, etc.), and the system ends (goal attainment, such as the production of automobiles or the creation of knowledge or the socialization of children).

Essentially the integrative problem is the focusing of relationships within the system so as to achieve solidarity, cohesion, stability, order, and the comparative permanence of the relational system. Since no actor is ever completely socialized, since no social system is perfectly balanced and congruent to the internal structure of relationships, since the private ends of actors may indeed be subversive to group goals and intentions, since there is never perfect adaption to the external environment, and since the human social condition seems inherently unstable and volatile, there is constant need to renew the integrative mechanisms. Indeed, two massive institutional complexes, religion and government, direct much of their societal energies and function to the integrative imperative.

Pattern Maintenance and Tension Management

As does the integrative necessity, pattern maintenance and tension management deal with the internal state of the social system. But whereas integration focuses on relationships between the system units (actors and subgroups), pattern maintenance and tension management center on the *condition* of the actors. The person, the social agent, is an occupant of the status/role unit whose primary form is determined by the characteristic configuration of normative expectations. Within the role system, however, the actor may be only tangentially or marginally socialized. He may not really believe in the ideational justifications; he may be "agnostic" and not a "believer"; in effect he may suffer from anomie and normlessness. If, indeed, there are many actors in a system who experience serious role conflict and normative incompatibility, the system will cease to be a congruent and harmonious integration of social forms, necessities, and purposes.

Thus, in order to integrate the actor more fully into structure, the system will devote considerable attention to appropriate socialization. It begins first in childhood, in the family, where the child is encouraged to learn and accept the ideational and normative formulas characteristic of the culture system. Later in life, he may participate in all sorts of training, indoctrination, and instructional programs within specialized institutional contexts in order to realize relatively complete cathexis to the social system. In this fashion, the college freshman will take some sort of "orientation" program, the child will receive religious instruction or go to a parochial school, the Army recruit will listen to "information and education" lectures, and the new employee will serve on the "training squad" for six months. The ultimate goal of all of these devices is to achieve a more complete cognitive integration of actor to the system's values, norms, and social structures.

Tension management is also a primary concern within any social system. The "actor," of course, is a sociological conception which underscores the "external" sources of a major component of personality. But there is an emotional dimension to personality as well. Within the social system, emotional tensions must be controlled or managed so as to not disturb the normal functioning of the system. For some systems tension management is quite critically maintained—particularly in those relationships guided by the pattern variable of affect neutrality. The bank manager or the Air Force colonel must not "break down" emotionally in his formal status/role capacity. Similarly, the football quarterback doesn't "lose his poise" when he is consistently rushed and tackled by the defensive linemen. On the other hand, there are limits to which emotional expression can be frustrated, suppressed, or controlled. As a result, the family as a social system permits a much wider range of tension display, thereby providing an outlet for emotional response and expression. By serving as a vehicle for emotional expression and tension release, the family system enables its members to perform more effectively in those social situations calling for strict tension management.

By way of summary, the four functional imperatives of all social systems— (1) goal attainment, (2) adaptation, (3) integration, and (4) pattern maintenance and tension management—are endemic and universal to all social systems. They are met by all enduring social structures. The first two, *goal attainment* and *adaptation*, are not unique to the human condition but are shared with all living things who enter into some form of social interrelationship and interdependence. The latter two functional prerequisites, integration and pattern maintenance and tension management, are uniquely human and emerge from the elemental plasticity of human kind. As a consequence, social systems and social structures sustained by human beings require internal devices and arrangements whereby the essential social forms are continually reformed, sustained, stabilized, and *integrated*.

INSTITUTIONALIZATION

Occasionally through our discussion we have used the term "institution," and it may be useful at this point to clarify this significant sociological concept. The idea of roles and status helps to focus the empirical observation that human beings engage in forms and types of behavior which are patterned and recurrent. Although we might primitively suggest that we occupy the status of "greeter" when we say hello to a classmate or colleague on campus, that position is relatively unattached to any other status. It is a sort of generic expectation that human beings confront when they see people they know. Similarly, the status of "boy friend" is isolated from systematic and formal relationships with any other series of status/role expectations—with the exception, of course, that if you are a "boy friend" there has to be a "girl friend." There are, in short, status/role positions that we occupy in the general context of communal or societal activities—"citizen," "car driver," "greeter," "host," and the like.

On the other hand, some roles are systematically and functionally interrelated with others, particularly in areas of significance to the society at large. An *institution*, accordingly, consists of a complex of interdependent and interrelated roles which are of strategic functional and structural significance to the social system. Institutions consist of combinations of roles with their attendant norms and constitute a more abstract sociological conception than "a" role, which comes closer to the level of empirical observation. Institutions generally appear at the more complex levels of social organization and are infused throughout the great associations of contemporary, urban industrial society.

Institutions are complex arrangements of interrelated norms.

Whereas gentlemen are expected to rise when a lady enters the room (a folkway), thus constituting a single normative act, institutions are *combinations of normative expectations* clustered about critical and strategic functions. For example, in many societies there is some sense of supernatural force extending mysteriously beyond the senses. This force may be related or attended to by any manner of isolated normative practices. A rabbit's foot may be an omen of good luck, a black cat one of bad luck. In terms of actual behavior, the person believing these to be true will behave accordingly. He will protect and preserve his rabbit's foot and avoid coming into close proximity with black cats. The resulting acts are normative but cannot be regarded as institutionalized. Religion, on the other hand, is largely institutionalized. Religion like superstition, entertains the idea of the supernatural, a force above and beyond the senses. However, in religion these practices are designed largely to satisfy a collective need and not the whims of the solitary actor. In essence, the host of beliefs, acts, roles, customs, expectations, attitudes, norms, ceremonies are institutionalized. An entire complex of interrelated norms centered around a strategic function (in this case, solidarity, integration, normative consensus) has become articulated in a series of mutually sustaining and reciprocal acts. Institutions are the social devices that organize and sustain complex normative relationships involving many actors and many roles in an enduring activity.

While many folkways consist of isolated normative expectations, institutions precipitate within the context of organized and complex groups. Institutions in underdeveloped, non-literate societies are largely undifferentiated and may often center on a single role, such as tribal chief, shaman (medicine man), and warrior. However, in complex urban societies these roles and the functions they subsume have evolved into great institutional complexes, such as government, medicine, and the military. Note too, the critical difference between institutions and associations, which are large, complex, rationally organized groups. Associations refer to the group—the interaction system—while institutions constitute the formalized and regularized procedures through which the group interacts and functions. An industrial corporation, such as the General Electric Company, is an association. Its primary economic activities are guided by the institutional complex we know as private enterprise. The New York Times is not only an economic enterprise within the private enterprise complex, but a newspaper and accordingly guided by the institution of journalism (ethics, technique, relationships). Thus while a hospital is an association, the institution of medicine guides part of the interaction in the hospital. While undergraduates are members of distinct colleges and universities as associations (Yale, Michigan State, UCLA), the institutions of the "application procedures," "registration," "lecture system," "examinations," "fraternity hazing," "dances," "commencement," "home coming," guide and organize the total associational activity and give to these extremely complex groups an order and symmetry which make their goals and functions possible.

Finally, it should be noted that institutions can be observed in terms of the inclusiveness of their normative definitions. Obviously "private enterprise" constitutes a broad set of expectations for economic activities. The practices, assumptions, and definitive procedures associated with private enterprise constitute an entire institutional complex —a series of interrelated institutions which form the total. Within the private enterprise system are the less inclusive institutions such as "buying on margin," "the board of directors meeting," "filing procedures," "overtime," "examination for promotion," "property rights," "chain of command," "collective bargaining," "evaluation procedures," "the inter-office memo," and even the "coffee break" and "Christmas office party." These entail the specification of role relationships through formal normative definition. Each becomes part of an ascending series of institutions until the ultimate institutional complex, in the case of our illustration, *private enterprise*, is reached.

THE FOOTBALL TEAM AS SOCIAL STRUCTURE AND SOCIAL SYSTEM

In the preceding discussion of social structures and social systems we have been admittedly abstract. But though the analysis of social systems seemed quite removed from sensory or empirical reality, we may have moved much closer to the ultimate features of social life than those immediate forms that we perceive through our senses. Through abstraction we may be actually simplifying events, although the language and ideas used are not as familiar. The general direction of theory is to move toward the ultimate and universal processes—in a sense, toward the "simpler" and more fundamental levels. And yet, if what we have had to say regarding the universal qualities of social structures and social systems are valid conceptual descriptions of these social units, then we should be able to observe them on the level of everyday experience. Concepts, no matter how abstract, should ultimately have references at the empirical level. At this stage of our discussion, therefore, we shall illustrate the utility and meaning of these terms by applying them to a social group with which almost every college student is familiar—a football team.

The first point to be noted is the ideational-normative context in which the football team is located, and in a sense, literally created. The football team is essentially the product of the game. The "game" is primarily a relationship between two teams in competition for "points" (the goal) on a fixed and determined locality (the field) over a period of time (playing-time 60 minutes) according to normative definitions establishing the nature of the game (the rules).

According to the National Collegiate Athletic Association's 1966 rules, there are ten primary rules to football, and each of these is broken down into many sections and articles. The norms (rules) are both prescriptive and proscriptive. There are things players must do and things players must not do. ("Players of opposing teams must wear jerseys of contrasting colors." "No offensive player while on his scrimmage line may receive a snap.") The rules also establish the size of the field (360 by 160 feet). Each team is allotted only four "offensive downs" to move the ball ten yards. If the offensive team fails to do this it loses its opportunity to score points and must give offensive possession of the ball to the other team.

These are merely some of the norms which define the game situation as a totality. However, they also define each status/role position within the team. The football team consists of eleven specific and formal status positions to be occupied by actors (players), such as "center," "right end," "quarterback," "lineback," "deep safety." The norms define what each status/role position may or may not do. An offensive player may not use his hands to hold back a defensive player. An offensive interior lineman is not eligible to receive a forward pass.

Recall that normative expectations are usually sanctioned negatively or positively. In football the norms are almost always negatively sanctioned. That is, if a norm (rule) is broken or violated, the team will be sanctioned (penalized) by the most precious thing it possesses in terms of the game—yardage. For the wide range of deviation from normative expectations, there is a wide range of penalties. For example, when a member of the offensive backfield moves forward before the snap of the ball, the team will be penalized five yards for an "illegal procedure." Similarly, if a kicker is even touched by a defensive player after he has kicked the ball, the defensive team will be penalized 15 yards for "roughing the kicker."

Note that in the football team we have identified the empirical referents to three basic units of social structure—norms, status, and role.

There is obviously the element of social interaction within the team and between the opposing teams. It is, indeed, in the quality and outcome of social interaction—the social relationships—that the primary interest of the game itself lies. Recall, too, that social relationships between actors have "a high degree of predictability and orient to the expectations of the other." Interaction cannot occur as a universal quality of social groups if order, anticipation, and predictability are not present.

Ideally, relationships within the team should be utterly predictable. Each actor orients constantly to the expectations of the others. The center "snaps" the ball to the waiting quarterback. He, in turn, "hands off" to the halfback, who "hits" off tackle through the "hole" opened up by the blocking guards, tackle, and left halfback. Each player moves exactly to the design of the play—each has a predetermined and established task to perform. Ideally, if each player (actor) performs exactly as he is expected to, the play is successful and a significant gain in yardage is effected. The play, which is a rationally designed series of specific acts, is identical to the concept of social institution that we noted previously. The point here is that the play is a complex series of role expectations organized around a strategic function of the social system—in this case, the football team's collective goal (to score points).

Note, too, that during the game, players are shuffled in and out of play. Individuals come and go, but the status positions (guard, end, halfback, etc.) stay out on the field. If a player is injured, another takes his place and the action continues. The same play may be used four or five times in a game, and three players who play, for example, left halfback, will perform. In this way, the interaction on the team calls for intensive predictability on the part of all eleven players; each must know exactly what the other is doing. Viewed in this fashion, the norms, statuses, and roles make predictive relationships the most dramatic quality of the football team.

But prediction occurs not only within the team but also *between* the teams. Recall that the norms define the situation for both teams and that certain facets of the game, certain conditions of play, bring about a response from the defensive team. For example, the offensive team is losing the game by 20 points with only six minutes left in the game. Furthermore, it has a third down with nine yards to go for a first down. Almost everybody watching the game knows this is now a "passing situation." Obviously, no one knows this better than the defensive team, which now adjusts its defensive arrangements to "protect against the pass." This protection may involve a "red dog" or "safety blitz," in which the linebackers, who normally wait until the offensive play develops before they commit themselves, attempt to break through the defensive line in order to tackle the passer before he gets a chance to pass. Now the offensive quarterback, knowing the linebackers may "rush" him, may adjust his own strategy to this expectation. Rather than passing, he may select a running play in the anticipation that the onrushing linebacks will have vacated their usual defensive positions, thereby leaving the valuable ground unprotected. Now the defensive team, suspecting that the offensive quarterback may be thinking along these lines, may . . . . Well, enough said on this point. It is clear that each team is constantly orienting to the expectations of the other. Indeed, part of the strategy of the offensive quarterback, as we have just noted, is occasionally to do something that is unexpected in terms of conventional or anticipated play.

The football team illustrates also the functional problems inherent in social systems. That is to say, the team as a social system must solve the problems of goal attainment, adaptation, integration, and tension management and pattern maintenance.

The football team must adapt to the physical environment, in terms of the climate, weather, and general condition of the football field. A dry field will critically affect the "passing attack." A muddy and wet field will affect the defensive team's general strategy to prevent scoring. Each team also has the critical adaptive problem of the other team—it is literally on how they "adapt" to each other in terms of offensive and defensive plays that the outcome of the game will depend.

Integration of the team involves conditions of the units—how well the defensive team holds back the enemy and how well the offensive team can move the ball and score touchdowns. Do the offensive linemen perform their obligations so that the ball carriers have adequate blocking? In short, is the status/role system intact and operative? Do the actors perform? Do they have spirit and "desire"—do they "cathect" to the norms of the situation? Are there integrative and cohesive bonds between the players? Without cohesion, solidarity, and integration of its essential units, the team cannot collectively pursue its goal. If a football team is not a *team*, not a collectivity of interdependent and interrelated units, if it does not cohere as a social system, it simply cannot win the game. Eleven *individuals* on a football field, no matter how strong and determined each individual may be, cannot cope with the situation as defined by the rules of the game.

Part of the integrative requirement will be met by tension management and pattern maintenance, for these, too, are concerned with the internal state of the system. So the coach will say, "Now, don't get discouraged, boys—don't throw the game away by beating yourself. No matter what happens stick to the game plan. Don't lose your heads and we'll beat them."

Similarly, players with "spirit" and "desire" will reinforce the patterns (role, status, norms) and maintain the essential social forms of the team. The quarterback will have a word of praise for a particularly effective block thrown by his defensive halfback. The linebacker who intercepts a pass will be surrounded by his happy teammates and pounded on the back in congratulation. The halfback who scores the touchdown on the long run will receive the warm praise of his teammates, but he will also point out the "key" block thrown by the offensive guard that made the dramatic run possible. The player who "dogs it" or who doesn't "put out" will find himself isolated and avoided. In this fashion the team itself maintains the essential forms of role expectations and the necessary psychological attitudes, the internal motivation that underscores the formal positions on the team. Without constant reinforcement of these needs of the system, the team as a social system could not function in the game.

If the team is successful in its adaptation to the physical and social conditions of the game, if it remains integrated, if the players perform their obligations and expectations, they will presumably be successful in "goal attainment." The goal, in the case of our illustration, is literally obtained by crossing into the end zone. If the team does this more often than the "enemy," it will probably win the game. In athletic events "goal attainment" is rather obvious. It is a simple quantitative matter, and the social system (the team) at the end of the contest knows whether or not it has been successful.

If the system has not functioned well, if it did not meet its goal (winning), then the coach and player will have to discover "what went wrong." Who failed to perform? Did the team "lose spirit" (integration)? Did the team lose its "poise" (fail to manage tension)? Did the team lose too much ground on penalties (normative sanctions)? Did the team play badly (pattern loss)?

LEVELS OF SOCIAL STRUCTURE

The idea of the functional imperatives implies that all enduring social systems, from the smallest, two-person relationship to society as a whole, must solve four basic problems if they are to survive. There are, literally, social systems within social systems within social systems. There are almost always substructures and subsystems within larger systems. For example, although *the economy* is generally regarded as fulfilling the adaptive function at the level of society, there are many subsystems within the total economic framework. If one conceptually pursues the subsystems from the societal level all the way through to a concrete, empirically observable economic group, he will move through six levels before finally arriving at the final and least abstract economic group.

Johnson, in this connection, notes six system levels: (1) the societal level, in which the functional subsystem charged with the adaptive needs is (2) the economy. Then follows (3) a functional subsystem within the economic subsystem, such as the investment-capitalization area of the economy. This is followed by (4) specific adaptive subsystems of the investment-capitalization area, such as one primarily concerned with the procurement of facilities. Finally (5) a total industry emerges, such as "the steel industry," which is in turn followed by (6) a particular industrial concern or corporation within the steel industry, such as "United States Steel."[1]

Note that, in spite of the drift toward empirical reality from the total economy to U.S. Steel, each successive unit of the system must also solve the four functional imperatives. It is critical, therefore, that though each social system must confront successfully the four functional imperatives, the level of a given social structure be kept critically in mind. Although economic "groups" are functionally related to the adaptive need on the level of the national society, there are substructures within economic groups whose functions may be purely goal attainment or integration.

Within the framework of any *society*, no matter how developed or "underdeveloped" institutionally, there are generally four major units of social organization; certainly these become sociologically visible and distinct from the beginning of cities (3500 B.C.) through modern times. These major social forms which comprise the primary anatomy of society are: (1) the polity or governance, (2) the economy, (3) religion, and (4) the family. There may be many more forms in the structure of modern societies, but these four still perform the vital functions necessary to collective survival. Again, at the societal level—the most inclusive system of functional interrelationship—the functional imperatives may be seen to relate directly to these primary institutional forms.

---

[1]Harry M. Johnson, *Sociology: A Systematic Introduction* (New York: Harcourt, Brace & World, Inc., 1960), p. 214.

Goal attainment on the societal level most clearly is subsumed by the polity, but the polity's functional concerns also center on integration and pattern maintenance.

Generally, sociologists view *the economy* as contributing basically to the adaptive needs at the *societal* level. It is adaptive because through essential economic activities goods and services are produced, distributed, and exchanged. Through economic norms and social structures an orderly system for the allocation of scarce resources is "institutionalized." These scarce resources (technology, capital goods, raw materials, manpower, systems of extraction and fabrication, etc.) can be *utilized* by the society in confronting any environmental situation—bombs for warfare, heat to keep out the cold, and food to sustain men as demanded by the biological environment.

While the polity strives to assure the successful pursuit of collective goals and the economy adapts to the environment, religion, through the articulation of the sacred, binds men together in an ethical-moral embrace. Through their statement of "moral values" and their primary concern with normative relationships, religious institutions contribute to the *integrative* function.

There is always the threat of widespread anomie and breakdown of the regulative systems but, through the church in all its forms in all cultural settings, integration, cohesion, and solidarity are sustained. By definition, a social structure has form, and the nature of that form is shaped by norms, status/role. Through religion the very basic forms of collective life—primary definitions of social reality, fundamental statements of the human condition, morality, values, indeed the ultimate ends of the actor (salvation, heaven, eternity)—are carefully nurtured and maintained. Since biology cannot integrate men in their social forms as it does ants, the forms themselves must assure integration, and to this imperative religion is a primary social response.

Certainly as Durkheim argued (*The Elementary Forms of the Religious Life*) religion contributes to the social solidarity of non-literate societies. With the emergence of contemporary social forms (cities, industrialism, open-class systems, rapid social change) the role of religion has shifted. Traditional authoritative, hierarchical, and formal ceremonial religions—highly *public* religious forms in short—have faded from the social scene and religions emphasizing "freedom of religious conscience" and in general the *privatization* of religious experience, have steadily emerged. Thus, from the standpoint of institutional dynamics, the formally public, liturgical, traditional restatement of the normative system recedes in modern times. In a sense, the almost revolutionary alteration of traditional religions today and the massive shift to the privatization of religious experience calls into question the capacity of institutionalized religion to survive. Some sociologists have already suggested that the end of public religion is almost at hand. Yet if this be true or not, or whether religion will simply assume a new, contemporary form, the functional concern for social integration and solidarity will persist. The real question is, what institutional form will it take—secular, or some continuation of the sacred?

When the level of social structure is society, there is an additional functional imperative that is not clearly subsumed in goal attainment, adaptation, integration, tension management, and pattern maintenance. Normally the recruitment of actors into social structures is accomplished through the mechanism of achieved or ascribed status. In medieval times, for example, a king was a king because his father was a king. Thus kings (a status essential to the polity) were assured through the mechanism of ascribed status. And so, all status/role units are filled either by ascribed-quality or achieved-performance considerations. Presidents, football stars, executives, professors, and the like enter into social structures through the vehicle of achieved status. But how does a society—the ultimate system—provide for new members?

The answer is not really sex and biology. In order to assure the proper reproduction, socialization, and nourishment of the child, a permanent relationship between a man and woman is institutionalized by society. In short, although General Motors, the Catholic Church, and the United States Navy are massive associations they are not societies because they cannot survive purely from their internal system of relationships. In these systems, achieved and ascribed status are the primary mechanism for recruitment into the status/role units. They depend for their human resources on other systems outside their sociological frontiers.

Society, on the other hand, no matter how small in numbers (e.g., Eskimo or Bushman groups), is functionally complete. A societal system can survive and endure forever, depending only on the internal system. Thus, on the societal level, another functional imperative, one that we have not encountered before, is the need to insure the orderly replacement of population.

The family system is the universal response to this functional need. Although the family system provides the society with the human materials for its continuity, the family also serves importantly in the needs of pattern maintenance and tension management. It is the family that first introduces the child into the prevailing system of normative expectations. It is the family that first shapes the actor's sense of self and social identity. It is the family that sanctions the first transgressions from the normative ideal. And it is the family that primarily defines the response to tension and the manner in which it is expressed and controlled. Later on, particularly in "developed" societies, the child moves from the home to the school, where "secondary socialization" occurs. However, in many societies almost the entire socialization experience in the early years takes place exclusively within the family framework.

The major and dramatic institutional forms of society have thus been seen as structural responses to the functional imperatives. But since all enduring collectivities must successfully meet the same needs, there are equivalent structures in the smaller units as well. For example, the organizational chart of a large corporation represents the formal articulation of the functional prerequisites into the major units of corporate form. The vice president in charge of manufacturing is clearly concerned with goal attainment; his task is to produce the goods and to attain the production goals set for him by the executives and committees charged with this responsibility. To this end, he directs the plant managers, the industrial engineers, the superintendents, the foremen, and finally the workers toward the goals.

Adaptation is most clearly seen in the comptroller, who essentially supervises the fiscal health of the corporation as an entity in the business world. The success of its general posture can be seen in profits versus losses. Adaptation to the external environment can also be noted in the sales division where the concern is adapting to the "sales climate," "customer image," "the market," and "the competition."

The general problems of corporate integration fall to the office in charge of industrial relations. Here the primary concern is with employment, recruitment, training, health and safety, employee services, and labor relations. The president of the corporation, though ultimately responsible for the total integrative health of the company, relies heavily on this special office. Here too, the particular patterns, the regulative norms, the successful operation of the basic status/role forms will be scrutinized and maintained.

Finally, *tension management* functions at almost all levels of corporate structure, and there seems to be no special sub-unit, apart from the industrial relations office, to cope with it. Usually, role breakdown or emotional responses that are held to be normatively excessive will be handled by the supervisory personnel charged with this sort of responsibility. A workman will be "talked to" by some of his peers or, if the matter is serious enough, by his foreman. Similarly, a vice-president who fails to perform to expectations (pattern maintenance) will be sanctioned by a gentle and informal suggestion that he improve or, in more serious cases, by a formal "separation."

The functional imperatives that we have been discussing here are abstract and analytic conceptions which reveal the *systemic* reality of collective life. They do not result from either the biology or the psychology of individuals but are rather generated purely from the internal necessities of social forms seen as systems. Since we often see "individuals" rather than the systems of relationships which are revealed only in the behavior of individuals, the unique reality of the sociological perspective often goes unrecognized. That is to say, social systems and structures are often obscured beneath the empirical behavior of concrete individuals; we cannot see the sociological forest because the individual trees are in the way.

Furthermore, the range of sociological observations is largely limited to what people say. Language, indeed, is the vehicle through which we might be able to see the operation of the functional imperatives on almost any level of social structure. For a moment let us turn to what people say. These are quite familiar situations and phrases, but perhaps for the first time you will see them as responses to system imperatives:

The Level of the National Society

1. "The purpose behind the American presence in Vietnam is to prevent a Communist takeover in Southeast Asia. We are there simply to prevent aggression."—Goal Attainment, Adaptation

2. "If we do not stop the dollar drain and the unfavorable balance of payments, the value of the dollar will be in serious jeopardy and our general position in the world economy threatened."—Adaptation

3. "Through the passage of this meat-inspection law the consumer will be protected as well as the honest and legitimate meat processor who does a good job."—Integration

4. "It is essential that management and labor work together as common partners rather than enemies."—Integration

5. "Ask not what your country can do for you. Ask what you can do for your country."—Pattern Maintenance

The Level of a Religious Denomination in the Community Setting

1. "Reverend Smith, you will simply have to do something about your sermons

on Sunday if you want to fill this church."—*Goal Attainment, and Pattern Maintenance*

2. "Did you know that we have lost three members of this congregation to the Lutherans this past year? I don't know, but something has happened to this church for the past few years. We don't seem to be going anyplace, and we are losing recognition in the community."—*Goal Attainment, Adaptation*

3. "Next week, as most of you know, the children of the Church School are putting on their annual Christmas pageant. I hope all of the parents will be here on Friday night to show the children how much we appreciate their efforts."—*Integration*

4. "Johnny, I understand when the collection plate was passed you took a quarter out rather than put one in."—*Pattern Maintenance*

5. "That was a mighty fine sermon, Mr. Smith, but personally I hate to see a minister cry."—*Tension Management*

The Level of the Family

1. "Well, if this family wants a new car next year, we are going to have to do something about expenses this year."—*Goal Attainment*

2. "The neighborhood has simply gone to pieces. The only thing we can do is move."—*Adaptation*

3. "Now I realize Johnny got in too late last night, but you spoke to him much too harshly. I think it would be a good idea if you two had a talk before things get out of hand."—*Integration*

4. "Tommy, nice little boys do not spit at their mothers."—*Pattern Maintenance*

5. "Mary, I don't want you to speak to me in that tone of voice and in that manner again—particularly in front of the neighbors."—*Pattern Maintenance, Tension Management*

MANIFEST AND LATENT FUNCTION

We have seen that social systems, if they are to survive, must be integrative internally and adaptive externally. When substructures contribute to the integration or adaptation of the system, we can sociologically define them as *functional*. On the other hand, when social structures or social actions weaken or impede integration or adaptation, they are essentially *dysfunctional* to the system. However, the actor in structure has very little sociological awareness of system needs. He pursues, rather, his own personal ends. We must therefore distinguish between the objective, sociological consequences of the behavior of the actor and his own motivations and subjective perceptions of the social world. The actor in church may be there in pursuit of "salvation," but collectivities of men sustained by the ritual liturgy and morality of the church may be functionally integrating the societal norm system. In short, the outcome of social relationships may be viewed from the subjective perspective of the actor or they may be seen in their full functional consequences from the standpoint of social structure.

The distinction between what the actor "thinks" he is doing and performing and what he is "actually" doing from a sociological point of view may be illuminated through the concepts of *latent* and *manifest* function. A manifest function is overt, public, ideological, obvious, natural, intended, and a manifestation of "common sense." The manifest function is the "purpose" or "explanation" the actor in structure employs to justify or explain a social act, group, or event. Hence, when a norm, a role, or an institution is publicly conceived to make positive contributions to a social structure, when it is avowed, intended and generally recognized, we identify it as a manifest function. It is the popular ideological-normative rationalization for anything that men do.

On the other hand, latent functions are those which are neither intended nor recognized by the actors in structure. Whereas manifest functions refer to the conscious justifications for social behavior, latent functions refer to the structural-functional consequences of such behavior, the socially unrecognized, unseen, and unintended.

The actor's end for going to church—in terms of manifest function—may be the salvation of his soul or the souls of others and eternity in heaven. Or it may be to live "the good and moral life." And although there may indeed be meaningful psychological rewards (peace of mind) for faithful religious devotion, those actors who participate fully in religious activity may be helping to integrate, stabilize, and maintain the necessary normative order. There are therefore two significant sociological dimensions illustrated here: (1) The personal ends which the actor pursues may be translated into functional requirements of the social order. That is to say, although only conscious, motivated, living creatures have ends or goals, a social system has structural and functional needs which are peculiar to itself and not to individuals. (2) The actor may justify his personal quest for ends and goals in the language of manifest function, whereas the objective sociological consequences of his behavior and that of his fellows may be revealed in latent function.

Note, however, that the distinctions between manifest and latent function are sometimes more difficult to observe and that there is often no distinct line between the purposes and goals of social activity (manifest function), and the unnoticed consequences (latent function). In the empirical sense it is often impossible to differentiate between the two—one actor may state, "I'm going to college to get a good education," while another might say, "I'm going to college to get a piece of paper, a diploma, so I can get a job." In one case the student's and the generally avowed purposes of education are congruent, in the second the student has dismissed the publicly manifest reason, but recognizes, and in a sense makes personally manifest, the latent goal.

I was doing research in an old, established New England community, which we shall identify here as Old Harbor. In this study I was gathering data on the class structure of the community and also on certain aspects of the voluntary associations—clubs, organizations, and the like. I was particularly interested in which social classes belonged to which particular organizations. In interviewing members of this community's upper class—those community members of great wealth, prestige, and power—I found that all of these upper-class people belonged to a club. We shall call it the "Cambridge Club."Now, although all of the upper class belonged to the Cambridge Club, I had difficulty in finding out what the club "did." In short, when I questioned my respondents about the manifest function of the Cambridge Club, they were almost evasive and quickly moved the conversation on to something else.

After several months of interviews, certain facts became clear: (1) only the upper class in Old Harbor were members of the Cambridge Club, and (2) the club didn't seem to "do" anything. It met once every two or three years for the installation of "new members." These members turned out to be young adults of upper-class families. But other than that, there were no meetings, no officers, no "function."

Beneath the upper class in Old Harbor there was another class of very rich "new" people. Some of them, according to the upper-class respondents, "had only been around for sixty or seventy years." Now, these "newcomers" lived generally in the same section as the old upper class. Their houses, in many cases, were larger and more luxurious than those of the old upper class. They were college-educated and the only thing they seemed to lack was a family line going back to the American Revolution. We will identify this stratum as the "Lower-upper Class." (We shall have more to say about class structure in general in a later chapter.)

The numbers of lower-upper class families had steadily increased in Old Harbor since the end of World War II. The community had become a suburb during this time, and its great natural beauty and proximity to the nearby city had attracted many new residents to the area. It was around this time, apparently, that the upper class became interested in the Cambridge Club, which had apparently lain dormant as an organization for over 100 years. (In the history of Old Harbor, the Cambridge Club had been an active club of sportsmen in the 1840's.)

During my interviews with the members of the lower-upper class, they often identified an upper-class family as being "in" the Cambridge Club. In short, it soon appeared that the lower-upper class was acutely aware of the Club even if they were not members of it. And although the two classes lived in the same general area of Old Harbor, went to the same high-prestige church, drove the same makes of car, sent their children to the same Ivy League colleges, and even went to some of the same parties and "socials," the one objective fact (other than ancestry in Old Harbor) that separated them was membership in the Cambridge Club. And recall that the club didn't "do anything"— that the members didn't seem to be able to describe it meaningfully. It is here that the distinction between latent and manifest function can be made.

In point of sociological fact, the Cambridge Club did not have a manifest function, and this is why the members were so embarrassed about it all. They were glad they belonged, but they could not explain what was *intended* or *recognized* about the club's activities. Of course, the club had a function that was entirely latent: *it existed simply to keep people out.* By keeping the lower-upper class out of the club and confining membership exclusively to the upper class, the club latently served to maintain class distinctions. Its function was to let the lower-upper class know they were lower-upper class and that they had not "arrived" at the top of the Old Harbor class system. And it became evident through my interviews that the latent function was dramatically operative. The lower-uppers were all aware of the club and were painfully conscious that they were not in it. Many of them revealed a strong fascination with the Club and would have gone to almost any lengths to be asked to join.

In my later interviews with the old upper class, I probed a good deal on the "functions" of the Cambridge Club. It was apparent that many of the people simply were not aware of what the Club did on the level of manifest function. There were attempts to describe the club as having "historical interests" or a concern with "preserving the charm of Old Harbor"—but when I asked how it did this, some of the upper class members simply lapsed into puzzled silence. Some confessed they really "didn't know what it did." The lower-uppers were equally confused regarding the manifest functions of the Club, though some were sociologically sophisticated enough to say, "Well, I'm not in it. . . ." But the unrecognized function of exclusion and the maintenance of class distinctions was brilliantly if latently executed by the Cambridge Club.

The Cambridge Club is unusual in that for many members only the barest sense of the manifest purposes, indeed, the latent function of maintaining class lines, were *manifest* to all. However, the distinctions between the publicly avowed and the unnoticed but actual, social consequences of behavior can be seen clearly in everyday social situations. The manifest function of regular attendance at religious services will be stated in terms of "salvation" or "worship," but the latent function may be to show off new clothes, socialize and meet people, or demonstrate class position by going to a "fashionable" church. Some young men *manifestly* go to college to get an "education" *latently* seeking to avoid the draft.

However, these illustrations refer to the personal and idyosyncratic behavior of individuals. Latent functions may also be seen in terms of a broad normative design. The "incest taboo" is a case in point. By the incest taboo we refer to the almost universal cultural standard that marriage and sexual relations may *not* occur within the immediate family of mother, father, and their children. There have been many explanations advanced by social scientists for the relative universality of this institution. Space does not permit an intensive discussion of the biological, psychological or moral factors traditionally put forward. But consider what would happen to the family system if free and easy sexual relations were permitted between the generations and among siblings. We might assume that the system would fail because *role obligations would collapse*, there would no longer be clear and definable roles, and there would be confusion as to who is responsible for who. It would also seem that paternity would be unclear and the critical role of the father go unspecified. The usual normative reasons advanced for the incest taboo are stated in moral and ethical terms, and not in the formal language of role conflict or ambivalence. The public or manifest reasons have nothing to do with the latent or sociological reasons. In short, the prohibition of incest among almost all people has really nothing to do with moral revulsion as a primary cause (the manifest), of the taboo, but with moral revulsion that has been acquired as a result of the taboo. Furthermore, the functions of the incest taboo are almost entirely latent in that the taboo exists to prevent family instability and particularly to prevent confusion as to role obligations. Without the taboo the structure of the immediate family in terms of status/role would be uncertain. Consequently the orderly replacement of population through the family system would become a highly erratic affair, a condition no society could tolerate over any period of time.

DYSFUNCTION

The primary thesis presented in this chapter has been that social structures, when viewed as systems, must maintain certain vital functions if they are to endure. And through the analysis in which functions are seen as manifest or latent, we have distinguished motive and goal on the level of the actor from the functional imperatives on the level of the social system. But the approach of functional analysis that we have presented here, while demonstrating the unique reality of collective life, sometimes gives the impression that a sort of perfect structural-functional harmony exists within social systems and with the coherence of the actors to the system. Such a condition has never existed, for social systems are never perfectly integrated or perfectly designed, and there is always a degree of tension between the actor as a psychological-biological system and the exterior social organization. Indeed, the pursuit of the functional imperatives, which generally aids in the integration and adaption of the system, may produce *dysfunctional* elements as well. We identify as a *dysfunction* those observed social consequences which hinder or lessen the integration and adaptation of the social system.

An illustration of the interplay between function and dysfunction may be seen in the dating and courtship practices of Americans as a basis for marriage. In many societies, marriages are arranged by parents, and children are expected to accept the mates their parents select for them. In the United States, however, with the decline of the extended family system and with the rise of great cities and a high degree of social and geographic mobility, it has been virtually impossible for parents to exercise this dimension of their traditional role. As a consequence, the individuals directly concerned make the decision for themselves. In view of the character of the times, there is probably no way for mate selection other than through some mechanism of individual choice between the two persons directly concerned. In this respect the current American dating and courtship practices are *functional*: they lead to integration and adaption. The family system *functions*: it reproduces children, they are socialized, they take their place in society, and the courtship, marriage, and child-rearing cycle goes on.

But there are serious dysfunctions in American dating-courtship institutions. The emphasis on physical attractiveness, the expectation of heady romance, the stress on cosmetic faces and personalities lead to a distortion of reality in the relationship between the dating partners. Romance, in short, which is the primary basis for marriage, leads to the masking and hiding of basic personality. Often, only when "the honeymoon is over" do the two people really discover themselves as persons and not as highly synthetic romantic prototypes.

The dysfunctions of the dating-courtship pattern can now be seen. Marriage and family relationships, if they are to endure, are built around the realistic appraisal of the participating actors. But the high rate of divorce in the United States (roughly 25 per cent of marriages end in the divorce court) suggests that the glorious expectations of marital life are not met and the functional structures and practices of dating-courtship patterns produce significant dysfunctions.

Another illustration of the interplay between function and dysfunction may be useful here. For almost the entire span of human existence, mankind has literally struggled to survive. Given the omnipresent problems of disease, famine, war, accident, infant mortality, maternal mortality, and the like, a high birth rate was the only way to keep population in any kind of balance. So it has been that all societies, through the norms and status/role system, encouraged a high birth rate.

It has been only within the past 300 years that a significant decline in the death rate has occurred and as a consequence population growth has soared. This spectacular gain has resulted not from a dramatic increase in births but from a steady decline in deaths. When the death rate began to fall because of elementary advances in science, medicine, and public policy in the seventeenth century, the birth rate continued high because its primary definitions were in the grip of the central mores. In the West, the very core of Church and "social" ideology advanced the cause of the large family because it was functional to do so. High births had to balance the high death rate. But today a point has been reached where many parts of the world face a serious overpopulation problem. India, increasing in population by 13 million people a year, could easily double its current population (over 500 million) within a generation.

It is here that the dysfunctional norms and practices can be seen. Where at one time a high birth rate was essential for survival (and the mores supported the high birth rate—indeed, made it possible) *the very same mores are now dysfunctional in many parts of the world. That is, a continual increase in population may so strain the already weak economies of Asian, African, and Latin American countries that they may collapse under the sheer weight of numbers, since resources to take care of them are inadequate.*

The press of numbers, in short, may so strain the social systems of these societies that loss of integration and adaptability will be the inevitable result. The large family, which was functional to these societies one hundred years ago, now threatens to destroy them. In the span of merely four generations function has become dysfunction.

It is interesting to note in this regard that the views of the Catholic Church, which have been supportive of the large family ideology and morality for so long (when it was functional) are now in the process of reconsideration. Note too, that while in 1968 the Pope restated the traditional Roman Catholic position regarding contraception and birth control, many American Catholics openly spoke in opposition. Indeed, during a Sunday service in which the officiating Bishop argued in support of the Pope's position in Washington, D.C. (September, 1968), half of the congregation walked out of church in protest and one member of the congregation attempted to rebut the Bishop openly in church. The time may come when the traditional morality regarding family size will be entirely reversed and married couples with one or two children rather than those with larger families will be the models for social approval. Indeed, if population continues to rise in the underdeveloped nations, the matter may be taken out of the hands of the informal norms and written into law. The time may not be far away when limits on family size may be written into legal codes.

THE OVER-SOCIALIZED MAN AND THE DREAM OF THE UNBONDED

Throughout this chapter we have stressed the structural and functional perspectives of social systems and social structures. It has been our basic purpose here to emphasize the unique forms of reality that social systems produce beyond the individual. To this end, we have attempted to demonstrate how individuals may be seen as the raw human stuff through which social systems endure. Similarly, we have tried to show how the ends actors personally seek to achieve may be functionally related to the imperatives of social systems. But in the attempt to demonstrate the emergent forms seen in the concept of social system, there is always the possibility of overemphasizing the group in contrast to the individual.

There is a peculiar paradox in the relationship of individuals to collectivities: a collectivity cannot survive without the human resources or raw materials through which it unfolds but, at the same time, no social system can so coerce the individual that it crushes him psychologically or physically. The individual, as a personality system, has needs, too, and no social system can survive if it completely subordinates the psychological requirements of the individual to its own functional requirements. Collectivities cannot survive without individuals, and individuals cannot survive without collectivities—that is, without association with other human beings and a stable group life. Neither psychology or sociology can be denied in the necessary interplay of functional system needs.

The answer to the issue of the individual versus the group is the inevitable, if rather unsatisfactory, conclusion that both live in a state of tension with one another. Neither individual nor group is completely satisfied in the relationship, because each may have to subordinate the full expression of system needs to the other. However, in spite of the lack of complete and full expression, both systems, psychological and social, manage to function and even to strengthen and grow.

Now, as we have seen, from a sociological point of view the individual is regarded as an "actor"—an actor because of the primary sociological units of norms, status/role, interaction, and social relationship. These combine in early childhood, largely within the framework of the family, to produce primary self-identity, an "ego," and a growing internalized amalgam of social expectations (ideas, beliefs, norms, roles, etc.) which becomes an organic part of the maturing psychic apparatus of the individual. Conscience, "superego," the "generalized other" in G.H. Mead's vocabulary, the "looking-glass self" in the system of C.H. Cooley, constitutes the psychologic-sociologic residue of systematic exposure to the organized social system.

And so we grow up to be "actors" locked in social structures, and often the very personal goals that *we think* are uniquely our own turn out to be the "pursuit of latent functional imperatives" far beneath the surface of visible society. It all seems very mechanical, impersonal, and quite possibly depressing. The individuality of each man seems utterly drained away by the functional point of view. Furthermore, each of us may feel terribly frustrated, trapped, coerced, manipulated, and controlled by the demands of the group even if we are not aware of latent sociological forces. Living with other human beings may, in short, produce frustrations of individual needs, of psychological needs, and of personal goals and ends.

To be joined with others in a permanent relationship—the family, the job, the community, the fraternity, the college, the church, the boy friend or girl friend—is to expose oneself to a constant condition of obligation. As son, father, employee, friend, neighbor, student, Methodist, "steady"—no matter what role or combination of roles we occupy—the essence of the role is defined by the prescriptive and proscriptive norms which give it its distinctive character. For all men, in all cultures and social systems, social life is an inevitable sequence of obligation. Through mutual obligatory relationships, through the principle of reciprocity, through specialization, through division of labor, through interrelationships and interdependence, the very essence of social life is distilled. To enter into social relationships with others (as we must), we submit to the inevitable obligations not only of the formal role structure, but also to the informal demands of interrelated human beings in other roles as well:

> John, on your way back from the store, would you return this library book for me? And while you are there, run down to the shoemaker. . . .

> Mary, after you finish typing the letter, I want you to get the Smith contract out of the files.

> Say, Charlie, I know it's 4:15 in the morning, but I'm out here on the freeway with a flat tire. I know it's a bother, but I haven't got a spare tire, so I wondered if you could. . . .

> Oh, yes, Professor Smith, I called you in this afternoon to discuss the grades given by your departmental staff. Do you realize that your department hasn't given an F grade in three years?

> There will be a full-period examination on Parts 3 and 4 of the course outline at the next class meeting. It's only fair to say that it will be quite comprehensive.

Of course, as demands are put upon us, so do we put demands on others. The core of association is reciprocity: both actors, or the multiplicity of actors, seek to gratify a number of ends through the relationship. Whatever it is that we seek through association with others (honor, love, power, wealth, friendship, redemption, etc.), the purposes and goals of others as well as our own must be satisfied in the relationship. Mutual interdependence and reciprocity are the key to it all. There is a congruence of ends in the reciprocal character of social relationships.

Furthermore, the psychic needs of individuals, many of which generate from interpersonal experience, must also be met. So there are egos to be established and sustained, self-identity to be fulfilled, personal ends to be secured. Group ends (latent and manifest) must be achieved, and the functional imperatives of social systems are to be satisfied. All of this is realized in the marvelous alchemy of sustained human relationships. In short, the ferment of enduring social interaction (from dyad to society) produces identity for the individual and, through the principles of mutuality and reciprocity, both individual and group ends are secured.

But there is a price to be paid. For, though men cannot live long apart from each other, the obligations of collective life may at times weigh heavy on all of us. Faced with the nagging, insistent, strident, relentless, obligatory demands inherent in life within "the system," there is inevitably the terrible moment when we want "out," when we have "had it up to here," when the most important immediate need is to escape from it all. In the course of every single lifetime, the burdens of reciprocity reach such an intense and relentless peak that the desire to "get out from under" is almost irresistible. But the elementary fact is that we do resist it, and the next day we are back "in structure" again.

When the burdens, problems, strains, obligations, contradictions, demands, and pressures of our everyday lives reach the point of serious stress, most of us develop devices of release. Certainly the "vacation" is a long-term, annual device to change the pattern of life and to restore the person both physically and psychologically. And for the week-in, week-out tension of life, there is the "party" on Friday night, the movie on Sunday afternoon, the cocktail before dinner, the football game on TV, the "chat" with the neighbors, and the inevitable "good" book. Note, here, that many of these "releases" from the routines and pressures of daily life are essentially middle-class forms; the upper and lower classes and certain ethnic subgroups have developed subcultural variations on the "escape" theme.

However, if a long and solitary drive in the country might serve to restore a suburban housewife from the monotony of her "four walls" and enable her to continue, there is currently a conspicuous social movement which seeks total release from the existing social order. I speak here of those highly visible bands of bearded, booted, long-haired persons identifiable on every college campus and in most large cities throughout the country. The hippies will not settle for a fleeting therapy or a momentary palliative from the obligations of social life. They want complete and total removal from society itself.

Some estimates put the total number of hippies in the United States at 250,000, but this figure does not differentiate between the "hard core" members and the "plastic" hippies who show up in uniform each weekend to "make the scene," only to return to the straight world each Monday morning. New York City Police have estimated that in 1967 more than 9,000 runaways were living the hippie life in New York and that girls were outnumbering the boys in running away from home.

Generally, hippies are recruited from the middle classes; they are not lower class in origin. Nonetheless, despite their "midstream" origins, they have vehemently repudiated almost every major social form characteristic of middle-class American society today.

In spite of their opposition to "the Establishment," the hippies are not a revolutionary group, in that revolutionaries, while striving for quick and often violent change from the existing order, seek to replace the "corrupt" or "decadent" system with a "new" society. The hippies are not really trying to change anything externally. The movement seems given to the search for new sensations and experience grounded on psychological rather than sociological change. Ideologically, they have largely removed themselves from society. They argue that the "rat race" and "gray-flannel-suit culture" and the "suburban thing" are beyond redemption. Thus, while repudiating almost everything middle class (personal cleanliness, competition, mobility, work, "responsibility") they have created a social ethic founded on sloth and the abrogation of middle-class "responsibility"—i.e., obligation.

Now, "responsibility"—that often despised term of the Establishment and the older generation—reflects to a certain degree the sociological concept of obligatory norm. To be "responsible" is to accept the normative obligations of an institutionalized status position. To be "irresponsible" is to be capricious and unreliable in the performance of role expectations. By rejecting institutionalized forms of responsibility, the central thrust of the hippie movement seems directed against obligatory society, formal expectations, and the primary organizational units of the contemporary social order. If the movement is against mass society and impersonality, it is for a communized, idealized, pastoral-slum world of the unbonded, in which the principle of total voluntarism takes place over the proscriptive norms.

Although the hippies resort to many physical and symbolic indicators of their alienation from the world of the squares—bizarre hair styles, speech forms, costumes (the flower children), personal decorations, and the like—the ultimate principle of their new order (total voluntarism) is all but impossible to sustain over a period of time. That is, to associate permanently in an enduring system, human beings must "define the situation," and this is achieved largely through the norm, status/role, interaction nexus. In time, status units bind to each other— or, perhaps more accurately, the persons who occupy the status units are bound in obligatory and reciprocal relationships. Eventually, groups and institutions arise to speed and harmonize and to direct the content of interaction. In short, formal social organization must inevitably emerge out of the initial, informal, and transitory relationships. But note that hippie culture centers on the "don't bug me" theme—"Don't hang me up," "Get off my back," and "Let me do my thing."

It is true that hippies have entered into a kind of communal living in their urban "colonies." And there are friendships and close bonds established between members of the community. However, the hippie life stresses the absence of institutionalized and formalized relationships; rather, the emphasis is on spontaneity and voluntarism, and this is the critical point in our discussion of the hippie phenomenon. Spontaneity and total voluntarism are not normative attributes around which sustained group relationships can survive. That is why hippie society must fade away and the escapees will somehow return to organized society. For if hippie society is to survive, it must become normative and obligatory. If it were to become normative and constraining (do this, do that) the salient values of spontaneity and voluntarism would be denied.

While sociologists generally avoid "value judgments" and taking sides in the humanistic or public policy issues of the day, it is nonetheless sociologically legitimate to point out that many non-hippie critics of the contemporary scene have also noted the "conformity," the "drabness" and the mass monotony, rigid institutionalization, and over-rationality of modern life. There seems to be legitimacy behind the hippie question as to the purpose of the "rat race." Why rush to the suburbs to buy a "little box" like everyone else's? Some responsible commentators have suggested that every new car bought constitutes another seduction by Detroit and the auto makers. "Where is it all leading to?" they ask.

"Make love, not war" is another hippie response. It may be, from the standpoint of a critical and ethical appraisal of the current state of affairs, that the hippies have more than a point. And though they will soon disappear from "the scene" that they have so desperately tried to "make," the questions or alternatives to blatant status struggle, to greed, to over-rationality, to materialism, to war and violence, to impersonality that they have asked will still be with us. Indeed, as the hippie cults run their course, the substantive moral-social issues they raised are increasingly incorporated into the questions asked by activist college students today. In the 1950's college students were called the "quiet generation," a description far from applicable at present. The issues and forces which led to the hippie reaction now seem to be at the very doorstep of higher education.

Apart from the relatively small number of hippies in their permissive utopias in the central cities, most people live their lives almost entirely within the framework of conventional expectations. And yet, as we have previously noted, everyday living carries with it a share of tension, frustration, and, most certainly, obligation. There are forms of release and momentary withdrawal from the "system," however, that are far more temporary and less spectacular than the hippie movement. For instance, the Western movie is a form of popular entertainment that now has almost universal appeal around the world. It is in the content of the Western film and its meaning to the common man that another form of brief respite from system demands may be seen.

Every week, millions of Americans sit before their television sets and watch a modern folk drama. Hundreds of thousands more Americans will see much the same thing in local movie theaters. But, more significantly, throughout the world, this very week, Arabs, Hindus, Japanese, Swedes, Pakistanis, Filipinos, Mexicans, Englishmen, Brazilians, Lebanese, Italians, and others, will trek by the millions to a movie theater or sit before their television sets and watch an old American cowboy film. In some cases, the local language will be dubbed in or subtitles will be used, but often the film is exactly as it was when it left Hollywood years ago.

The basic plot of the film, the principal characters, the primary issues, the essential ethical and moral message, and the ending are all a familiar and foregone conclusion. The incredible fact about the Western film is the way in which it cuts across cultures and apparently has value and meaning for everyone. Indeed, the Western has become so widespread and so universal an "art form" that it is being made in Japan and Italy purely for the local markets.

In spite of the very real differences in cultural values and beliefs, what is there about the Western that has such universal appeal to Arabs and Israelis, Italians and Puerto Ricans, Britons and Japanese? Part of the answer may be found in the basic form of the Western. Although there are endless variations on the primary theme, certain features reoccur again and again in each film. Perhaps the major constant is the character and social status of the hero—the cowboy. Although the heroes may show minor personality differences, they all share a common social dimension. The Western hero is essentially a totally *unbonded man.* Like the hippies, he seems to base his life entirely on the principle of voluntarism. He usually stands outside of formal, obligatory, institutional and organizational relationships. He represents the form and spirit of rugged individualism.

The prototype Western hero is never married, and rarely is there the suggestion that he will be. That is why he rides off into the sunset at the end. Furthermore, he is generally outside the church, although he is kind to nuns and generally tolerant of clergymen. The saloon rather than the church is his hangout. Ideally, he shouldn't have a job, but it would be expecting too much of the audience to suggest that he has a substantial inheritance to live on. So he is often seen as a ranch hand or a "hired gun" or perhaps just a "drifter" moving through town. And behind it all there is the expectation that whatever job he has is temporary and he will move mysteriously on. This suggestion is almost always necessary, for the Western hero is the spirit of unbonded freedom and his mobility must be established.

Finally, though a believer in "law and order," he is often peripheral or tangential to the law. It is true he is sometimes cast in the role of the marshal or sheriff, which does represent institutionalization, but more typically he is totally unbonded to anything permanently. Or he may be the classic cowboy figure—a soft-spoken, utterly free soul, who rides into the troubled town, confronts evil, shoots evil down in the inevitable confrontation (good versus evil—the morality play), and then rides off leaving a teary-eyed heroine (society) watching him race the tumbleweeds out of town.

Not only is the Western hero an idealized prototype of the totally free man, not only is he tangential to society in all institutional forms, but he has a common and fascinating psychological dimension. Central to his personality is not only total independence from others but the suggestion of violence. With his six-gun and fists, he is also the Angel of Death. And, irrespective of the cultural setting, there is always a fascination with death.

However, death is usually meted out to evil, and when evil presses the hero enough, he will act with quick and brilliant technical skills to destroy it. It is for the classic confrontation of good (the hero) and evil (the villain) on Main Street at "High Noon" that the audience patiently waits. They know it is coming, because that is part of the morality play endemic to the Western. It is only the idiosyncratic circumstances that vary with each film. It is not a Western if there isn't at least one shoot-out, and it is the shoot-out that is illustrative of the personal, individualistic but nevertheless volatile and potentially violent character of the Western hero. He settles his own affairs in his own way.

Now, why do the Japanese, the Arabs, and the Italians love the Western so? The hero is usually a white Anglo-Saxon "Protestant." The physical setting and the cultural issues are so removed from the daily lives of most people throughout the world as to be almost meaningless—or so it would seem. Recall that most "actors" live out their lives totally within the status/role nexus. And yet each person must have his moments when the desire for total escape is intense. Can it be that for a few hours in the darkened theater or living room, the social man, the bonded man, the obligated man, finds some brief catharsis, some momentary respite from the burdens of the day, through *identification* with the very spirit of freedom—the Western hero?

Arabs, Japanese, and Italians live in societies with particularly intense and demanding norms. Can the cross-cultural appeal be so strong that all men find in the Western film momentary release from the lives they live? For a brief moment or two, "Everyman" rides the wide and open range with the power of life and death strapped firmly to his hip. And can the inevitable violence appeal, in spite of cultural differences, to some latent and slumbering aggressive force generic to the human personality but often covered up and disguised through socialization and normative definition? And note, too, that the violence is purely vicarious and not real. It is symbolic and transcendental, and it is directed against evil. That is what makes the Western socially acceptable as well as psychologically enjoyable.

The Western film offers positive, if temporary, release from the obligatory demands of social systems. With the Western hero all men may ride the range for an hour or two, seeking adventure, romance, and the heady wine of combat. Afterwards we all return to the system and tomorrow's bout with obligations, norms, and expectations—bosses, wives, husbands, fathers, professors, students, girl friends, ministers, papers, reports, telephones, examinations, sales charts, memoranda, bills, Draft Boards. . . .

SUGGESTED READINGS

ARENSBERG, CONRAD M., and SOLON T. KIMBALL, *Family and Community in Ireland*. Cambridge: Harvard University Press, 1940.
> *Social system perspectives applied to the study of the Irish peasant family.*

JOHNSON, HARRY M., *Sociology*. New York: Harcourt, Brace & World, Inc., 1960.
> *An introductory text in which the theme of functional analysis and social system is a critical concern. Chapters I through III are particularly relevant.*

LEVY, MARION, *The Structure of Society*. Princeton: Princeton University Press, 1952.
> *The analysis of society viewed from the structural-functional perspective.*

MERTON, ROBERT K., *Social Theory and Social Structure*. Glencoe: The Free Press, 1957.
> *A collection of Merton's principal papers in which the functional theme prevails. Chapter I contains his formulations on latent and manifest function.*

PARSONS, TALCOTT, *The Social System*. Glencoe: The Free Press, 1951.
> *The basic and definitive source of social system analysis but difficult to read, especially for the introductory student.*

chapter 5

GROUPS

If you were to ask a knowledgeable person what sociology was "all about," he would probably reply that it was the study of "groups." Such a reply is generally correct. But whatever we may finally decide to be the definitive sociological qualities of groups, we could not really understand them without knowing about (1) the actor, (2) norms, (3) status/role, (4) social relationships, (5) social interaction, and (6) social systems. In short, the formal anatomy of social groups involves all six subsidiary concepts, and that is why it has taken us so long to get here.

Groups are social systems, but they are something more. The concept of social systems and social structure deals with the primary functional imperatives and units of social organization. All groups solve the functional imperatives of integration and adaptation. They could not long survive if they did not. Similarly, all groups involve social relations and some form of interaction— certainly cooperation and possibly competition. But social groups, besides being social systems, interaction systems, are also concrete and empirical. The functional imperatives are *analytic constructs*. Groups, however, are visible; they exist in time and place. That is why, when we discuss social groups, we often refer to "a" family or "General Motors" or "the United States of America"

or "the gang." These are groups that have solved the functional imperatives. They have structure and interaction. They are empirically verifiable.
But they are also different from each other: and this is where our
discussion of groups really begins. The concepts that we previously
developed (social system, structure, etc.) largely demonstrated what collectivities *had in common* as forms of social reality. Essentially what we
are saying here is that sociologists have done two things regarding group
phenomena: (1) they have stressed their similarities, largely through
functional-structural analysis, and (2) they have pointed out their differences. It is to the latter concern that we shall now turn our attention.

One of the prime requisites of scientific procedure is the organization of knowledge. Hence the scientist's concern with classification.
Astronomers classify stars and planets. Biologists classify living things
by gross and minute differences. But how are groups to be classified?
What variables are critical or definitive in determining the final social
character of groups?

This question has led sociologists down many paths. It is a
complex issue and one that is not entirely answered today. But there is,
nevertheless, a pattern in the way in which sociologists have set out to
answer the question. We may find a clue by considering how two sociologists of the past approached the problem.

GEMEINSCHAFT AND GESELLSCHAFT

In 1887 the German sociologist Ferdinand Tönnies published *Gemeinschaft und Gesellschaft*, in which he argued that there were two basic and
fundamental forms of social relationship common to all mankind. These
two generic forms, he argued, rest on two types of "will," which he
identified as *Kurwille* (rational will) and *Wesenwille* (natural will). Essentially Tönnies maintained that two definitive forms of social relationships stemmed from this psychological or volitional source.

Today we no longer accept Tönnies' conclusion that the source
of social relationships is psychological, but his analysis of the types of
relationships per se, irrespective of their origins, was a major contribution
to the theory of social groups. The terms *Gemeinschaft and Gesellschaft*,
which refer to the distinctive forms of relationships, have no direct trans-
lation into English and that is why sociologists today continue to use
Tönnies' original terms. There is a primitive English equivalent in the
terms "community" (Gemeinschaft) and "society" (Gesellschaft) but by
no means do they represent the same thing in the two languages.

For Tönnies, the two types of "will," natural and rational, become expressed in a general and shared "collective will." That is to say, groups may characteristically emphasize one of these forms of will, so that it produces the predominant and pervading kind of relationship throughout the interaction system. The "collective will" grows out of each individual's predisposition for one of the two types and becomes the model for all relationships within the group.

According to Tönnies, major social units can easily be distinguished by their characteristic emphasis of *Gemeinschaft* or *Gesellschaft* tendencies. *Gesellschaft* can be illustrated by a simple commercial transaction. If you were buying a car and entered into a relationship with the seller, you would both view each other "rationally." That is to say, the seller has a car he wants to get rid of, and he desires money in its place, and you have money but want a car. Each of you would *calculate the other as an object and means to further you toward your own goals*, a car or money. Each actor considers the other actor as a means with which to achieve an end. The entire relationship is infused with rationality and the careful, deliberate calculation of the appropriateness of means to ends. For Tönnies, this is the essence of the principle of *Gesellschaft* —rationality, calculation, formality, specificity, the absence of emotion and regard for the other persons.

On the other hand, there are those relationships in which other persons and relationships are viewed not as instrumentalities but as *ends in themselves*. Such relationships are unconditional and sought after for their own sakes. The family, the gang, the collective reality of the dating couple is valued simply for its own sake. A mother who sits up all night with her sick child doesn't ask, "What am I getting out of it?" She preserves the child because the child is part of the familial relationship predicated on *Gemeinschaft* principles. By contrast, although the classroom may offer great intellectual satisfactions to both professor and student, it is rarely viewed as an end; it is rather, a means to further some longer-range goal of both. In those relationships that are "natural" rather than "rational"—in the family or the local community, for example —there are intrinsic rewards and satisfactions. In a sense, we often enter into the calculation and rationality of the world of *Gesellschaft* in order to preserve the relationships we find in the *Gemeinschaft*. Viewed in this way, *Gesellschaft* may be a means to assure *Gemeinschaft*.

For Tönnies, *Gemeinschaft* and *Gesellschaft* define social relationships not only at the level of the actor but in groups and total societies. Thus, corporations embody the *Gesellschaft* force, and it will also be found characteristically in cities rather than small towns. Whereas the family, extended kinship, and the local community are groups sustaining

Gemeinschaft forms, the state, the capitalist system, the city, and commercial transactions emphasize the *Gesellschaft* principle. Whereas the unit of wealth in *Gemeinschaft* societies is land, in *Gesellschaft* it is money. Whereas mores, folkways, and religion bind persons into the *Gemeinschaft*, convention, contract, and legislation are the normative forms of *Gesellschaft* groups. The characteristic *Gemeinschaft* figure (status/role) is woman, who acts through sentiment and particularism. The characteristic figure of *Gesellschaft* is man, who acts through rationality and calculation.

Now the question is, what is the primary unit of differentiation that Tönnies employed in his classic distinctions between *Gemeinschaft* and *Gesellschaft?* Note that it appears originally as "will" at the level of social relationships. If we discount the issues of will and psychological factors, we can ask, "What sets the pattern of relationships at this level?" Recall the concepts of status and norms. It is here that Tönnies sociologically establishes his distinctions. That is, the norms shape and give form to status positions, and these in turn guide the content of social relationships and interaction. The Tönnies system is essentially an analysis given over to normative differences, which in turn establish critical distinctions in status positions, which in turn shape the character of interaction, *Gemeinschaft* or *Gesellschaft*.

If we were to examine the Tönnies concepts, which are now more than eighty years old, in the language of the pattern variables (see p. 85), these differences will become clear. The *Gemeinschaft* principle is expressed clearly in the pattern variable of quality rather than performance (ascribed status over achieved), particularism over universalism, affectivity over neutrality, diffuseness over specificity, and collectivity-orientation over self-orientation.

Using the family as the prototype model of *Gemeinschaft* relationships, we can see the emphasis on "quality" rather than performance: the key distinctions are "son," "daughter," "father-mother," "male-female," "wife-husband"—all statuses firmly anchored in the principle of quality arising out of sex and age differences. It is true that "husband-wife" is essentially achieved, but nonetheless most family statuses link most critically to the factors of ascription and quality rather than of achievement and performance. Furthermore, family members treat each other as "particular" individuals rather than relating to each other by the same (universalistic) standard of "treating everyone equally."

The family system encourages the expression of emotion and affect between members (love, loyalty, friendship, tenderness, compassion, sympathy) rather than the "coldness" and affective neutrality characteristic of relationships in the corporation. In addition, family roles are generally diffuse rather than specific. The expectations, obligations, rights, and privileges of family life range through an almost limitless and diffuse number of experiences. There is no "rule" or specific norm which says that the mother must stay up with her sick child all through the night. There is no *Gesellschaft* "contract" which specifically and formally enumerates the rights and responsibilities of each "party."

Lastly, the role system of the family, with its generic *Gemeinschaft* orientation, causes each family member to think in terms of the collectivity, the family as a totality, rather than in terms of his own self-interest. In the corporation or the state—in the *Gesellschaft* group—the individual rationally calculates his own self-interest against that of the collectivity. If he comes to feel that self-interest is not compatible with that of the organization, he may rationally elect to resign. The *Gemeinschaft* group, however, encourages actors to identify with the total inclusive group and to regard the interests of the organic whole as identical with their own.

As Tönnies pointed out, the *Gemeinschaft* group is a "ship of fate," in which all of the members share the same ultimate fate within the social system. What happens to one happens to all. It is a community of collective interest rather than a collectivity of distinct persons pursuing private and personal goals.

In laying down the critical formulations of *Gemeinschaft* and *Gesellschaft*, Tönnies was establishing the first comprehensive sociological statement of the nature of social groups. His analysis focused directly on the norm and status systems of collectivities, although he did not use these terms. And from these two major forms of social interaction he established basic distinctions regarding the nature of social groups, communities, and societies. Note, too, that Tönnies was concerned with group differences rather than similarities. *The differences are essentially in the interaction and relationships growing out of major and fundamental differences in normative expectations and the status/role system.*

PRIMARY GROUPS

Twenty-two years after Tönnies presented the view of social relationships shaped by "natural" or "rational" influences, the American sociologist Charles Horton Cooley formulated the concept of "primary group." Cooley was particularly concerned with the essential sociological character of small groups, and the similarity of his conception of the primary group to Tönnies' *Gemeinschaft* notion will be readily apparent. However, Cooley was not so interested as Tönnies in the dichotomous character of social relationships. As we have seen, Tönnies' ideas ranged from "will" to monumental social systems such as the state and society. Cooley, however, confined his interest to small groups, and this was largely compatible with his intellectual interests. He was actually one of the first social psychologists in the United States, and his interest in primary groups resulted from concern with the growth and development of personality. According to Cooley, primary groups are characterized by:

> ... intimate, face-to-face association and cooperation. . . . they are fundamental in forming the social nature and ideals of the individual. The result of intimate association . . . is a certain fusion of individualities into the common whole, so that one's very self, for many purposes at least, is the common life and purpose of the group. . . . it is a "we"; it involves the sort of sympathy and mutual identification for which "we" is the natural expression.[1]

It was Cooley's view that primary groups are the central and crucial unit of social organization down through the ages and in all societies. They are the common social precipitate of all culture systems. They are fundamental because they express and respond to a universal "human nature." They are primary because they are "the primary phase of society." However, the sociology of 1909, particularly that of Cooley, was not so conceptually rigorous or so systematic as it is today. There is a "softness" in his general language, a certain amount of moral judgment running through much of his commentary, in addition to a lack of hard, formal, and systematic conceptualization. Nonetheless, in Cooley's primary group we note one of the significant intellectual achievements in the literature, for he pointed out that no matter how great and complex a society may be, no matter how massive and formidable the institutional apparatus, primary groups will always have form, meaning, and significance to those who participate in them. It was Cooley who suggested that primary relationships are absolutely essential for social life and that no matter how rational, formalistic, and associative a society can grow, the need for small, informal, responsive, personal, affective, inclusive, and spontaneous relationships will always exist.

In order to develop the essence of Cooley's notion, in spite of the semantic difficulties, it would be best to approach the matter from a systematic framework. Accordingly, we will consider primary groups from the standpoint of (1) physical conditions, (2) role characteristics,

---

[1]Charles H. Cooley, *Social Organization* (New York: Charles Scribner's Sons, 1909), p. 23.

(3) social interaction and social relationships, and (4) the concrete social context in which they may be seen and illustrated.

Cooley notes that primary groups are intimate and face-to-face relationships. They are small groups characterized by a common spirit, sympathy, common standards, and mutual aid. Now, the context in which intimacy and face-to-face relationships occur, in terms of the physical requirements for such relationships, suggests that primary groups are physically small and that the members are in close, rather continuous interaction over a long period of time. That is to say, the bonds of tenderness and sympathy, the mutuality of interests, cannot occur quickly or suddenly or among large numbers. These forms of relationships, and the psychological involvements they entail, suggest smallness and continuity. Thus, primary relationships are most likely to occur within a family, a peer group, a neighborhood, or a small community.

The roles within the primary group, as we noted in *Gemeinschaft* groups, cluster clearly in one direction in terms of the pattern variables. From Cooley, we note that there is a "fusion of personalities in the common whole," which he characterizes as the "we" feeling. This is a clear indication of collectivity orientation over self-orientation. In addition, the primary group, with its characteristic emphasis on love, sympathy, vanity, resentment, etc. (Cooley's terms), suggests the dimension of strong affect and feeling. The primary group is expressive rather than being

TABLE III

GEMEINSCHAFT AND PRIMARY RELATIONSHIPS: THE PRINCIPAL SOCIAL FORMS

PHYSICAL CONDITIONS	ROLE CHARACTERISTICS	SOCIAL RELATIONSHIPS	TYPICALLY FOUND IN:	
			Dyad	Group
Small number	Affective	Largely cooperative	Husband-wife	Family
Long duration	Diffuse	Identity of ends	Friend-friend	Peer group
Physical-spatial proximity	Particularistic	Relationship and end	Parent-child	Neighborhood
	Collectivity-oriented	Spontaneity		Small community
	Quality	Personal		
		Inclusive		
		Informal controls		

SOURCE: Kingsley Davis, *Human Society* (New York: The Macmillan Company, 1958), p. 306. Modified with permission of the publisher.

purely instrumental—cool, detached, controlled, and emotionally neutral.

Role obligations within the primary group are characteristically diffuse. That is to say, members interact in terms of broad, normative understandings rather than specific, contractualized obligations. The range of interaction within the primary group is so diffuse and covers so broad a spectrum of social activity that formal specificity to role obligations would be impossible.

In addition, roles are generally linked by particularistic expectations—the fact of personality and the distinctiveness of each human being within the primary framework is simply too powerful to allow universalistic standards to serve as the basic mode of orientation. The father, for example, may believe in equal justice before the law (as a judge) but, when it comes to his own son, there are always "extenuating circumstances." Finally, primary groups emphasize the generic quality a person brings to the role rather than performance. Primary relationships hinge on distinctions like son, daughter, mother, father, boy friend, girl friend—indeed, a complex of expectations that center on factors the individual cannot control.

In terms of the pattern variables, the primary group's fundamental and characteristic role expectations are essentially *affective, diffuse, particularistic, collectivity-* and *quality*-oriented. The basic mode of interaction within primary group is cooperation. The members generally share collective goals and through cooperation may share in the success of combined effort. Although cooperation is probably the most powerfully developed form of interaction within primary groups, Cooley does note that internally the group is "differentiated" (subgroups) and that competition does occur. There is struggle for scarce goals (mother love, father's attention, status, praise, etc.,) that cannot be equally shared. In short, within the broad cooperation of primary relationship, competition is by no means unknown.

The cooperating actors, however, share an identity of ends. These ends clearly depend on the nature of the primary group. If the group is a family, then the ends may be simply the preparation of the evening meal, a summer vacation, or the move to a new house. This, again, is the *Gemeinschaft* "ship of fate" notion: the primary group is a social vehicle, an inclusive system of interaction in which the participants share the ultimate ends of the system goals.

One critical system goal involves the preservation of the parties, the individuals who effect the interaction. Hence, the primary relationship involves not only a mutual identification of collective goals by the participants but also a positive feeling about the intrinsic value of the other persons involved in the relationship. In addition, because primary relations involve small numbers of persons over long periods of time in close physical proximity, there is ample opportunity for the participants to acquire wide and inclusive knowledge about the others within the group. Cooley identified the mutuality of interests and ends within the primary group as the "we" feeling, which expressed the "mutual identification" and sympathy generated in the group. "One lives in the feeling of the whole," he wrote, "and finds the chief aims of his will in that feeling."

Not only is the primary group founded on the sharing of and identity of ends but the relationship, as with Tönnies' *Gemeinschaft*, constitutes an end in itself, Friendship is valued "for its own sake," not because it will "make a dollar." From a rational and calculating point of view, what value is there in a child? Parents securely locked within the primary-*Gemeinschaft* system would be shocked and offended by the question. The basic characteristic of primary relationships, one that makes them unique in our rational, associative, and calculating world, is that it is a relationship which for most persons constitutes the ultimate end of life itself. It is true that men may give their lives for God and country, or even capitalism or "white supremacy" or "black power." But for most men, for whom lofty ideological national or philosophical issues have little everyday meaning, the final referent which underlies each day's activity is "home"—the primary group of the family.

Relationships within the primary group are personal, inclusive, and spontaneous. They are personal because they deal with persons and not things. Persons are viewed as having intrinsic value, as do the relationships which bind them together. People react to each other as "total persons" rather than role segments, such as one encounters in the *Gesellschaft* pattern.

Because of the general diffuseness of role expectations there is a greater range for personality to express itself in the primary group and consequently a freedom and spontaneity of response between the participants which does not occur in more formally organized groups. This is not to suggest the absence of restraints within primary groups. Roles and statuses, norms and expectations, apply here as well. The role of "daughter" within the family group relationship is one thing, the role of "girl friend" in another primary group is quite a different matter. It is simply that the spectrum of legitimate response and the situations encountered within primary relationships do not admit of specific or formalistic definitions.

Lastly, the primary relationship is inclusive. It surrounds each actor in a totality of experience. Within the primary group a person is probably his most complete "self." In *Gesellschaft*, or associative relationships, we may be just a social security number, a claim number, an employee personnel form, a series of punches on the IBM card. In the primary group, we are relatively total persons, surrounded by other concrete individuals and participating in an enduring relationship.

All groups are "organized" in patterned and predictable relationships, and interaction is characteristic of all sustaining social forms. It is in the manner in which relationships are organized, however, that the differences between primary and "secondary" (Gesellschaft—associative) may be seen. We are essentially concerned here with the functional problem of integration. The social organization of a group continues if it remains integrative and cohesive. In primary groups, integration is achieved informally. That is to say, the essential form of the group is supported by the basic norms as articulated through the status/role system. When patterns are not maintained, the group through its leadership structure (parents in the family, "leaders" in the gang) will act to reintegrate the deviant or wayward member through positive or negative sanctions. The amount of sanctioning, from a frown or raised eyebrow through expulsion from the group ("Never darken this door again!"), will depend upon which norm or complex of norms has been violated. Thus, primary groups maintain the integration of the essential social structure largely from reliance on informal controls.

SECONDARY GROUPS

Cooley discussed only primary groups. Tönnies, on the other hand, was concerned through the Gemeinschaft-Gesellschaft conception, with a fundamental dichotomy in social relationships. In a sense, the opposite of primary groups would be "secondary" groups, just as the opposite of Gemeinschaft is Gesellschaft. If primary groups are small in size, of long duration, and physically and spatially proximate, then secondary groups are large in size, of short duration, and physically and spatially distant. This does not mean that secondary groups are "short-lived" in contrast to primary groups. Indeed, the opposite is true. Primary groups last only as long as the lifetimes of their members, but the relationships within the system are intensive and long lasting. Secondary groups, on the other hand, may last as concrete entities hundreds of years—e.g., the United States Navy, the Roman Catholic Church, Columbia University, the A & P—but they bring people together in formal, specific, and relatively short interactive situations (the eight-hour day). Lastly, whereas primary groups are characterized largely by cooperation, secondary groups—or, as they are also called, *associations*—though also cooperative (no group can exist without cooperation) strongly emphasize the competitive dimension as well.

TABLE IV.

GESELLSCHAFT AND SECONDARY RELATIONSHIPS: THE PRINCIPAL SOCIAL FORMS

PHYSICAL CONDITIONS	ROLE CHARACTERISTICS	SOCIAL RELATIONSHIPS	TYPICALLY FOUND IN Dyad	Group
Large number	Neutrality Specific	Cooperation and competition	Manager-salesclerk	Corporation
Short duration	Universalistic	Disparity of ends	Salesclerk-customer	Nation
Physical-spatial distance	Self-oriented	Relationship is a means	General-private	Army
	Performance	Formalistic	Actor-theater goer	Religious denomination
		Impersonal	Congressman-constituent	
		Exclusive		Trade union
		Formal controls		

SOURCE: Kingsley Davis, *Human Society* (New York: The Macmillan Company, 1958), p. 306. Modified with permission of the publisher.

Characteristically, roles in secondary groups are dominated by affect neutrality and specificity. Emotion and feeling are buried beneath the role segment (Vice President in Charge of Development, Associate Professor of Chemistry, Sales clerk, Able-bodied Seaman), which dominates the formal interaction within the system. Relationships are universalistic, self-oriented, and performance-(achievement-) directed.

> I'm sorry, but it's impossible to change your grade. I clearly told the class that everyone would get a grade of C if they had an average between 70.5 and 79.5. Yours is 68.6 even with the 82 on the final examination.

> Sorry, Miss Smith, but you are classified as a clerk-typist Grade 4, which means you are not qualified for a salary increase until you are reclassified to the 3 Level. I must also say that there are a lot of people coming up for reclassification this year who are very well qualified. . . .

These two statements indicate characteristic *Gesellschaft* formality and specificity. Note the emphasis toward universalistic standards rather than the particularism of a primary relationship. Consider, too, in the last statement, the competitive implication that rewards cannot all be shared. Characteristically in the secondary association, however, there is the possibility of status change on the basis of performance ("reclassification"). Note also that when Miss Smith asked for a raise she showed that her relationship with the company (secondary group) was based on the calculation of rational self-interest and self-orientation. If the company does not come through with the raise, Miss Smith may feel that the goals of the company and her own are no longer congruent and she may leave.

If the pattern variables as seen in role expectations differ diametrically between primary and secondary groups, so do the characteristic modes of social relationships. Whereas identity of ends is maximized within primary groups, there is within the secondary group a plurality and disparity of ends among the actors. For example, an "up and coming" salesman may feel his boss is "standing in his way." Relationships, as Tönnies indicated, are infused with calculation and rationality and are viewed by the actors as means rather than ends. The actors may be individually seeking status, power, or wealth. They may view each other as conditions or obstacles to further advances. Competition may be intense. Furthermore, the high degree of role specificity introduces formality into relationships in contrast to the freedom, expressiveness, and spontaneity of the primary group.

Lastly, the secondary group is characterized by its exclusivity—the narrowed range of role possibilities and the intense focus on specific and rationally articulated goals. ("Listen Charlie, don't make any mistake about it. Television is a business; we aren't out to educate anyone. We are selling products. And if we don't sell, we're out of business!") The secondary group is rationally conceived to achieve known goals. It does this through the articulation of formal, impersonal, and exclusive focused relationships.

If control in primary groups is informal, within the secondary group it is heavily institutionalized and formal. If an actor fails to perform to a minimum standard, he is simply removed from the status position. Since achievement is the primary mechanism for filling status positions, the lack of expected performance is the chief factor in removal. Secondary groups have, however, devised all sorts of mechanisms to remove persons with some consideration for the person. A man may be "kicked upstairs" to a vice-presidency which is not sensitive to organizational purposes. A man may be "promoted" to some distant branch office which is so unattractive that he will do the expected and resign. Or, indeed, if the situation warrants, an actor may be simply forced out of the secondary group by "firing," or by excommunication from the religious group, or by a dishonorable discharge from the military, or "separation" from the university for poor academic grades.

In the primary group, with its small numbers and ascribed roles, there is much more difficulty in removing the actor. Mothers are not fired, nor are fathers dishonorably discharged, nor are friends publicly unfrocked or "drummed out" of the relationship. If the primary group ceases to satisfy or to function—as in the case of a peer group or a gang—it may simply cease to exist. If one person is "the cause" of the "trouble," the group may, indeed, find some informal device to remove him or discourage him from the relationship. For example, the members may cease to recognize or respond to the deviant. He gets the "cold" treatment. If he "gets the message," he may conform to the collective expectations; or, if the group no longer has value and meaning to him, he will leave. On the other hand, a family with serious internal problems—a neglectful mother, an alcoholic father, an errant child—has serious difficulties. Society does not like to see the family broken up and the members scattered to take up isolated lives. The national concern with divorce clearly indicates the ethical, moral, and normative disapproval involved in breaking up the family as a primary group.

Primary and Secondary Groups as Ideal Types

We have spent considerable time distinguishing between primary-secondary groups and the *Gemeinschaft-Gesellschaft* dichotomy. It is clear that although Tönnies and Cooley may have emphasized different dimensions of the sociological character of small groups, they were essentially dealing with the same generic force in collective life. Cooley had strong social-psychological interests, and for him the primary group was particularly fascinating for its contributions to personality and the sociology of the self. Tönnies had massive institutional interests and was concerned with the "unfortunate" drift of modern society from the natural bonds of *Gemeinschaft* relationships toward impersonal, calculating *Gesellschaft*.

At this juncture of our consideration of social groups, it is important for the student to realize that all that we have said regarding the ultimate character of group forms has consisted of idealized exaggerations of empirical reality. We have summarized the distinctive forms of primary relationships, but in the real world we can never find an empirical, concrete group which perfectly duplicates or completely reflects all of the variables of primary groups. The primary group described on these pages is an "ideal type"—the logical and perfect summation of all primary relationships. The best that we can do with the concrete world is to contrast empirical, operating, extant groups with the conceptual model. We will find that families, peer groups, and small folk communities lean toward our conceptual ideal. But even here we will find elements of *Gesellschaft*, or secondary relationships. Sometimes family members do consider each other as means and not ends. Sometimes there is not an identity of ends. Sometimes achievement rather than ascription may be a powerful reality within primary groups.

The fundamental distinctions between primary and secondary relationships are the conceptual and ideal-typical prototypes of two basic group forms which have no total empirical fit with the real world. In the extant social world, however, there are operating groups which spread out along a continuum from one pole on the primary side to a pole on the secondary side.

Real groups may be systematically observed by the extent to which they sustain primary or secondary forms. Families in the United States, as a totality, will unquestionably range toward the primary side of the scale. Certain specific families would almost reach the primary "ideal"; a few would probably have almost classic secondary characteristics. On the other hand, the giant corporations, the great associations, would fall out along the secondary side of the scale. Some corporations, however, might be further along the secondary side than others. Indeed, in this fashion, entire societies might be observed by the extent to which they reflect primary or secondary relationships. Note, however, that the concepts that we have just been discussing are idealized conceptual extensions which reflect but do not completely describe the empirical reality of the sociological world.

THE SOCIOLOGY OF HUMAN GROUPS

At the beginning of this chapter, we posed the issue of the classification of groups, pointing out that the classification system depended on the conceptual units upon which the classification was based. In the intervening pages, we have discussed the two classic formulations of social groups that have appeared in the sociological literature. But what is the ultimate basis of classification? We shall return shortly to the Tönnies-Cooley constructions, but note that sociologists have employed many other "definitive" variables in the classification of groups. For example, groups could be classified in terms of "function," either latent or manifest. We could discuss "educational" groups, "political" groups, and "economic"

FIGURE 3

Primary and Secondary Groups Viewed as a Continuum From the Conceptual Ideals Through the Range of Empirical Possibilities

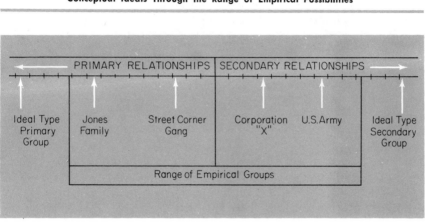

groups. Size has occasionally been a unit of comparison, for, as we have already seen, the physical characteristics of a group (large-small) can help to establish certain social relationships. A large group, *viewed as a large group*, cannot sustain primary relationships.

Groups, or collectivities, can be distinguished on the basis of one factor alone, such as age of over 65 years—an element of ascribed status. Or collectivities may be differentiated by a certain trait or characteristic acquired from the social structure, such as being a "New England Yankee" or a "Westerner" or a "college graduate." There are, in short, many devices and concepts which sociologists have employed in the determination of "groups," but let us return to the Cooley-Tönnies formulation.

The ultimate character of groups, as viewed by either Cooley or Tönnies, emerged from the *characteristic relationships* of the groups—primary or *Gemeinschaft*, "secondary" or *Gesellschaft*. It is clear that, for both Tönnies and Cooley, the determining and definitive variables on which their conceptualizations were based are generic differences in relationships which distinguish primary from secondary groups. Therefore, it is in the *bonds*, the *linkages*, the *essential forms of interaction* that the final sociological quality or distinctiveness of groups may be seen. It is in the essential manner in which actors relate to each other as defined by the status/role system.

It is assumed that social groups bind men in interaction and that a necessary element of the interaction is cooperation. Furthermore, it is assumed that a complex of normative, ethical, evaluative, and ideational justifications has infused the norm, status, and role linkages with enough satisfactory meaning so that the occupant actors have cognition and cathexis as to what the relationship and group are "all about." In short, actors have "identity," "understanding," and "meaning" in the relationship, and, indeed, all group members share through these devices a "consciousness of kind." A psychological affinity for the group and relational system has emerged out of the complex of cultural and social forces which have shaped the essential quality of the relationships and, subsequently, the group itself. We may conclude, therefore, that *social groups are organized systems of interaction and that concrete groups may be differentiated from each other largely through the quality (primary-secondary) of the relational-interactive forms.*

REFERENCE GROUPS

If social groups are interaction systems whose reality is found in the patterned empirical linkages between persons, reference groups, on the other hand, are social-psychological in that the locus of their reality reduces to the subjective perceptions, aspirations, and motivations of the solitary actor. Social groups are external and can be observed by sociologists through any number of methods and techniques; reference groups, however, are a component of the person and are imputed from his unique behavior.

A reference group is exactly what its name implies; it is an external social point of reference for the actor. It is often a "real" group in the sociological sense (Democratic Party, U.S. Navy, Split Rock Golf Club), but the term has been extended to include a wide spectrum of social phenomena—classes, ideologies, norms, values, and the like. In short, a reference group may not refer to an organized interaction system. These external social events are internalized as a positive value by the actor and become a significant anchor or referent for his identity and self-image. Reference groups thus fuse with the ego to become a major social dimension of the personality system. The actor relates and identifies with some social entity or group. He aspires to be a part of it. He adopts the norms, values, social forms, and roles (if possible) of the reference group. A component of his identity closes about it and it becomes a part of him.

Since its introduction into the sociological and social-psychological literature in the early forties, the concept of reference group has been extremely useful. In the phenomenon of *anticipatory socialization*, for example, we can see the internalization of reference groups in small children. When little children dress up in their parents' clothing, and in their attic or backyard "living room" play out parental roles and situations, we observe the internalization and expression of the adult world. The child is *anticipating* his social roles as an adult. Similarly, when a high school student wears his older brother's college fraternity jacket, he is visibly anticipating his status as a future college student. And when the ten-year-old in the urban ghetto begins to adopt the language, dress, and swaggering, aggressive values of the older boys of the street gang, anticipatory socialization via reference group is under way.

Note that while a reference group and a viable (empirical) group can coincide, such as a young man who wants to be a Harvard student and *is* a Harvard student, a reference group may not eventuate in a membership group. For example, an objectively identified member of the working class (unskilled worker, seventh grade education, income below the national median) may *aspire* to the middle class, but he may not actually enter the middle class. However, upward mobility would not be possible were it not for persons who *aspired* for it and who internalized the values and life style of the class they wished (consciously or unconsciously) to become a part of. Indeed, there is probably a good deal of frustration for many millions who have internalized references for which they have little realistic chance of converting into membership groups.

If *anticipatory socialization* is a useful concept to help explain the adjustment of persons into new roles and groups, the concept of *relative deprivation* also utilizes the idea of reference groups. Relative deprivation occurs when a person feels deprived, *relatively deprived*, of something valuable in terms of his reference orientation. In research conducted during World War II, for example, the concept of relative deprivation in terms of reference groups became an important analytic tool. It was found that morale was lower among troops permanently based in the United States than among noncombatant soldiers overseas. It was also found that Air Force personnel, for whom promotions in rank were frequent, were more disgruntled and unhappy about promotions than were infantry soldiers who had little opportunity for promotion. Furthermore, research found that highly skilled blue-collar workers were often more annoyed and upset by being drafted than were white-collar workers and liberal arts college graduates. In all three cases the forces of reference groups and subsidiary concepts of relative deprivation were found to be at work.

In each case, it was found that the soldier felt relatively deprived in terms of his reference group. In the Air Force, where promotions and rank were easy to come by, morale was low because the men wanted to be promoted faster. In the infantry, on the other hand, where promotions were not rapid, the soldier felt he was being treated just like everyone else. Few were promoted, no one felt relatively deprived. As for the non-combatant service troops permanently based in the United States, their reference group was the civilian workers in the nearby defense plant who had more money than they and greater freedom. However, the service troops overseas, who objectively were living a much more uncomfortable and hazardous life than the United States service troops, had higher morale. Why? Their reference group was the combat soldiers and the violence of the battlefield. In comparison, the noncombatant overseas soldier felt he had a "good deal." Similarly, the skilled worker who got drafted felt relatively deprived since many of his friends with similar jobs had been given draft deferments because of the high order of technical skills demanded by the job. He felt deprived because his reference group was anchored in a "no-draft" occupational category.

Relative deprivation may also be a useful concept to explain racial violence and civil disorders in the cities. Until the last ten years, the American Negro was ascribed a fixed and lowly position in the class-caste system. All blacks were treated alike and if you were black you accommodated yourself to the existing order, or you suffered the retributive consequences of the system—in some cases, violence and death. And when race relations were most repressive to the Negro, there was no concerted or mass action (such as exists today) on the part of the black population to change it. But, with the rise of the civil rights movement and the dramatic alteration of race relations in recent years, there has also come about an ideological change in the black population—*they now feel relatively deprived. They compare their own life fate and opportunities with whites and feel outraged.* In the past, only a few Negro intellectuals or persons sensitive to the issues felt relatively deprived, but now, increasing numbers of blacks feel it.

In a sense, the appearance of civil disorders on a wide scale may be seen as a positive response of the black population to the means-ends framework of American society. Negroes want full participation (means and ends) in the system, and see themselves as possessing an equal and legitimate claim on it. There is at present, therefore, an all-pervading sense of relative deprivation, whereas a decade or two in the past most blacks simply accepted the class-caste system and the allocative institutions as inevitable—their life chances were determined as inferior to whites' in all ways. There is something of a bitter irony in all of this because, in some respects, the conditions of blacks in America have improved greatly in recent years—higher incomes, better jobs, greater educational opportunity. Yet, in spite of these gains, the sense of being *relatively deprived* (with white society as the reference group) grows stronger each year, as does violence and civil disorder.

THE ASSOCIATIONAL SOCIETY

From the time of Tönnies and Cooley, sociologists have continued to employ these basic distinctions. However, whereas Cooley's interest centered on the small, primary groups of society, the most dramatic social change occurring in Western civilization—certainly since the time of industrialization—has been the rise of massive, formal, secondary groups. Indeed, this was the major source of Tönnies' concern—the steady erosion of *Gemeinschaft* through the triumph of rationality and the *Gesellschaft*.

These same distinctions have been rephrased with slight conceptual modifications by a host of scholars interested in the major changes in social relationships and group forms in Western society. Durkheim, for example, was aware of the transition, though he used the terms "mechanical solidarity" versus "organic solidarity" to identify the primary-secondary dichotomy. Similarly, in the contemporary literature, the distinctions are also identified by such terms as "folk-urban continuum," "sacred versus secular," and "community versus society." And though interest in the sociological nature of small, primary groups continues, much attention is given to the analysis of the character of modern society and contemporary social organization. Terms often employed to summarize the social character of contemporary Western society are the "multi-group society," the "pluralistic society" or the "associational society."

All of these conceptions reflect a social condition that has arisen only in the past two hundred years. These concepts suggest a type of societal structure that is highly differentiated, segmented, and pluralized into a larger number of complex and specialized groups. Indeed, associations are rationally organized collectivities oriented toward a specific purpose or function. They are essentially secondary groups as we have already discussed them. For almost the entire span of the million years during which human beings have occupied this earth, the exclusive mode of relationships and group life has been primary. However, the rise of large-scale industrialization, urbanization, popular democracy, and national states was accompanied by a steady drift toward the associational type of organization. It is the dramatic confluence of these huge, specialized, rationalistic units of social organization that has remade the basic structural units of society itself. And these remarkable contemporary social forms are still in the process of emergence and development. It is because of their comparative recency that social scientists are still trying to understand what they are, what their significance is, and what the implications are for the future development of society.

Tönnies, of course, deplored the rise of *Gesellschaft* rationality and calculation. However, the rise of associations in the business, political, economic, educational, and religious contexts has steadily continued. Where perhaps only two hundred years ago the lives of all human beings on this earth were spent exclusively within the framework of primary groups, today we spend most of our time in the specific, formalistic, rational, emotionally neutral world of associations. Ours is the "associational society"—a world of bureaucracy in which millions of persons each day are caught up in social structures so vast and complex that no one individual, not even the corporation president, the general, the Cardinal, or the President has full understanding or, indeed, "control" over what is happening. Some call it the "mass" society—a world of mass production, mass recreation, mass communication, mass consumption—even the "massification" of tastes, styles, and appetites.

In a later chapter, we shall attempt to "explain" the force behind the steady rise of specialization and associationalism in modern society. At this point we simply wish to call attention to what has literally been a revolution in social organization—a revolution still going on. From the dominance of primary relationships over the past few hundred years, modern society has seen the triumph of urbanism over the rural village, the corporation over the master craftsman, the trade union over the guild, indeed, the almost universal dependence on secondary relationships. Our lives are increasingly shaped and affected by millions of unknown others who perform a multitude of services upon which we depend. Increasingly, we live in a social system of accelerating interdependence and interrelationships. The mechanism of that interdependence is the association, the secondary group, the bureaucracy, the formally organized group.

SUGGESTED READINGS

BALES, R. F., *Interaction Process Analysis: A Method for the Study of Small Groups*. Reading, Mass.: Addison-Wesley Publishing Company Inc., 1950.
> *A highly systematic presentation of a conceptual system for the analysis of interaction in small groups.*

COOLEY, CHARLES H., *Social Organization*. New York: Charles Scribner's Sons, 1909.
> *Often quaint and moralistic by the standards of today's sociology, but nevertheless a powerful statement regarding the character of small groups.*

GANS, HERBERT J., *The Urban Villagers*. New York: The Free Press, 1962.
> *A study of "peer group society" set in an urban neighborhood.*

GREER, SCOTT A., *Social Organization*. New York: Random House, Inc., 1955.
> *A brief but useful analysis of the social group on terms of functional interrelationships.*

HOMANS, GEORGE C., *The Human Group*. New York: Harcourt, Brace & World, Inc., 1950.
> *Now a classic formulation of the essential and recurrent characteristics of small groups.*

TÖNNIES, FERDINAND, *Community and Society (Gemeinschaft und Gesellschaft)* (trans. and ed. by Charles P. Loomis). East Lansing: Michigan State University Press, 1957.
> *Tönnies' basic distinctions of Gemeinschaft and Gesellschaft are faithfully translated, and his essential contributions to sociology are related to those of other pioneering figures such as Durkheim and Cooley as well as to contemporary sociologists.*

WHYTE, WILLIAM F., *Street Corner Society* (rev. ed.). Chicago: University of Chicago Press, 1955.

> *Now a primary study set in the 1930's of the structure and organization of a street corner group of young men.*

chapter 6

COMMUNITY

In both primary and secondary groups, the principle of social system is implicit. That is to say, groups, if they are to survive, must solve the problems of integration and adaption. But neither primary nor secondary groups are "survival" systems; both are *dependent upon a larger system of relationships* beyond the borders of their interaction. If entirely dependent on the relationships *within the system*, they would eventually disappear, if only because the actors in the group must one day die. Consequently, the relationships defined by status/role and norms within both primary and secondary groups are not designed to be internally self-sufficient or sustaining, to the extent that all of the "needs" of both actors and social systems can be met purely within the group. Occasionally, in these groups, actors "go outside" or engage in and depend on systems external to the immediate group.

In our own social world, for example, family members have jobs outside the family, are educated formally outside the family, seek recreation outside the family, and indeed, spend much of their lives in groups beyond the family. The family, though a vital and significant primary group, is dependent upon relationships and systems beyond it.

Similarly, all the great associations and secondary groups,

though vast and complex in terms of people and institutions, are dependent upon exterior systems. Such great corporations as Dupont, General Motors, U. S. Steel, and General Electric could not function were it not for an organized system beyond their social borders. The business world—indeed, the entire economy—is dependent upon government as a system and also upon the family as a system of institutionalized relationships. Despite all that we hear about the strain between government and industry, business looks to government for the coinage of money, for enforcement of contracts, and indeed, for "regulatory" practices that stabilize and strengthen the economy. Were it not for the United States government, the business world as we know it could not exist or function. Similarly, vast and complex though the giant corporations may be, they cannot last beyond the lifetime of a single member unless they recruit from the "outside" and see to it that a supply of human raw materials fills the status/role structure continually.

Although all the groups that we have encountered so far have been essentially "dependent" systems, the concept of *community*, as we shall now present it, refers to a system of relationships that is relatively self-sustaining and inclusive. A community is a survival system in that as a social system it can endure, theoretically, forever, and all the needs of both actors and social systems are met *within* the system.

A community is a social group and can be viewed as a social system. That is to say, integration, adaptation, goal attainment, and tension management will be solved internally. Indeed, the great associations, family, economy, polity, and religion, which form the basic social anatomy of both community and society can be viewed as substructures which serve to satisfy the functional imperatives for the community.

Community and society share analytically the distinction of social completeness, relative functional independence and social self-sufficiency. And though society may be an abstract conception of functional autonomy as a total system of relationships, community more closely approaches the empirical in that it can be observed operating in extant situations. We may talk of London or New York as urban communities with greater empirical precision than we can of English or American "society."

Community possesses locality. We may have a sociological "idea" about community in terms of functional completeness, but it also is a place. Community, in short, involves specific locality and territorial proximity. We can fix certain territorial limits to community, be it a small, nonliterate community of Bushmen in Africa, a band of Eskimos, or a village in Mexico.

Note again, however, that both community and society refer to systems of relationships that are inclusive and functionally self-sustaining in that the internal system of relationships as a total system can survive beyond the lifetime of individuals. Community and society endure and relationships on this level make it possible for substructures like General Motors or the Roman Catholic Church to possess a degree of social immortality as well.

Whereas community develops substructures to answer the functional imperatives (such as government responding to the needs of integration and economy responding, at least in part, to the needs of adaptation), community faces a functional problem that is unique. It must solve the problem of replacement of population internally and not externally. Note that General Motors supplies itself with new members through its personnel office and that the United States Army replenishes itself through the draft board, the recruiting office, and the college ROTC programs. As formally organized hierarchical and institutionalized groups, all associations look outside themselves for members. But a community, as the first inclusive system, cannot; it must arrange for replacement from *the internal system.*

The universal, or virtually universal, device by which the community arranges for the orderly replacement of new members is the family. That is why the community, in terms of moral, ideational, ethical values—indeed, the entire complex of normative forms—is so critically concerned with family relationships. Were it not for the family system, sustained within the community, there would not be an orderly, stable, functional organization of adults prepared to accept and care for the new child.

The family system is actually not a coercive device to control sexual relationships between adult men and women so much as it is concerned with the consequences of free sexual access—pregnancy and childbirth. It is the *responsibility* for the care and socializing of the child that is the center of the community's concern. Through the family system, therefore, a permanent stable relationship, generally between an adult man and woman, satisfies the community's vital need for replacement of population. Hence, the emergence of a family system in all community forms throughout the world. The community as a survival and yet inclusive system of relationships faces a functional problem (replacement of population) from within that was not characteristic of the groups we have discussed thus far.

To this point we have defined community as a social group whose system of relationships is such that it can survive through time purely from its internal relational system. That is to say, a community internally replaces its membership through the family system. In addition, it organizes economic activities through the institutionalization of property concepts and through procedures for the production and distribution of goods and services. It stabilizes the internal substructures and subsystems through integrative devices found in forms of governance, religion, and social control. Patterns are maintained and tensions controlled initially in the family system, but almost all groups, primary or secondary, develop their own integrative and controlling mechanisms.

In addition, through the possession of a common normative, symbolic, ideational tradition, the members share mutual systems of actions, relationships, and common definitions of reality. Lastly, a community is socially self-sufficient in that its needs for continuity and indefinite survival (the functional prerequisites) will be met within the system. All of this happens in a physical locality where the interaction is bounded by territory and physical proximity. A community is a place.

Since men have lived on this earth for a million years in cumulative social development, it logically holds that human communities go back that far as well. But the character of community has developed in many ways from the simple bands of Paleolithic hunters of a half million years ago. Indeed, the Neolithic village of 7500 B.C., which was a classic *Gemeinschaft* group, has evolved into the giant metropolitan area of today. Although New York City, the ancient Mesopotamian city of Eridu (3500 B.C.), and the Neolithic village of 7500 B.C. are all sociologically communities, they are all "different."

But how are they different? We face again the thorny issue of classification. We know that somehow the giant metropolis is different from the rural village—but how? One of the obvious answers is the size and density of the population, and indeed this has traditionally been a major factor in the classification of communities. However, the manner in which the population is bound together in mutual interdependence through specialization and the division of labor is also significant. And the extent of heterogeneity and difference within the population also differentiates communities. In short, (1) the size and density of population, (2) the degree of interdependence and specialization, and (3) the differentiation and heterogeneity of the population are essentially what distinguish folk communities from contemporary urban forms.

THE FOLK COMMUNITY

Historically, the first cities appeared around 3500 B.C. in the "Fertile Crescent"—the eastern area of Mesopotamia and particularly the river valleys of the Tigris and Euphrates. Until that time, for about a million years of human-social development, the characteristic mode of community life was the small, isolated, homogeneous settlement. There are many terms used to describe the modal community forms that preceded the rise of cities. Tönnies' notion of *Gemeinschaft* critically applies. Certainly these communities were primary groups in Cooley's sense of the term. For our purposes we shall identify these community forms as the "folk community," after the conception originally introduced by Robert Redfield.[1]

Folk communities as we shall describe them are, of course, ideal conceptions, much in the manner that primary and secondary groups are "idealized" conceptions of group forms. Similarly, the folk community is "ideal," a mental construct to which no empirical society or community completely corresponds. There are, of course, many communities which approach the polar ideal of the folk community but never completely empirically reach it. And, note, too, that we are dealing with a continuum of conceptions. At one pole stands the ideal-typical folk community and, ranging through a host of intermediate forms, at the other end of the conceptual extreme stands the contemporary metropolis, the extension of urbanism in all its incredible complexity and process.

Although the metropolitan region may be regarded as the conceptual opposite of the folk community, folk communities are by no means a rarity today. American society is moving steadily toward the complete dominance of the metropolitan area as the modal community form (more Americans live in metropolitan areas than in any other community form), but most of the world's population remains, and will remain for some time to come, within the folk rather than the urban framework. Although large cities and urbanism are growing in importance throughout the world, the so-called "underdeveloped" areas and countries of Africa, Asia, and Latin America are still characterized by the dominance of folk settlements and villages.

Our generalizations about folk communities, therefore, do not apply only to the past and pre-urban society. Probably most human beings today live out their lives on the folk side of the continuum rather than the urban. Of course, as industrialism proceeds at its present rate throughout the world, the eventual spread of the urban way of life seems almost inevitable.

The folk community is small and relatively isolated. It is characterized by *Gemeinschaft* and may be regarded as a series of interlocked primary groups living within a locality or territory. The family is the basic and key unit of social organization, and much of the actor's identity

[1]Robert Redfield, "The Folk Society," *American Journal of Sociology* (January 1947), pp. 293–308.

and the roles he occupies within the community flow from his family's general position within the community.

The division of labor and degree of specialization are limited. The basic factor in the division of labor is sex, and there is some truth to the assertion that if you know well the life of one man or woman in the settlement you know the lives of all the men and women. They all engage in essentially the same task, although the differences in the status/role structure for men and women may be significant.

Within the small, isolated, slow-changing, relatively static world of the folk community people know each other well. The social world has a familiar and regular rhythm to it. And because of the great visibility of community forms and the people of the settlement, social control is primarily informal and very effective. The normative system is monolithic and unyielding. The role/status and ideational choices are few, and so the community acts in concert to sanction deviants from the expected pattern of things. Gossip, visibility, and group consensus oriented from the central mores are generally enough to reinforce the essential normative forms, and thus integration and stability are easily maintained.

Classically, folk communities are nonliterate and economically self-sufficient. They are not "market" oriented, and the indigenous economy is designed to supply local needs and purposes. In terms of the three major units of community analysis that we enumerated earlier, the folk community (1) is small and lightly settled, (2) sustains a simple division of labor and minimal interdependence and specialization of functions compared with the urban community, and (3) is homogeneous and comparatively undifferentiated in social structure and social organization. It is, in short, an undeveloped and simple community.

In terms of the culture system and social organization, the folk community is relatively static and unchanging. Each generation is born into quite the same world as the preceding generation. Furthermore, both the normative and social order are characterized by massive unity and integration. The folk society offers few ideational or role alternatives to its members. Tradition, custom, sameness, regularity, and repetition are its principal concerns. In sum, a folk society is a local community, static and unchanging, homogeneous and unified, sacred and undifferentiated, small and familistic, isolated and self-sufficient, nonliterate and visible, *Gemeinschaft* and primary.

Although folk communities in the ideal-typical sense reflect these qualities, it is doubtful whether any but a few extremely isolated bands or settlements empirically duplicate them. Many folk communities still continue to function in relative isolation today, but they are almost always located within some larger, if for them meaningless, political society. They may be part of an entity called "Brazil" or the British Commonwealth, though the national government has little effect on the lives of people in highly isolated folk settlements. However, their economic self-sufficiency is probably giving way almost everywhere. The world market and international trade, or even trade within the larger "nation," is eroding the local economy and propelling the folk community into a larger system of relationships. As the local economy becomes integrated within a larger economic system, the inroads of industrialization, urbanization, and the associational society will have begun; indeed, it has already begun in many underdeveloped areas of the world.

In briefly outlining the salient features of folk communities, we have identified the essential community features that shaped the social condition of man for a million years. Moreover, the folk community still prevails as the modal community form in the underdeveloped parts of the world. By 1950, almost 21 per cent of the world's population were living in cities of 20,000 or more in population.[2] This was a spectacular increase in urban growth from 1800, when only 2 per cent were living in cities of 20,000 or more.[3]

Conversely, however, even by 1950 approximately 80 per cent of the world's total population were living in settlements and villages of less than 20,000 and, although data for places below 5000 in population are impossible to obtain on a global basis, it seems certain that the majority of the world's population still lives on the folk-society side of the community spectrum. Indeed, approximately one-third of the world's population in 1960 was living in urban places of all sizes, leaving two-thirds to the circumstances of folk or rural society.[4] Such a condition is probably limited to the next generation or two, however, because the forces of urbanization and industrialization unquestionably will render the folk community virtually extinct except in the most inaccessible and isolated places.

THE RISE OF CITIES

A folk community is almost entirely preoccupied with the search for food. Rarely is there a surplus for any period of time, although there may be

[2]Kingsley Davis and Hilda Hertz, "The World Distribution of Urbanization," *Bulletin of the International Statistical Institute*, XXXIII (1953), Part IV, 3, p. 230.
[3]Kingsley Davis, "The Origin and Growth of Urbanization in the World," *American Journal of Sociology*, LX (March 1955), 433.
[4]Kingsley Davis, "The Urbanization of the Human Population," in the *Scientific American* volume *Cities* (New York: Alfred A. Knopf, Inc., 1965), 4.

fleeting moments of plenty and prosperity resulting from a successful hunt or bountiful harvest. Cities consume food and do not produce it. Therefore, urbanization had to wait until agricultural surpluses were possible. Consistent surpluses were not obtained until the first cities appeared in ancient Mesopotamia.[5] Here the Neolithic villages in the rich alluvial valleys of the Tigris and Euphrates had evolved into a level of social organization which made possible the surpluses necessary to support an urban population.

Furthermore, these settlements had evolved into a sort of feudal, preindustrial level. The division of labor had elaborated under the food surpluses, enabling men to specialize in a wider base of economic roles. A more complex class structure had evolved from the expanding division of labor, resulting in more sophisticated leadership and the beginning of rational control over the physical environment, such as irrigation systems. Advances in metallurgy made possible the invention of the bronze plow, which increased the agricultural surpluses even further. By this time the wheel had appeared, which further facilitated the exchange and distribution of goods and services.

So it was that about 3500 B.C. some Neolithic villages began to shift into a newer type: they were becoming cities, and a dramatic reworking of the generic human community was under way. One may wonder why scholars and students of these ancient urban settlements called them cities and how they were critically different from the folk villages and hamlets that surrounded them. We can return to our three critically differentiating variables of community: (1) size and density of population, (2) specialization and differentiation, and (3) characteristics of the population. These settlements were larger than the villages and they were unquestionably more highly specialized in terms of division of labor, institutional-associational forms, and heterogeneity of population.

A city is made possible by special modes of social relationships and social structure. This is seen not only in the manner in which agricultural surplus is achieved through more rational social organization but also in the manner in which surpluses are distributed. The surplus had to be gathered, transported and stored, and eventually distributed. This called for a variety of full-time specialists and a class structure; certainly a ruling elite had to give the commands and oversee the necessary arrangements. In short, in these early cities we see the articulation of complex forms of social stratification and the emergence of formal institutions and procedures.

The early cities of Mesopotamia were often dominated by a ruling

[5]For a more complete account of the rise of early cities see Gideon Sjoberg, "The Origin and Evolution of Cities," *Cities*, op. cit., pp. 23–39.

priest class. But rulership of this sort, even if emerging from a more rationalized religious system, can be viewed as the institutionalization of political authority. That is to say, the state as a rational system of political-governmental power can be seen as an organic development and consequence of urbanism. Indeed, some of the ancient cities have been called "polis"— the "city-state"—indicating the governmental forms that were necessary in the more complex and heterogeneous world of the early cities.

Thus, in these ancient cities we find embryonic indicators of social forms that were unknown and unneeded in the folk community: the rationalization of agriculture, the emergence of the state and the beginning of formal law, the rational organization of the "marketplace" for economic exchange, the articulation of formally organized religion, and the development of a complex system of stratification. These localities were cities because they had produced a social structure far more complex than the folk community; they set in motion for the first time those social groups which were to form the anatomy of modern urban society—the rational economy, the state, the formalization of social controls in organized religion, and a ruling elite who had the power to regulate and administer these complex settlements and, in the process, took the lion's share of everything for themselves.

All of this occurred in a setting in which agriculture was relatively easy. In ancient Mesopotamia the soil was unusually fertile in the wide alluvial river valleys and the climate beneficent. Wheat and barley sprouted from the rich earth opened up by the bronze plows. Surpluses emerged and dense settlements of socially heterogeneous populations began. But one final factor had to appear—literacy. Without the written word, the technical administrative procedures of the new economy, the marketplace, and the governmental and religious order would be impossible. Records had to be kept and orders transmitted. Writing was an indispensable element of urbanism because it not only made philosophy, science, and scholarship possible but facilitated the necessary principle or force from which urbanism could develop—rationalized authority and procedure and formal social structures.

In urbanism, we see for the first time the elements of bureaucratic social organization: the rationalization of procedures centered on formally articulated goals. The state, the coinage of money, the marketplace, the church and priestly class, laws and the dispensing of justice, and the bureaucratization of the military could not have taken place without the innovation of the written word. What we are saying here is that with the city, "civilization" began: secondary groups developed, *Gesellschaft* appeared, and the still immature institutional alignments of modern society were set in motion. It took mankind almost a million years to build the first city, but cities have taken mankind to the present state of social development in just five thousand years.

From Mesopotamia, city culture spread to (or developed independently in) Egypt. There may have been urban settlements in the Nile Delta by 3100 B.C. By 2500 B.C., in the valley of the Indus River (in contemporary Pakistan), the cities of Mohenjo-Daro and Harappa were prosperous settlements. About 1500 B.C. the Yellow River in China supported urban communities. The force of urbanism emerged in empire building in the early centuries of the Iron Age. From Persia in the sixth century B.C., the principle of empire expanded into western Turkestan. Thence, urbanism flowed to India at the end of the fourth century and through all of Asia. Similarly, during the second millennium, the Phoenicians moved westward to carry city forms and culture to North Africa and eventually to Spain. In the New World, Mesoamerican cities have been discovered as settlements of the ancient Mayans, Zapotecs, Mixtecs, and Aztecs, the earliest dating probably before the birth of Christ.

Urban culture shaped the course of human history even in classical times. Both Greece and Rome began as city-states, and each in its own time dominated the known world. Indeed, from the time of the first urban settlements of Eridu and Ur, the balance of power and dominance shifted from the village settlements to the cities. It was the cities, with their comparatively massive organization of men, their technical efficiency and knowledge, that came to dominate the rural hinterlands. The folk communities simply fell before the superior social organization of cities, even though the cities constituted only a small proportion of the total population. Indeed, as the centuries passed, the cities always remained in the numerical minority. Athens or Rome represented a form of social organization that could exert superior social, military, or political power over an atomized rural area or a less vigorous city-state.

Although cities came to dominate and control vast hinterlands, the statistical triumph of urbanism *as a mode of community life* which embraced the majority of a nation's population did not come until long after the Industrial Revolution. Although cities appeared more than 5500 years ago, the "urbanized society" did not make its appearance until 100 years ago. Before 1850, cities may have culturally and politically dominated the world, but the majority of men lived on the land and followed out a way of life shaped by the folk community. Before 1850, no *society* could be legitimately regarded as urbanized, and by 1900 only Great Britain statistically showed an urban majority.[6] In 1801, 16.9 per cent

[6]Davis, "The Urbanization . . . ," *op. cit.*, p. 8.

of England's population was classified as urban; by 1891, over 53 per
cent was urban.[7] In the United States, on the other hand, 6 per cent
were urban in 1800, whereas 35 per cent were so defined by 1890.[8] In the
past 100 years, however, the growth of cities throughout the world has
been spectacular. If present trends continue, by 1990 more than half
of the world's people will be living in cities with populations in excess
of 100,000.

THE PROCESS OF URBANIZATION

By urbanization, we refer to the proportion of a society's total population
which is living in cities and urban settlements. We are not referring
here merely to the growth of cities, because cities can grow without appreciable urbanization if the rural population grows as rapidly as the
city or urban population. A "total" population consists generally of the
rural-urban combination. We may say that urbanization within a society
is increasing if the urban proportion is increasing over the rural.[9]

In addition to the concept of urbanization, which is the ratio of
growth of the urban population to the rural, we shall be dealing with
several other basic concepts from this point on. Because there is no
technical sociological definition for the term "city," we shall use it almost
interchangeably with the term "urban," which describes a community
with a large, dense, heterogeneous population linked to highly differentiated institutional-associational social structure. If a folk community is
sparsely settled, simple and undifferentiated structurally, with a homogeneous population, an urban community, at the other end of the
spectrum, constitutes the conceptual opposite—dense, complex, and
heterogeneous.

In a sense, the term "city" is a recognition of the physical condition of urbanism in terms of size and density. A city is a large and dense
settlement, whereas "urbanism," in the sociological sense, constitutes the
modal social structure: the groups, distinctive processes, and forms of
cities, the heterogeneity, differentiation, specialization, and complexity.

Over the years, the U. S. Bureau of the Census has struggled to
develop definitions of urbanism based upon the size of population within

[7]Peter Hall, *The World of Cities* (New York: McGraw-Hill Book Company,
1966) , p. 17.
[8]Noel P. Gist and Sylvia Fleis Fava, *Urban Society* (New York: Thomas Y.
Crowell Company, 1964) , p. 50.
[9]The over-all approach taken in this section will be found in much more
detail in Davis, "The Urbanization . . . ," *op. cit.*, pp. 3–24.

localities. For decades the Census Bureau regarded as *urban* any incorporated place of 2500 or more. In 1950 the definition was altered to include unincorporated localities of 2500 as well. However, it is clear that an incorporated "village" of 3000 is a quite different community from New York City with its population of 8 million, although both are "urban" in the formal statistical definition used by the Bureau.

In order to identify and gather data for the larger urban units within the country, the Bureau has developed two relatively new categories for population enumeration in the 1950 and 1960 census counts: the "Urbanized Area" and the "Standard Metropolitan Statistical Area" (SMSA). Essentially, Urbanized Area refers to "one or more cities of 50,000 or more and all the nearby closely settled suburban territory or urban fringe." The SMSA concept focuses essentially on a city of 50,000 or more, the county in which the city is located, and contiguous counties if they meet certain formal specifications in terms of work force and place of work and residence.

Urbanism is a social condition of differentiation, heterogeneity, and specialization, but it also emerges from the factor of physical size. It is the size of population that has most often been the convenient statistical guide to the urban condition; however, the number of persons within a locality defined as urban is quite arbitrary. For example, in a study of world urbanization Davis used a figure of 100,000 or more, whereas the Bureau of the Census defines a locality as urban if it has a population of 2500 or more, and an "Urbanized Area" as a city of 50,000 or more. It is important for the student of urbanism to be aware of these inconsistencies of definition, for data and conclusions may often appear to be inaccurate or contradictory unless the statistical cutting points are made clear.

Generally, city growth has been accompanied by urbanization. Certainly this occurred in Western (European and North American) society, where cities in the eighteenth and nineteenth centuries grew by drawing the rural population off the land and into the urban areas, which were the focal points of industrialization. In short, men left the farms to take jobs in the burgeoning cities. Hence, urbanization and city growth accompanied each other. But, as Davis points out, urbanization is finite and limited. Since urbanization constitutes the proportion of urban to rural within a society, there is just so much rural population that can be drawn into the cities before a point is reached at which there may be hardly any rural population left.

In the United States, for example, more than 70 per cent of the population is now urban. Between 1920 and 1959, the net migration from farms in the United States was 27 million—an average of 700,000 a year. As a consequence, the farm population dropped from 32.5 million in 1916 to 20.5 million in 1960 although total population continued to grow. By 1964, utilizing a stricter definition of farm families (those families actually earning their livelihood from farming), the farm population was down to 13 million, constituting about 7 per cent of the nation's total.

Part of the urbanization process, of course, is the rise of industrialization accompanied by dramatic improvement in agricultural techniques and practices. As the farmer became more efficient and produced more with less effort on less land, the excess rural population was drawn to the cities, where new jobs were opening up in the factories. Hence, there was a functional congruence of economic forces in the West, and urbanization constituted a healthy tension between changing agricultural, technical, industrial forces and a shifting mode of community life.

As urbanization proceeds in the industrial nations, it tends to slow down. The process of urbanization, indeed, follows what the sociologist or demographer calls an S curve. At the early stages of urbanization, at the bottom of the S, growth is comparatively slow. However, once the bottom of the S is turned, growth is spectacular and attenuated. As the proportion of population classified as urban exceeds 50 per cent of the total population, urbanization slows down and the curve reaches the top of the S and flattens out. At this point, there is no longer enough rural population to mount a significant migration to the cities.

In addition, by this point the great metropolitan growth characterized by advanced industrialization and urbanization dramatically increases the process of suburbanization. In effect, the urban population begins to migrate toward the thinly populated fringes around great cities. The Bureau of the Census is consequently faced with a dilemma of classification: Are the new suburbanites "urban" dwellers or should the suburban villages be classified as "nonfarm"? At any rate, urbanization comes to an end when there is simply not enough rural population left to affect critically the urbanization ratio and when the dense populations traditionally characteristic of urbanism and cities start to thin out in the suburbanization process.

Davis points out that in the underdeveloped nations urban growth is taking on a pattern quite different from that just outlined for the industrial countries. While urbanization for the advanced and developed nations is slowing down, the underdeveloped nations are urbanizing at a rate slightly faster than did the industrial nations during the period of rapid urbanization in the nineteenth century. In data gathered by Davis, 40 underdeveloped nations had an average gain in the urban proportion of the population of 20 per cent per decade. In 16 industrial

FIGURE 4

S Curve

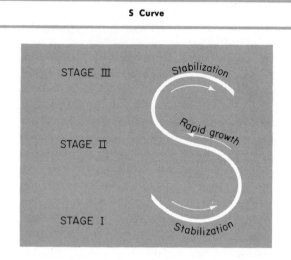

countries, during the time of their rapid urbanization in the nineteenth century the average gain in the urban proportion was 15 per cent per decade. Although the urbanization rate for the underdeveloped countries today is just slightly higher than the rate for the Western countries during their time of intensive urbanization, the cities of the underdeveloped nations are literally bursting with population. There has been an incredible growth of cities in the underdeveloped countries although the rate of urbanization is just slightly higher than the case for the developed countries in the nineteenth century.

There appears to be a contradiction here. But recall that urbanization is a ratio of the rural to urban population and that urbanization increases only when the rural population goes down. With the tremendous city growth in the underdeveloped nations (they are expected to double their population every 15 years), there has also been a significant increase in the rural population. It is this critical phenomenon, the growth of both urban and rural populations in the underdeveloped countries, that changes the pattern of community growth from that previously established in the industrial countries. In short, the well-publicized "population explosion" in the world today, particularly in the underdeveloped lands, has critically affected the urbanization ratio: both rural and urban populations are increasing significantly.

Since 1940, the underdeveloped nations have been increasing in population twice as fast as the developed nations, and this growth is much greater than it was in the industrial, Western countries during the period of their rapid growth. Whereas the industrial nations urbanized by drawing off the surplus rural population to the growing cities, the underdeveloped countries today are characterized by tremendous city growth resulting from the sheer increase in population. In Costa Rica, for example, only 20 per cent of the growth in cities and towns can be regarded as a result of urbanization *per se*. On the other hand, 44 per cent of the city growth, Davis calculates, was due to Costa Rica's general population growth, and the remaining 36 per cent was due to a combination of natural increase (births over deaths) and urbanization. In the same fashion, 50 per cent of the increase in the urban population in Mexico during 1940–1960 was due to the general population increase and only 22 per cent is attributable to urbanization alone.

The problem of the underdeveloped lands is that their population is growing significantly beyond their institutional capabilities and social design. Cities are filling up with starving populations, and the economic order has not kept pace. There are not enough jobs in the still primitive economies to support the burgeoning population. Recall the functional tension between the declining rural population in the industrial countries and the rising job opportunities in the new and growing cities. There is no such equivalent force in Asia, Africa or Latin America.

Until the nineteenth century, city populations in Europe were decimated by plague and famine. Urban populations were recurrently reduced through the lack of medical knowledge, unsanitary conditions, slums, crowding, and the like. But the costly lessons in sustaining urban population were eventually learned, and the cities of the underdeveloped lands are not going through those bitter experiences, although famine and malnutrition are still major factors. The result has been that city populations in these areas are reproducing themselves at a rate unprecedented in the experience of the West.

But these problems are complicated from still another source—the rapid increase of the rural population. With limited land and resources, the poor countries face the nightmare of unemployed and inactive farmers as well. If they do not move farmers into the cities (urbanization), the rural areas will not be able to support the sheer numbers in their midst. Yet, if substantial numbers of the rural population enter the cities, they will simply swell the jobless, homeless masses already there.

The case of Caracas, Venezuela, is illustrative of the problem. The city's population increased from 359,000 in 1941 to 1,507,000 by 1963. However, the Venezuelan farm population from 1951 through 1961 increased by 11 per cent. Agricultural density became even worse as the amount of cultivated land decreased. In 1950, approximately 64 males were engaged in agriculture per square mile of cultivated acreage in Venezuela. By 1961 there were 78 men working each square mile of agricultural land—compared with 4.8 for the United States, 6.8 for Canada, and 15.6 for Argentina.

The conditions in Venezuela are being duplicated throughout the underdeveloped lands. Cities swell through natural increase, and slums spread over the face of the city. Squatters camp in parks and public places. People die on the sidewalks. Not only is the inner city transformed by rapidly rising population, but along the fringes, where suburbs normally rise in American cities, there are junk towns, reed shack villages, hand-built shanty towns devoid of sanitary facilities and the normal Western amenities.

However, while the underdeveloped nations struggle with run-away populations and inadequate institutional forms and resources to cope with their emergent needs, Western society, which is essentially urban society, has had to face a new series of problems. In the course of 35 or 40 years the prime unit of nineteenth-century urbanism, the city, has given way to a new and still puzzling community form which has thrust up a host of complex issues and contemporary problems—the contemporary metropolis, which has remade the face of the Western world.

SUGGESTED READINGS

GIBBS, JACK P. ed., *Urban Research Methods*. New York: D. Van Nostrand Co., Inc., 1961.
> *A useful collection of papers dealing with specific methods employed in urban research. The book deals with the major methodological-theoretic problems of cities and suggests methods for their analysis.*

GIST, NOEL P., and SYLVIA FLEIS FAVA, *Urban Society*. New York: Thomas Y. Crowell Company, 1964.
> *A substantial textbook in urban sociology covering the major areas of this field.*

HATT, PAUL K., and ALBERT J. REISS, Jr., *Cities and Society*. New York: The Free Press, 1957.
> *An outstanding collection of papers dealing with the major forms and processes of urban life.*

MUMFORD, LEWIS, *The Culture of Cities*. New York: Harcourt, Brace & World, Inc., 1938.
> *A broad and sweeping overview of the emergence and significance of the city in human society.*

PARK, ROBERT, ERNEST W. BURGESS, and RODERICK D. MC KEN-ZIE, *The City*. Chicago: University of Chicago Press, 1967.
> *A republication of the 1925 book which established the ecological view of the city. The definitive essays of Park, Burgess, and McKenzie are well worth reading today.*

REDFIELD, ROBERT, *The Little Community*. Chicago: University of Chicago Press, 1965.
> *The culmination of this scholar's concern with small folk communities.*

SANDERS, IRWIN T., *The Community*. New York: The Ronald Press Company, 1966.
> *A current text largely designed for undergraduates which summarizes the generic characteristics of human communities.*

SCIENTIFIC AMERICAN. *Cities*. New York: Alfred A. Knopf, Inc., 1965.
> *An extremely useful collection of articles dealing with the origin, development, and current state of cities and urbanism in the world.*

SJOBERG, GIDEON, *The Preindustrial City*. New York: The Free Press, 1960.
> *Scholarly and careful presentation of early city forms.*

VIDICH, ARTHUR, and JOSEPH BENSMAN, *Small Town in Mass Society*. Princeton: Princeton University Press, 1958.
> *The primary issue in this case study of a small town is the persistence of the rural myths of "independence" which continue to prevail in a community sorely dependent upon the mass society outside its borders.*

chapter

THE
METROPOLITAN
COMMUNITY

THE RISE OF METROPOLITAN COMMUNITIES[1]

Community life in the United States has gone through two major revolutions within a single lifetime. The first which began in the last quarter of the nineteenth century, was the almost incredible burgeoning of cities; the second, which we are witnessing today, is the rapid and thorough spread of urbanism far beyond the physical limits of the city.

    The nineteenth century in America was a time of intense population growth and city-building. Immigration squeezed additional hordes into the already overburdened and deteriorating city wards. Steam power was a critical force in the compacting of the nineteenth century industrial city. Because it could not be easily transported, it was served *in situ*, like Molloch, and impacted commercial, industrial, residential, and public functions in grossly inadequate land areas. "Insensate industrial towns," as Lewis Mumford calls them, precipitated around factories.

    Much of the hope for a good new life, which drew millions to the great cities from the farms and small towns of America and from bitter circumstances abroad, foundered on the slag heap, the city slum, and the company town. Yet in spite

[1] This section is a revision of material originally appearing in the author's, *Class in Suburbia* (Englewood Cliffs, N.J.: Prentice-Hall, Inc., 1963), pp. 3–4; 143–157. Used with permission of the publisher.

of all of the terrible social consequences and injustices that stemmed from city life, cities continued to grow: for every 2 people living in the city in 1800, 31 lived in rural and wilderness areas, but a hundred years later 21 people lived in the city for every 31 who lived in rural areas. In 100 years the city had grown 1000 per cent.

How did the city make room for the torrent of migrants who swept across its borders? For a while it simply got taller and darker: it put more floors on apartment buildings; it built them closer and on little plots carved out of farmland or playgrounds or refuse heaps. It partitioned large rooms into cubicles and entire city neighborhoods sprang from the "backyard" plot of a farm wife's table garden.

By 1920, the urban triumph was statistically clear; more of the population was living in cities than in rural areas. But the nineteenth-century city—cramped, dark, dirty, the victim of its terrible dynamism—was changing its form. It began to grow outward. Interurban railroads and the automobile allowed the congested city populations to escape into the sunlight from the grime, noise, and darkness of the cramped commercial, industrial, and residential areas, yet retain cultural and economic ties with the city. Suburbs and a "suburban way of life" along with a string of industrial satellite cities were changing the character of urban America.

A generation earlier, the city had eclipsed the rural community as the mode of American community life; now the highly concentrated city was similarly challenged. The super city, the *metropolis*—a new, rangy complex of central city core, residential suburbs, industrial satellites, and sprawling, voracious urban fringe all bound together by the steel and concrete sinews of the rail and roadway systems—was in the making. Metropolitanism had become the American way of life and the suburbs the new Promised Land, where a man could realize the American Dream —his own house and his own piece of land.

In 1900, metropolitan areas claimed 31 per cent of the total population. Today, 2 out of 3 Americans live in urban places, but over 60 per cent of the total population lives in metropolitan areas. Census forecasts suggest that by 1975 the population of the United States will exceed 220 million, an increase of roughly 40 million over 1960, 63 per cent of whom will live in metropolitan areas.

The growth of metropolitan centers, however, is merely one facet of the urban revolution of the last sixty years. Although metropolitan areas have demonstrated amazing growth, the component parts are by no means growing at the same rate. In 1900, for example, the population of the *central cities* of metropolitan areas constituted 61.9 per cent of the total metropolitan unit while the suburban and fringe areas outside of the cities were only 38.1 per cent of the total area. By 1960, however, the picture had changed. Central cities claimed barely half of the total population of metropolitan areas.

The 1960 Census for the New York Standard Metropolitan Statistical Area dramatically illustrates the national trend. While New York City lost a total of 109,973 persons between 1950 and 1960, its suburban counties were registering spectacular gains. Nassau County increased 93 per cent over the decade, Rockland 53 per cent, Suffolk 141 per cent, and Westchester 29 per cent. While New York City lost about 1½ per cent of its population during the decade, its suburbs increased by 75 per cent.

Between 1900 and 1920 central cities were growing faster than their tributary rings.[2] However, in each decade since 1920 the rings have been growing faster than the central cities. Between 1940 and 1950, rings grew almost two and a half times as fast as central cities. The result has been that the suburban population alone is estimated at more than 50 million. The trends in the New York metropolitan area are clearly reflected on the national level. According to the 1960 Census, about 84 per cent of the 28 million population increase during the decade 1950–1960 occurred in the nation's metropolitan areas.[3] However, the increase in these areas, from 89,316,903 in 1950 to 112,885,178 in 1960 (26.4 per cent), saw the suburban rings growing at a much faster rate than central cities. The increase of central cities in the decade (5.6 million) to a total of 58 million by 1960 constituted a 10.7 per cent increase; in contrast, outlying suburban areas grew from 36.9 million population in 1950 to 54.9 million in 1960, an increase of 48.6 per cent.

The growth rates for central cities are clearly continuing to decline. Indeed, the trend is for the central cities of the largest metropolitan areas to have even slower rates of growth than the central cities of smaller metropolitan areas. New York City lost population during the 1950–1960 decade. In the five metropolitan areas of 3,000,000 or more, the growth in central cities was only 1 per cent. In contrast, however, the growth of the suburban rings of these great metropolitan centers was 71 per cent. As size declined, the growth rate of central cities increased in relation to the suburban areas. In the case of the smaller metropolitan areas of less than 100,000, the growth rate (29 per cent) exceeded the suburban rate (11 per cent).

[2]Donald J. Bogue, "Urbanism and Metropolitanism," in W. M. Dobriner (ed.), *The Suburban Community* (New York: G. P. Putnam's Sons, 1958), p. 25.
[3]*United States Census of Population 1960, United States Summary,* Number of Inhabitants, PC(1) 1A, U.S. Department of Commerce, Bureau of the Census, pp. XXIV-XXVII, *passim.*

It is clear that population is moving toward the suburbs and the claim of central cities is decreasing. For the country as a whole, the outlying rings of metropolitan centers accounted for about two-thirds of the total U.S. population increase since 1950 and for more than three-fourths of the total increase within metropolitan areas. Furthermore, the trend of central city loss and suburban gain is expected to continue. By 1975, the Committee for Economic Development estimates, the central city population will have dropped to 42 per cent of the metropolitan total, whereas the suburban and fringe areas outside will have grown to 57 per cent of the entire metropolitan complex. This almost reverses the central city–suburban population proportions established for metropolitan areas at the turn of the century.

Like *urbanism* and *the city*, the term *metropolis* is subject to varied interpretations. Although there are literally hundreds of experts today dealing with the many facets of metropolitan matters, both scientific and practical, no one is quite sure what a metropolis really is. The many faces of metropolitanism seen by the specialists serve only to illustrate the significant point that *metropolis* and *metropolitan* are conceptual entities—constructs which categorize certain emergent and dominant properties of modern urban life. Accordingly, definitions of the critical features of metropolitanism will vary as each specialist abstracts out of the total empirical context those patterns that have particular relevance to his investigation. The metropolitan area, therefore, will be viewed by the Bureau of the Census in terms of its needs for clear statistical delimitation between community forms—rural and urban. Then, too, metropolitanism may be conceptualized in terms of an area of economic dominance from the core city outward into its hinterland. The metropolitan area may be thought of as a transportation network without regard for political boundaries. On a more complex level, the metropolitan area may be regarded as a vast spatial structure consisting of functionally interdependent economic, political, and social subsystems. The result may be a super-organized concentration that takes in portions of two or three states in a highly specialized and differentiated functional integration of areas that go well beyond the political limits of the core city.

Indeed, the process of metropolitan growth has proceeded so far that the unit "metropolitan area" in the aforementioned sense may no longer apply to the larger, integrated metropolitan aggregates that are flowing into each other across the nation. The boundaries of metropolitan areas are fusing to form super-metropolitan entities that have been called "strip cities" or, as Jean Gottmann has termed the integration of metropolitan areas from southern New Hampshire all the way to the Appalachian foothills in Virginia, "Megalopolis."

According to a study made by *U.S. News and World Report*, the thirteen major "strip cities" in the United States—Boston to Washington, Albany to Erie, Cleveland to Pittsburgh, Toledo to Cincinnati, Detroit to Muskegon, Chicago-Gary to Milwaukee, St. Louis to Peoria, Seattle to Eugene, San Francisco to San Diego, Kansas City to Sioux Falls, Fort Worth–Dallas–San Antonio–Houston, Miami-Tampa-Jacksonville, and Atlanta to Raleigh—contain half the population of the country (89,395,469) and have increased more than 25 per cent since 1950. Of the total 212 metropolitan areas in the nation, 119 fall within 13 giant strip city patterns. Not only did half of the population live within these super-metropolitan constellations, but 109 billion dollars in retail trade, or 54.7 per cent of the total consumer market, was expended here.

Terms such as "metropolitan district" and "standard metropolitan area" are the arithmetic constructs through which the Bureau of the Census gathers data on the metropolitan areas of the nation. They were designed as convenient statistical guides suitable for the purpose of the Census. For other purposes the Census concept of metropolitan area might not usefully apply.

We are primarily concerned with the metropolitan area as a spatial structure, one which reflects the underlying functional specialization and integration of the area. On this level, the units of analysis go considerably beyond the demographic and political variables used by the Census, such as size of population or city or county lines. In the main, social scientists, who have watched the growth and development of metropolitan areas until they have become the predominant expression of urbanism in the United States, conceptualize the area in terms of three interrelated "rings," "zones," or "belts." These three units of the metropolitan area stand in a peculiar spatial or ecological relationship to each other. Although their language varies, ecologists, demographers, economists, sociologists, and political scientists *think* of the metropolitan area in terms of three differential zones each of which is characterized by not only differences in demographic characteristics but metropolitan function as well. We shall identify these zones as, (1) The Central City Core, (2) The Suburban Zone and, (3) The Rural-Urban Fringe.

The Central Core

The Central Core of the metropolitan area is usually the old nineteenth-century urban settlement that went through the characteristic period of intensive growth during the time of great industrialization and urbanization. It was the center of business, residence, and industry before the advent of suburbanization. We shall spend some time discussing the current problems faced by the core cities in a subsequent section of this chapter.

The suburbs have been centers of great growth, particularly from 1945 to the present. It has been the unprecedented growth of suburban settlements that has remade the urban character of the United States from a condition of dominance by central cities to the present metropolitan unit in which central cities *and suburbs*—the metropolitan area—is the characteristic mode of urban expression and form.

Finally, the fringe consists of that marginal, interstitial area where the new suburbia is penetrating into the rural and agricultural area. It is that ecological zone where the metropolitan area of industry, residence, and commerce passes on to agriculture and the rural village.

The Suburban Zone

The Bureau of the Census does not provide a definition of *suburb*, even for its own limited statistical purposes. Neither has the term received much formal attention by sociologists. The idea of the suburbs has been around a long time, but only a few writers in recent years have begun to question whether the idea of the suburbs in terms of structure and function within the metropolitan complex has much meaning and usefulness. Within the past decade, the term *suburb* has been heavily reappraised.

Boskoff defines suburbs as "those *urbanized nuclei* located outside (but within accessible range) of central cities that are politically independent but economically and psychologically linked with services and facilities provided by the metropolis."[4] In addition, he stresses the "economic and social . . . bonds of dependence" between suburb and central city. According to Walter Martin, "*Suburb* refers to the relatively small but formally structured community adjacent to and dependent upon a larger central city."[5] Fava writes: "Suburbs . . . refers particularly to the residential or dormitory variety, characterized by dependence on the city occupationally and for various specialized types of shopping and recreation. A working definition would comprise the area outside the legal city limits but within commuting distance."[6]

[4]Alvin Boskoff, *The Sociology of Urban Regions* (New York: Appleton-Century-Crofts, 1962) , p. 133.
[5]Walter T. Martin, "The Structure of Social Relationships Engendered by Suburban Residence," *American Sociological Review*, XXI (August 1956) , 446–453.
[6]Sylvia Fleis Fava, "Suburbanism as a Way of Life," *American Sociological Review*, XXI (February 1956) , 34–37.

FIGURE 5

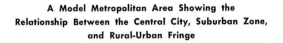

**A Model Metropolitan Area Showing the
Relationship Between the Central City, Suburban Zone,
and Rural-Urban Fringe**

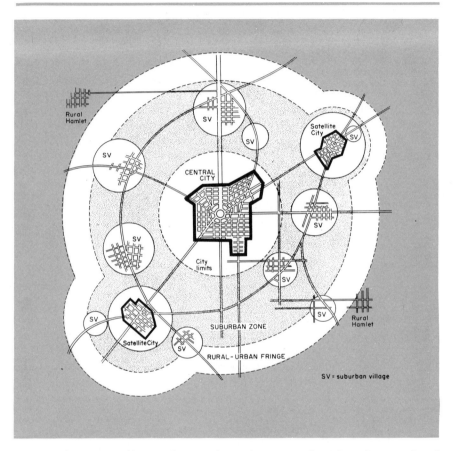

A metropolis consists, at least in part, of a densely populated highly urbanized core surrounded by a belt of politically independent but economically dependent suburban communities. At least, this seems to be the prevailing view. However, the term *suburban* is meaningful when applied to many species of community. The varieties, kinds, and types of suburb dealt with literature go back at least 40 years. Taylor first discussed the character of "satellite cities."[7] These were centers of

[7]Graham R. Taylor, *Satellite Cities* (New York: Appleton-Century-Crofts, 1915).

production and employment and were not residential. Later, in the 1920's, Harlan Douglas differentiated suburbs as *residential, industrial,* and *mixed* types.[8] For Douglas, the two basic modes of suburban life were the "centers of consumption" (the residential suburbs) and "centers of production" (the industrial suburb). Taylor's satellite city and Douglas' suburb of production are essentially one. Still later, and moving into the contemporary tradition, Harris distinguished between housing or dormitory suburbs and manufacturing and industrial suburbs.[9]

Schnore has recently contrasted the characteristics of residential suburbs and "employing satellites."[10] In *spatial* terms, according to Schnore, both satellites and suburbs are "indistinguishable from adjacent areas" and must be viewed as "constituent parts of a larger urban complex —the metropolitan area." Continuing his distinction, Schnore maintains that "goods and services tend to flow out of the employing satellites to other areas . . . while persons are attracted into these for employment." The residential suburbs, Schnore maintains, "tend to receive an influx of goods and services for the consumption of their inhabitants." In terms of their characteristic functions within the metropolis, the residential suburbs are "suppliers of labor and consumers of commodities," whereas the employing satellites are "consumers of labor and suppliers of commodities."

Satellites tend to be older than residential suburbs and are found most often in industrialized sections of the Northeast and North Central areas of the nation. In addition, suburbs and satellite cities tend to have contrasting types of populations. In general, satellites contain younger populations than do residential suburbs with a trend toward the lower socioeconomic class and status groups. Along similar lines, the population of satellite cities, contrasted with a model residential suburb, have a lower average education, lower average rent levels, high proportions of foreign-born whites, higher fertility rates, higher percentages of tenant-occupied buildings, and a work force in which two out of three workers are in the blue-collar occupations.

Schnore demonstrated that the residential suburbs were growing almost twice as fast as the employing satellites. Furthermore, the suburbs were becoming even more residential in character, while the satellite areas, like the central cities, were becoming more industrialized.

The significant differences in both the functions of suburbs and

[8]Harlan Douglas, *The Suburban Trend* (New York: The Century Co., 1925), *passim.*
[9]Chauncey D. Harris, "Suburbs," *American Journal of Sociology,* XLIX (July 1943), 1–13.
[10]Leo F. Schnore, "Satellites and Suburbs," *Social Forces,* 36 (December 1957), 121–129. Reprinted in Dobriner, *op. cit.,* pp. 109–121.

the kinds of people who characteristically live in them has been demonstrated, again by Schnore, in a study utilizing data from the 1960 Census.[11] In this research, suburbs were classified as "residential," "employing," and "intermediate." Employing suburbs were defined as those localities with *less* than 25 per cent of their work force employed *outside* of the county of residence. Places with 37.5 per cent of the labor force working across the county line were defined as residential suburbs, and the intermediate suburbs were regarded as those in which intercounty commuting involved between 25 and 37 per cent of the working population.

Five basic categories for analysis were selected; (1) age and ethnic composition, (2) fertility and dependency, (3) socioeconomic status, (4) population growth, and (5) housing characteristics. From these broad

TABLE V

SOCIAL AND ECONOMIC CHARACTERISTICS OF SUBURBS IN THE 25 LARGEST URBANIZED AREAS, 1960

| | | TYPE OF SUBURB | |
	Employing	Intermediate	Residential
A. Age and Ethnic Composition			
1. Percentage foreign-born	10.5	8.5	7.7
2. Percentage nonwhite	7.0	6.2	2.4
3. Percentage aged 65 or more	9.7	9.0	9.1
B. Fertility and Dependency			
4. Nonworker-worker ratio	1.41	1.44	1.44
5. Fertility ratio	421	437	422
6. Percentage with children under 6	27.8	29.2	28.2
C. Socioeconomic Status			
7. Percentage completed high school	43.2	48.2	55.8
8. Percentage in white-collar occupations	44.6	49.8	58.5
9. Median family income	$6,869	$7,510	$8,210
D. Population Growth, 1950–60			
10. Median rate of increase	6.0	18.1	26.9
11. Percentage of places losing population	30.4	24.2	16.2
12. Percentage migrant 1955–60	13.8	16.7	17.4
E. Housing Characteristics			
13. Percentage built between 1950 and 1960	24.1	29.4	31.6
14. Percentage owner-occupied units	57.7	63.1	71.4
15. Percentage one-family units	62.3	68.2	75.9
No. of suburbs	102	99	99

SOURCE: Leo F. Schnore, *The Urban Scene* (New York: The Free Press, 1965), p. 178. Used with permission of the publisher.

11Leo F. Schnore, *The Urban Scene* (New York: The Free Press, 1965), pp. 169–183.

categories, 15 specific variables were systematically compared (see Table V). The analysis was based on data from a sample of 74 suburbs in the New York area and a group of 300 suburbs within the 25 largest Urbanized Areas in the country.

Schnore found a patterned change in the values of the variables from one suburban category to the other. The most obvious differences among the suburbs were in socioeconomic status. Income, education, and occupational characteristics scored highest in the residential suburbs and lowest in the employing suburbs or satellites. There were significant differences, as well, in the other variables with a status or honorific dimension, such as the proportions of foreign born and nonwhite and the proportions of owner-occupied and single-family dwellings.

These differences clearly suggest that the burgeoning suburbs are by no means identical and homogeneous centers. Indeed, continued research and study in the suburbs has indicated that they are highly variable. Communities are not "all alike," as their critics have often claimed. Note that the residential suburbs had a median family income almost $1400 higher than the employing suburbs and contained 12 per cent more residents who had completed high school and 14 per cent more in the white-collar occupations. Note, too, the significant differences in population growth between the residential suburbs (28.9 per cent) and the employing suburbs (6.0 per cent). These data suggest that the residential suburbs are more characteristically middle-class, whereas the employing suburbs tend toward a working-class population.

The Rural-Urban Fringe

In the zonal view of the patterning of metropolitan areas, Zone I consists of the densely populated and highly commercialized and industrialized core. Zone II consists of a belt of rapidly growing suburban communities and industrialized satellite cities. Of the two, suburbs and satellites, the suburbs seem to predominate slightly on the national average. Beyond the suburban belt lies the third zone of the metropolitan area, which goes by a variety of names—"the rural ring," "urban fringe," "the outer ring," "the rural-urban fringe," and the like. We have called it the "rural-urban fringe," and by that we identify it as the last belt or area in which metropolitan or urban patterns are still evident.

Essentially this belt consists of a geographic area in which the prevailing use of land is neither clearly urban nor clearly suburban (residential, industrial, commercial) nor clearly rural (agricultural). It is that area where the expanding metropolis is currently waging its imperialistic war. This is the belt where the new suburban colonies and satellite cities will emerge in a few years. Thus, from an ecological view, the rural-urban fringe represents that spatial dimension of the entire area in which new urban functions, largely in the form of suburban residential areas and employing satellites, eat into the rural countryside. As such, it is a heterogeneous area of instability and change.

On one side of the illusive and fragmentary boundary of the urban fringe lies the ring of suburban villages and satellite cities; on the other, beyond suburbia and the interurban railways, past the commuter railroad, the expressway and parkway systems, the mass-produced subdivisions, the land opens up and the signs of the city fade. Beyond the volatile and unstable rural-urban fringe lie the small villages, the pokey economies, and the sleepy roadways of rural America.

THE MYTH OF SUBURBIA

If metropolitanism has transformed the urban character of contemporary American society, it was during the decade 1950–1960 that the major thrust occurred. Millions of city people moved to the suburbs. And since the movement was such an obvious one, it was inevitable that journalists and popular writers would take note of it and pass judgment on it. As Bennett Berger subsequently noted, a "myth of suburbia" mounted in the early 1950's.[12] The essential features of the myth identified the "new suburbia" (as they often called it) as basically middle-class, matriarchal and child-centered, a compulsive and frenetic center of outgoing participation, transient and formless, haplessly conformist, and a conversion center in which urban Democrats became suburban Republicans and agnostic freethinkers were fashioned into conservative and liturgical religionists.

The myth was fostered by urban intellectuals and cosmopolitans, for whom the mass-produced, post–World War II tract subdivisions were simply a shameless retreat from the urban and cultured world. By the mid-1950's the myth was full-blown, and at about this time serious sociological investigation of the suburbs began. From that point on, the more extreme elements of the myth began to crumble.

The central thesis of the suburban myth presented by the popular writers was based on a legitimate sociological assumption—the power of the social environment to shape and critically influence behavior. The issue which eventually separated the "sociology of suburbia" from the

[12]Bennett M. Berger, *Working Class Suburb* (Berkeley: University of California Press, 1960), pp. 1–14.

myth was the identification of the influencing social forces. The fundamental assumption behind the myth was that "suburbia" in some massive and mysterious way changed the behavior of the urban migrants. It was the "suburban situation"—the new community—that was doing it all. Sociologists, however, were really not sure what "suburbia" was, if it existed at all, and they were not at all certain that the suburban rings were critically influential in changing people who had lived in the central cities. There were certainly the obvious differences of less density, greater home ownership, the single-family dwelling, and generally higher socioeconomic status. But did this make suburbia so powerfully different from life in the core?

There are two terms in this issue that need clarification. Suburbs, as we have noted, are politically independent towns, villages, and even small cities surrounding a large central city. Although these suburbs are probably becoming more self-sufficient economically as more businesses suburbanize, there are still sizable numbers of suburbanites who commute into the central city to work. (However, more and more city dwellers are "commuting" to the suburbs these days, although, of course, their number is comparatively small in terms of the total suburban commuting population.) If suburbs are communities, "suburbia" seems to be the general life style practiced by residents of suburbs. It is "suburbia" and supposedly suburban life styles that concerns us here—not the reality of the suburban rings and the characteristics of the suburban population, for which there is ample empirical evidence.

Probably the most serious flaw in the myth was the gross oversimplification and generalization about suburbs being "all the same." The essential fact of the matter is that the 50 to 60 million persons living in the suburban situation around central cities are not all conforming to a single, monolithic life-style.[13] Somehow the writers who created the myth all managed to interview or observe a handful of families in generally the middle- or upper-middle-class tract suburbs. This is probably the source of the white-collar, young-executive elements of the myth. In addition, these suburbs were newly built, and the young newcomers were all caught up in the novelty of the experience; therefore, neighboring and informal socializing—elements of the myth—were maximized.

Anyone who spends much time in the suburban rings around great cities cannot help being aware of the vast differences in the price of houses. There are suburbs for the $10,000 house buyer and suburbs for the $50,000 buyer—and even for the $100,000 buyer. There are great tract subdivisions, such as the Levittowns. There are also small, rural

13See, for example, the researches of Gans and Berger as noted on p. 211.

villages on the borders of the rural-urban fringe which suddenly fill up with suburbanites and become "reluctant suburbs." There are the old, established, high-status suburbs "closer in," where every house is different.

Although the racial characteristics of the suburbs have not changed radically in recent years, there is nevertheless a steady increase of nonwhites, and the appearance of the "black suburb" is not far off. Then, too, there are suburbs that consist of minorities of blue-collar workers—the industrial suburbs and employing satellites. There are, in short, suburbs whose inhabitants show significant religious, ethnic, racial, and class differences. It is virtually impossible to find a major element of life style which they all universally share and which shapes a primary dimension of their lives.

Even within the so-called homogeneous suburbs there are significant differences in the backgrounds of the residents. On a single street in Levittown, Long Island, in the late 1950's I counted the following: a Catholic second-generation Italian plumber, a Protestant "old American" salesman, a Catholic third-generation German blue-collar worker, a Protestant "old American" skilled worker, a Jewish, third-generation factory foreman, a Jewish second-generation clerk, a Catholic "old American" research physicist, a Catholic third-generation Irish semiskilled factory worker, a Protestant "old American" Wall Street "customer's man," and a retired elderly couple who had just moved into the neighborhood. The ideologies, beliefs, customs, life styles, aspirations, child-rearing practices, and the like seem to deny the crucial role of suburbia in every way.

After living for eight years in a similar suburban neighborhood, I was hard pressed to find any single massively unifying "suburban" force in the social life of the street. On the other hand, one could not help but be impressed by the influence that the traditional forces bore on behavior—religion, class, ethnicity, and the like. In short, those variables which sociologists have found to be crucial in affecting people's lives continue to critically influence them in the suburbs. As to the overpowering role of "suburbia," it was simply not there.

It is in terms of these variables that the myth dissipated. People simply carried their backgrounds to the suburbs. It is true, of course, that suburban life is not the same as city life. There is the home rather than the apartment, flat, or second-story walk-up. There are neighbors to be gotten along with and "property values" in which one has a personal stake. There is the relative lack of public transportation in the suburbs, which means that almost everything beyond the neighborhood involves the automobile.

Then, too, the units of suburban government are smaller and

require greater participation from the citizenry (a public library or no public library, street lights or no street lights, garbage collection or no garbage collection, a village-sponsored swimming pool or no swimming pool). In addition, there is the school system and the vote for "trustees" and the school budget each year. All of these make differences in a person's or a family's life in the move from city to suburb. But the notion that suburbia works some powerful alchemy on each urban migrant is simply not valid. Suburbs are essentially urban communities with less density. They are the city spilling outward along with its people and many of its institutions as well. It may be that "the city" as we knew it in the nineteenth century is obsolete and that metropolitanism and the metropolitan unit is the new form of urbanism in the second half of the twentieth century. But suburbs actually constitute the new form of urbanism with differentiation and specialization and growing interdependence now cast over a great physical area.

THE CENTRAL CITIES:
Race, The Ghetto, and Flight to the Suburbs

Until the first quarter of the twentieth century the central cities were the locus of urbanism. They had grown steadily and were the undisputed centers of economic and cultural dominance in the nation. By the 1930's, the rise of suburbs and the expansion of urbanism into the metropolitan area were growing phenomena. The decades following World War II, as we have already noted, saw the explosion of population far beyond the political boundaries of the central city and the subsequent dramatic rise of suburbs. However, as suburbs grew in population, retail trade, and industry, the old core cities, once the sole expression of the urban community, were faced increasingly with serious internal problems.

Originally, suburbanization was a middle-class movement. It was the economically comfortable, white-collar, middle-class city dweller who could afford the comparatively costly suburban single-family house, and it was the middle-class family that sought out the suburban house to better realize its goals of child rearing, privacy, fresh air, sunlight, "nice neighbors," and the like. During the decade 1950–1960, however, working-class whites also followed the suburban trail out of the city, and the middle-class ethos of the suburbs began to change. Working-class, middle-class, and upper-class suburbs were clearly visible in the population rings surrounding the great central cities.

Urban Racial Changes

But while the largely white exodus from the cities was going on, Negroes from the South were entering the central cities in great numbers, particularly the cities of the Northeast and North Central states. For example, four of the central cities of the five largest metropolitan areas of the country—New York, Chicago, Philadelphia, and Detroit—all experienced a total population loss during the decade 1950–1960.[14] But the losses were in the white population. New York lost 6.7 per cent of its white population, Philadelphia 13.3, Chicago 12.8, and Detroit, 23.5.[15] However, the losses of whites were balanced by the entrance of nonwhites, with nonwhite increases in the same decade of 47.2 per cent in New York, 41.2 in Philadelphia, 64.4 in Chicago, and 60.4 in Detroit.[16] Los Angeles, which had a gain in white population of 17.2 per cent in the decade, saw a nonwhite increase of 97.2 per cent. The geographic and social distribution of races within the United States was now significantly changing. The rural, Southern Negro was becoming a resident of the central cities outside the South.

During the decade 1950–1960, 70 per cent of the metropolitan areas of the country saw increases in the nonwhite population. Outside the South, 90 per cent of the metropolitan centers saw nonwhite increases. In addition, Census data indicate that the 50 largest cities in the United States all had increases in their nonwhite numbers.[17]

Gathering comparative population data on cities, particularly over periods of several decades, is complicated by the fact that their borders may change by annexation. Thus, although a city appears to have grown in population from one decade to another, the "growth" may have been due to annexation of neighboring localities rather than an actual population increase within the same geographic area. However, in the 12 largest metropolitan areas—New York, Los Angeles–Long Beach, Chicago, Philadelphia, Detroit, San Francisco–Oakland, Boston, Pittsburgh, St. Louis, Washington, Cleveland, and Baltimore (in order of size), there have been no significant annexations since 1920; hence, it is possible to gather data over time.[18]

These large metropolitan centers contain at least 1.7 million

14Noel P. Gist and Sylvia Fleis Fava, *Urban Society* (New York: Thomas, Y. Crowell Co., 1964) , p. 74.
15Schnore, *The Urban Scene, op. cit.*, pp. 282–283.
16*Ibid.*
17*Ibid.*, pp. 256–257.
18*Ibid.*, p. 258.

TABLE VI

PER CENT DISTRIBUTION OF THE COMBINED POPULATION OF THE TWELVE LARGEST STANDARD METROPOLITAN STATISTICAL AREAS (1960), THE CENTRAL CITIES, AND THE RINGS, BY RACE, FOR TOTAL POPULATION OF THE UNITED STATES: 1930–1960

The Twelve Largest SMSA's, Central Cities, Rings, and Remainder of the United States	Total Population				PER CENT DISTRIBUTION BY RACES: 1930–1960 White				Nonwhite			
	1960	1950	1940	1930	1960	1950	1940	1930	1960	1950	1940	1930
Twelve Largest SMSA's (1960)	26.3	25.6	24.6	24.4	25.8	25.7	25.4	25.4	29.7	24.2	17.6	15.5
Central Cities	(13.2)	(15.7)	(16.5)	(16.8)	(11.6)	(15.2)	(16.7)	(17.3)	(24.7)	(20.2)	(14.5)	(12.5)
Rings	(13.1)	(9.9)	(8.1)	(7.6)	(14.2)	(10.5)	(8.7)	(8.1)	(5.0)	(4.0)	(3.1)	(3.0)
Remainder of United States	73.7	74.4	75.4	75.6	74.2	74.3	74.6	74.6	70.3	75.8	82.4	84.5
Total United States	100.0	100.0	100.0	100.0	100.0	100.0	100.0	100.0	100.0	100.0	100.0	100.0

SOURCE: Leo F. Schnore, The Urban Scene (New York: The Free Press, 1965), p. 259. Used with permission of the publisher.

people, and their combined populations constitute slightly more than a quarter of the United States total. As can be noted from Table VI, these centers now claim a somewhat larger proportion of the total population than they did in 1930, although their suburban rings have almost doubled in their percentage of the total metropolitan population. Note, too, that the proportion of nonwhites has doubled in the thirty-year period. Whereas the white population in the rings is now slightly larger than that in the core cities, the relative growth of nonwhites in the suburbs has not been significant over the three decades, going from 3 per cent in 1930 to 5 per cent in 1960. The movement of nonwhites into the large central cities did not occur only in the 1950–60 decade. Indeed, the largest percentage increase of nonwhites was in the 1940's, whereas the heavy white exodus from the cities was most noticeable during the 1950's.

The data on race distribution within the metropolitan areas indicate the steady movement of nonwhites into the core, the old central city area, and the out-migration of whites of all economic groups to the suburbs. Thus, while central cities are becoming increasingly nonwhite, the suburbs have remained virtually the same in percentage of nonwhites over the past 30 years—now roughly 5 per cent of the total.

Washington, D.C., is the only clearly black city in the United States, Newark is probably over 50 per cent and Gary, Ind., and Richmond, Va., are near the halfway point. Although the movement of nonwhites to the core will continue, there is no expectation that the majority of large cities will become predominantly black within a short time. Only five of the country's 25 largest central cities and 10 of the cities with populations over 100,000 will have nonwhites in excess of 40 per cent by 1970.[19] According to the *Report of the National Advisory Commission on Civil Disorders*, however, the following major cities will have populations over fifty percent Negro by 1984: New Orleans (1971), Richmond (1971), Baltimore (1972), Jacksonville (1972), Gary (1973), Cleveland (1975), St. Louis (1978), Detroit (1978), Philadelphia (1981), Oakland (1983), and Chicago (1984).

The problems faced by the central cities because of the distribution of races within the metropolitan area are intense. The central cities have lost much of the stable, tax-paying, supportive middle class to the suburbs. In addition, they have lost tax revenues from retailers who have followed their affluent customers to the suburbs. In New York, almost all the great department stores have suburbanized. In addition, manufacturing and industry have moved to the suburbs to take advantage of lower

[19] Herbert J. Gans, "The White Exodus to Suburbia Steps Up," *The New York Times Magazine* (January 7, 1968) , p. 90.

suburban taxes, cheaper land, less traffic, in some cases a better labor supply, and possibly easier rail access.

But while the middle-class depart, along with tax-paying industry, the cities continue to absorb unskilled, largely poverty-stricken newcomers who place additional strains on the cities' municipal services. Thus, the costs of welfare, police, sanitation, fire protection, education, etc. all soar as the result of a population which is essentially dependent on the city rather than supportive of it. Through this process, the cities become bankrupt while the suburbs, with their simple governmental units and relatively affluent populations, prosper.

The predicament of the old, large central cities, therefore, is essentially declining revenues coupled to large increases of unskilled, uneducated dependents. Although this population is basically nonwhite, Chicago, for example, has seen the beginning of a migration of poor, rural white families from the declining economic areas of Appalachia.

Growth of the Ghettos

The old pattern of residential segregation that has characterized city growth in the United States continues as the incoming Negro migrants move into the already crowded and inadequate black neighborhoods— the Negro ghettos of the central cities. Although for many life in the city may be an improvement over what they knew in the South, the crowding, the poverty, the brutality of the streets, the transience, the instability, the broken homes and shattered families constantly tear and erode at any semblance of middle-class life style.

It should be clearly noted that the ghetto is not a "voluntary" community; migrating poor blacks have no other housing choice when they enter the city. The pattern of residential-racial segregation in American cities has concentrated uneducated, relatively jobless, marginal blacks in the urban ghettos. In turn, as the black population increases and the ghetto grows, the public (neighborhood) schools shift from white to black. Thus residential segregation, through the process of housing discrimination, changes the character of urban neighborhoods and schools, which in turn speeds up the white exodus to the suburbs.

Like the whites, those blacks who can, escape to the suburbs. However, the patterns of residential segregation face the Negro in the suburbs, too. Even in the suburban rings there are Negro suburbs. In the New York City area, for example, the suburban communities of Hempstead, N. Y., and Plainfield, Orange, East Orange, Montclair, and Englewood, N. J., saw a significant growth of nonwhite population during the 1950–1960 decade. Hempstead, for example, went from 8.9 per cent nonwhite in 1950 to 22.4 per cent by 1960.

A large-scale movement of Negroes out of the core ghettos is not likely, if only because of limited income. The suburban house requires a minimum income of $7500 (in 1967 dollars), which is substantially higher than most nonwhite incomes. Hence, the bulk of the urban black population will remain within the ghettos and the central city, at least for a decade or more.

The conditions of ghetto life are so brutalizing, so disruptive, and so alienating that it is remarkable that violence has remained suppressed for so long. However, the civil rights movement has made concerted Negro action and protest a legitimate cause. During the past ten years, black demonstrations have become commonplace. Increasingly, the demonstrations become less passive and more militant and activist. By the summer of 1965, civil-rights demonstrations had passed from organized public protest sponsored by civil-rights organizations into unplanned and spontaneous rioting and violence.

These urban riots are the consequence of a powerful combination of structural forces and strains building in the national society over a span of 300 years. The ultimate causal factor, according to the *Report of the National Advisory Commission on Civil Disorders*, has been the "racial attitude and behavior of white Americans toward black Americans." The Commission study goes on to indicate that "white racism" has led to three interrelated forces which significantly contributed to city racial disorders: (1) pervasive discrimination and segregation which led to black migration to the cities coupled to (2) the white exodus to the suburbs and (3) finally the emergence of the black ghetto. Once the teeming ghettos had become a major component of the central cities, from about the 1950's on, the forces of segregation and poverty "intersected to destroy opportunity and hope and to enforce failure." Rather than serving as the urban locus for an improved life, the ghettos became centers of hopelessness and despair, of men without jobs, families without fathers, violence, crime, and normative collapse. Schools merely served as points for the assembling and management of children. Thus, according to the Advisory Commission, the black ghettos acted to catalyze three powerful disruptive forces—*frustrated hopes* came into line with a growing sense that *violence could be legitimately exercised* in an ethos of *powerlessness* and *alienation*.

In an earlier chapter, it was pointed out that the sense of *relative deprivation* is particularly acute among blacks. Two or three decades ago, the sense of deprivation was strong, *but it was not relative to the white population in terms of reference group*. Then too, the hopes and aspirations aroused among blacks as the result of both legislative and juridical gains in recent years eventually led to frustration and cynicism as the gap between reality and promise continued. The continuing separation between promise and fulfillment in the ghetto, attentuated by a sense of powerlessness, was eventually fused to the legitimation of violence.

Free and spontaneous violent action is not new to the Negro. For centuries the blacks had been the object of white terrorism, particularly in the South, in which the administration of justice had clear racial implications. The traditional precepts of "due process of law" and "freedom and justice for all" really applied only to whites. Furthermore the recourse to mob law and to violent acts against Negroes, in which "law and order" values apparently had no meaning then, established a tradition for which eventually the ghetto blacks could also utilize violence legitimately. Simply put, the black sub-culture knew violence well. Eventually, it was turned back on those who first used it.

With all of the festering and intertwined frustrations of ghetto life, the critical point of contact with white society and institutions has been the police. Crime and social disorders are rife in the ghetto and the police are ever present. It is the symbolic confrontation of the police and the ghetto that usually sparks or triggers, a riot. Whether the police were acting properly or improperly in the specific incident is immaterial. The causes of the riots run much deeper than the arrest of a black man by a white policeman. The ghetto sees the incident as another expression of the white "power structure," another indignity, another indication of racial contempt.

In terms of the primary forces, the urban disorders were ultimately caused by the racist ideology of white America. These, in turn shaped the norms and patterns of discrimination and segregation. In recent years, this led to large migrations of blacks out of the rural south and into the cities of the industrial states. In the ghettos a culture of poverty and anomie eventually led to violent acts which were essentially directed against the institutions of white society. For many young Negroes, all of whom responded in some way to ghetto conditions and the general circumstances of the Negro in the United States, the violence on the streets was in no direct or rational manner connected to the civil rights movement. It was apparently an unconscious response to life in the ghetto, and in the final reckoning it was a violent attack on the primary institutions of white society. Of the urban ghettos, which are the immediate source of civil disorders, the language of the commission is perhaps the most revealing, "White institutions created it, white institutions maintain it, and white society condones it."

The Pull of the Suburbs

The question has often been raised as to why whites have left the central cities in such great numbers. But we should first note that not all central cities are losing populations. Generally, it has been the suburbs surrounding very large and relatively old central cities that grew the most rapidly during the 1950–1960 decade. In addition, they generally stand higher in most socioeconomic measures than do the central cities. That is to say, their populations have higher median incomes, higher education, and better paying and more prestigious jobs. On the other hand, the smaller central cities continued to grow more rapidly than did their suburbs and to have higher socioeconomic characteristics.

Probably the principal reason for suburbanization is that most people simply prefer a single-family house in which to raise their children. Since cities are dense and crowded, the single-family house, the yard, and "privacy" are more likely to be found in the suburbs. And this desire for a piece of property and a house is not confined to the middle class; the poor would unquestionably leave the central city if they could afford it. The rich have always lived in the best of two possible worlds— the "town house" or apartment in the city and the "estate" in the rural-urban fringe on weekends. But aside from the rich, most people have had to make a choice, and they have been choosing the suburbs over the city.

There may be something in the American character or the American tradition which makes home and land so attractive. Possibly it may be due to relatively easy access to land in the United States in contrast to traditionally land-starved and upper-class-dominated Europe. Also, deep in the culture of American society is the agrarian tradition where land and land ownership are historically intertwined. In addition, in the stratification system, honor and status has gone to the property and land owning class. Whatever the causes, life in the suburbs seems to have great appeal.

Not only is the cultural tradition of the country generally supportive of suburbanization but affluence, government financing, and the lack of available land in the cities also encouraged the movement outward. Certainly these factors acted to "pull" city dwellers to the suburbs. But changes within the city also acted to "push" them out as well. As we have noted, the large central cities saw a significant change in racial composition in the decade 1940–1950. The intensive suburbanization of whites is clearly evident in the decade 1950–1960. There is really no "hard" evidence to show how many whites left the cities because of changing racial balances, but unquestionably many did. Furthermore, the public schools in the great cities were steadily taking on a nonwhite, lower-class character. This resulted not only from the increases of Negroes in the cities but from the loss of whites to parochial schools and the tendency for urban upper-middle class and upper-class to send their children to private schools. Over the years the socioeconomic characteristics of the school population drifted steadily downward, and this further hastened the loss of middle-class whites to private schools or to the suburbs.

As the black ghettos grew in size, they also intensified the problems faced by the city. Crime, prostitution, illegitimacy, broken homes, drug addiction, violence in the public schools, dwindling student performance, the increase in welfare costs, and a general deterioration of life in the city unquestionably led to the movement of many families across the city limits. In addition, the social, racial, and economic problems of cities are such that they are failing to hold persons who would normally be expected to stay. For example, after the phase of child rearing, older persons, who might find the conveniences of the city more appealing than the now empty seven-room suburban house, are not returning to the city. The movement of suburbanites back to the core areas has simply failed to materialize. Should racial violence and crime continue to increase, even the "hard-core" urban cosmopolitans, who have been stridently antisuburb over the years, may reluctantly come to find life in the suburbs preferable to that in the city.

If the present trends continue, the old and large metropolitan areas will witness not only increasing race polarization between central city and suburb but also class polarization as well. The cities will be inhabited by low-income, poorly educated, lower-class populations while the suburbs will reflect the relative prosperity and affluence of white America. Note, again, that suburbs are attracting blue-collar whites in great numbers in recent years and that consequently the suburban rings will reveal a greater spread in lower-middle to upper-class strata.

Problems of the Cities

Obviously, conditions in the central cities are regarded as the major internal problem of the country. This is true not only because of tragic waste of human potential in the ghettos but also because violence could eventuate in racial warfare throughout the country. Hitherto the attempts to deal with the cities' problems have met with little success. Legislation designed to achieve racial integration both in terms of housing and education has thus far failed. Urban schools become blacker as nonwhites spread through the core areas and whites move to the suburbs.

Thus far the urban-renewal program has not brought the white middle class back to the city through middle-income housing. Attempts at dealing with *metropolitan* problems through the development of metropolitan governmental units have not succeeded. Suburbanites apparently desire no political or governmental affiliation with the city. Some will argue that this is why they left the city in the first place.

Success in rebuilding the cities will depend largely on the introduction of massive Federal funds into the core areas and also on the sociological wisdom employed in their expenditure. Since a major problem of the core cities is dwindling income in the face of rising costs, the financial need is obvious. Perhaps the basic need is to convert the ghetto population from a state of social and economic dependency into one of self-reliance, capability, and productivity. This calls for the dramatic improvement of ghetto schools and new concepts in ghetto education and approach. Most standard educational practice in the United States is designed to serve and reinforce the white, middle-class norm; the ghetto child simply lives in another world.

Since wide-scale racial integration within the metropolitan area seems physically impossible within the next five to ten years, the remaking of the ghetto school to serve the ghetto child and his particular needs is a primary concern. In addition, since the ghetto child often comes from a fatherless home, a broken home, or a home with a working mother, he needs special preparation in his preschool years for formal education. The middle-class child, from the relatively stable home and community, may very well have had books read to him by his parents, but the ghetto child may not even know what a book looks like, and reading itself may be a mystery to him. Government-sponsored projects such as "Head Start" are designed to prepare the ghetto child for the discipline and self-control he will need in his capacity as a student.

But although improvement in the ghetto schools is an obvious need along with the massive improvement of housing in the central cities, perhaps the greatest over-all need of the cities is the viable *integration* of the races. It is clear, however, that the majority of whites are not prepared to accept integration at either the school or the neighborhood level. However, as Negroes move through the educational system and finish college, as they take white-collar jobs and move upward in executive positions in industry—in short, as *they become mobile in the class system*—they will functionally integrate into the mainstream of American society. With educational, occupational, and the attendant class and life-style characteristics (dress, speech, manners, etc.), residential integration will proceed more rapidly.

The massive concentration of marginal, poverty-stricken, uneducated, and anomic blacks in the core areas is the greatest immediate problem of cities. Over the next generation, the process of educational-occupational integration as just outlined, followed by residential integration, will undoubtedly take place. But what is to be done about relieving the torments of ghetto existence now? The Negro would unquestionably like to leave the city slums now, just as the German, Irish, Italian, and Jewish immigrants and newcomers to city life did generations before. But the lack of money to support a suburban house is a major factor keeping Negroes in the ghetto, along with housing discrimination in the suburbs.

One partial solution to this problem is Federal rent subsidies to the poor which would enable them to become property owners either in the cities or suburbs. Although suburbanites may resist racial integration, strict juridical action and enforcement of open-housing laws have proven to be helpful in the racial integration of suburbs. It is difficult to enforce open-housing laws in the older established middle-class, white-collar suburbs, but the new large, tract developments which depend on Federal funds are far easier to integrate. Furthermore, if Negro families are among the first to settle into these suburban tract subdivisions, the usual concern with falling property values can be avoided. In this fashion, blue-collar ghetto families can embark on the suburban trail themselves, while the growing number of black professionals, executives, and the like will be quietly integrating the more affluent upper-middle-class suburban villages.

To sum up, the primary problem of central cities is the crush of poor nonwhites in the core. In order to hasten the viable integration of Negroes into American society, a dramatic improvement of ghetto education and ghetto housing is immediately required; this must involve billions of dollars of Federal money. Secondly, the ghetto population must be dispersed, and this can be achieved by making it a capable, self-reliant, producing population rather than a "welfare" population. (By 1968, one million people in New York City's eight million were receiving welfare benefits). The dispersion can be effected by rent subsidies, by job-training programs—in short, by the assimilation of nonwhites into the class structure. From that point they will physically and socially integrate into American society.

THE URBAN PRINCIPLE

In this chapter, we have seen that community constitutes a form of social organization that can survive theoretically forever and that all other units of social structure—no matter how vast and complex—must rely ultimately on the inclusive character of community and its distinctive organization of relationships. Furthermore, we have seen how, for most of man's existence, the basic form of community was the folk type. Essentially, the folk community is small, isolated, primary-group-dominated, and economically self-sufficient. However, around 3500 B.C. urban settlements began to appear. Their unique characteristic, at least in the beginning, was not necessarily the size of population but a distinctive mode of social relationship. The essence of that difference was in the dramatic increase and elaboration of the division of labor within the community, the rise and growth of specialization, and the general thrust of institutional-associational differentiation. In time cities became far larger than the rural Neolithic settlements, and therefore size and differentiation became the physical and social characteristics of urbanism.

From the time of the first cities, the folk villages were doomed as the prevailing and functional prototype of the human community. It is true that folk villages and settlements probably still numerically dominate the world today, but the rise of cities and urbanism is now so rapid that another generation will see the triumph of the urban community almost everywhere. The question arises as to why cities and urbanism have swept the folk society aside in such a comparatively short time in the development of human society. What principle underlies urban society that seems to make its universality such a foregone conclusion?

Up to this point in our discussion, we have been on relatively firm conceptual and empirical ground. That is to say, the historical, conceptual, and statistical materials that we have employed thus far have been firmly anchored in the sociological literature of communities. From now on, however, we must be speculative, and the order of proof will be rational rather than empirical. As the scope of the question increases, the degree of statistical (empiric-quantitative) control decreases.

Why does the continual growth of urbanism seem inevitable and why must the folk settlement give way before it? The urban principle would seem to suggest that cities represent a form of community more congenial to some generic need of the human condition. But what is that primary force, that fundamental imperative to which the human community is constantly responding? One answer may be that the essential force of association itself (on the level of community and society) is simply the elaboration and proliferation of the division of labor—the degree of specialization and differentiation (status/role) which is articulated in a constantly expanded group structure. In short, the principle that may underlie the expansion of cities is that in these large and dense population areas, people are bound to each other in increasing inter-relatedness through the expansion of the division of labor.

Recall that in the folk community the division of labor was simple and was based largely on sex differences. In short, the social division of labor was anchored in the original division of labor established in nature by the sexual reproductive pattern—male and female. However, human society is a system of mutually interrelated and functionally interdependent groups. It is, in short, an elaboration of the division of labor and the augmenting of specialized tasks far beyond a simple "state of nature." Indeed, the social evolutionary process has been marked by one salient condition: the increase in interdependence and the steady elaboration of the division of labor.

From this perspective, one can see the functional significance of the city and urbanism. It is a form of community which facilitates and continually expands the division of labor and the degree of specialization, which, in turn, fuses mankind (certainly the urbanite) into increasing dependency on others. The urban principle is *simply the societal principle set into the community situation*. Cities grow and dominate the world because they maximize the central thrust of society itself—men are bound to each other increasingly in larger systems of interdependence through specialization and differentiation.

Out of the extreme specialization promoted by the city have come all of the conditions of modern society—science, democracy, knowledge at an incredibly expanding rate, and a rising standard of living made possible by the rationalization of production. Only men bound together in what Durkheim called an "organic" fusion of specialization and interdependence could make this possible. It is here perhaps that the sociological dominance of the city may be found over all other community forms. It is simply that the principle of interdependence is possibly the primary force of human social life. Men bound together create a reality that is more powerful and greater than anything one man can achieve alone. It is perhaps the old Aristotelian dictum that man is basically a "social" animal and by living in organized societies there is literally no limit to what men in association may aspire to and achieve.

Urbanism not only may represent a basic principle of society itself in the idea of a locality of intense interdependence but it gives to each person within the community a freedom that is impossible in the folk community. The sheer size of population characteristic of cities, the proliferation of statuses based on performance, the articulation of complex institutional forms and associational groups all make it possible for each man to find a social situation far more compatible with his individual desires and needs. The folk community, with its emphasis on the sexual division of labor, limited ascribed roles, and simple primary groups coupled to a traditional and monolithic normative system, leaves little room for personal choice and incentive. Cities, from their very beginning, allowed greater personal freedom, and in their steady growth over the centuries they have reached a point where it is quite clear that urban man is simply a freer and more liberated human being. In the Middle Ages, it was a commonplace that "city air makes a man free." And it was during this time that runaway serfs, if they could manage to stay within the walls of the city for a year and a day, could be declared "freemen."

But the city is more than simply a community of greater political freedom. It creates a condition of personal freedom because its very social structure must be based on choice and the relative abundance of alternatives. In a sense, freedom exists to the extent that an individual has alternatives—choices. Typically, the city presents greater alternatives (statuses, roles, jobs, norms, groups, etc.) than the folk community and the current rural village.

It seems ironic and even paradoxical that the modern metropolis —built around the dingy and bankrupt core cities—is a center of comparative freedom. And yet that is why the Southern Negro has migrated so heavily into the cities—basically for freedom. The cities have more jobs, better schools, more enlightened social services, and simply more choices over existing conditions than either the urban or the rural South. Such a condition may not always prevail, but it is the search for a fuller, better, freer life that draws many to the cities. And it has almost always been so. It was jobs opening up in the cities that attracted farmers in the eighteenth and nineteenth centuries. And it is the opportunities, the excitement, the chances and choices that continue to draw Americans from the small towns into the metropolitan areas.

The paradox is that rural areas *seem to be freer.* They are free *of* people and full of empty land and space. But in the sense that we have defined freedom—realistic alternatives—only social structures can create this kind of freedom. Rural man may be free of congestion, noise, and air pollution, but what are his realistic choices? What are the job opportunities in a small town? What kind of "future" does the farm boy have if he doesn't want to farm? Generally, he heads for the city—for the noise, filth, congestion, and gross inconvenience that hundreds of thousands of human beings create when they live together in great density— but there he finds the alternatives, created by the social structures, that only urban forms can produce.

So it may be argued that urbanism represents the current community form which most appropriately fulfills the societal mandate of interdependence. And yet, although some teleological societal force may be acknowledged here, the individual man, in spite of density and all of the problems associated with cities today, may find a greater measure of freedom and spontaneity within the urban social system. It may be that in the cities of tomorrow these two principles, interdependence and freedom, can be more fully joined. They seem on the surface contradictory, but in the manner in which we have presented the issues here, they represent the societal and individual facets of the same phenomenon.

SUGGESTED READINGS

BERGER, BENNETT M., *Working Class Suburb*. Berkeley: University of California Press, 1960.

A critical analysis of a working-class suburb which dispels many of the popular illusions of life in the new suburbia.

BLUMENFELD, HANS, *The Modern Metropolis*. Cambridge: The M.I.T. Press, 1967.

A series of selected essays dealing with the origins, growth, characteristics, and planning problems of contemporary metropolitan areas.

GANS, HERBERT J., *The Levittowners*. New York: Random House, Inc., 1967.

Probably the best single study of a contemporary mass-produced suburb. Gans uses the method of participant observation in his analysis of Levittown, New Jersey.

GOTTMAN, JEAN, *Megalopolis*. New York: Twentieth Century Fund, 1961.

An exhaustive analysis of the urbanized area stretching from southern New Hampshire to northern Virginia. The interrelationships among the social and economic processes of the area is a basic concern.

GREER, SCOTT, *Urban Renewal and American Cities*. New York: The Bobbs-Merrill Co., Inc., 1965.

A survey of the broad scope of the urban renewal program currently in effect in hundreds of American cities. The discussion includes an organizational analysis of the program on local public authority.

JACOBS, JANE, *The Death and Life of Great American Cities*. New York: Random House, Inc., 1961.

A critical evaluation of urban renewal and other programs designed to halt central city decay.

HALL, PETER, *The World of Cities*. New York: McGraw-Hill Book Company, 1966.

> *An analysis of metropolitan growth on a global basis, with case studies of London, Paris, Randstad Holland, Rhine-Ruhr, Moscow, New York, and Tokyo.*

HOWARD, EBENEZER, *Garden Cities of Tomorrow*. London: Faber & Faber, Ltd., 1945.

> *This classic originally appeared in 1898 and was the first major statement pleading the cause of rational urban and town planning.*

Report of the National Advisory Commission on Civil Disorders. New York: Bantam Books, 1968.

> *A major government report of a sociological nature commissioned by President Johnson to study the causes and solutions of civil disorder largely in the cities.*

SCHNORE, LEO F., *The Urban Scene*. New York: The Free Press, 1965.

> *With the use of census materials, major trends in urban and suburban areas are analyzed. A primary source in the empirical analysis of contemporary metropolitan areas.*

chapter  8

STRATIFICATION
AND SOCIETY

In dealing with groups in an earlier chapter, we considered a social structure that subsumed the sub-units beginning with actor, norms, status/role, social relationship, and social interaction. In a sense, *group* constituted the conceptual nexus built up from these ancillary ideas. Similarly, the concept of community subsumes the notion of group but also adds the idea of social inclusiveness—the ability of the system to survive theoretically forever purely from the internal relational forms. Community utilizes the basic primary-secondary dichotomy within the substructure but adds the subsequent variables of population size and density, social heterogeneity, and differentiation.

The social reality of groups is such that the participating actors share a psychological affinity for and understanding of the group members. This can be seen not only in the "we" feeling arising out of the primary group (the *Gemeinschaft* sense) but, indeed, simply in the awareness that all members of the United States Army or General Motors as "soldiers" or "employees" have that they are "part of it." There is a reality to group structure (norms, status/role, interaction) that becomes a part of the personality system of the persons that compose it.

STRATIFICATION

When we deal with social stratification we are no longer in the realm of organized relationships and groups. We are considering a form of social reality that emerges from interaction and that to a degree can be found in all groups but is not in *itself a group form*. Social stratification is largely a condition that builds in a community after a certain level of development. Indeed, it constitutes a dimension of social experience that is best understood at the communal or societal level. Stratification, as a form of social reality, is not an organized interaction system (a group); it is, rather, the allocative system developed by a society (or community) for the distribution of scarcities. Social stratification, in short, is essentially the *organization of inequalities* within a society, the distribution of rewards, the allocation of scarcities, and the *formalization of positions in some hierarchical order*.

Although the phenomenon of stratification is best seen as a condition arising from community and society, even the simplest human groups have a dimension of hierarchical structure (informal leader—informal follower). Primitive folk bands and villages have an equally primitive stratification system, with no great differences in life style or consumption patterns. There is a tendency for general sharing, and need is often the principal criterion for *who* receives *what*, but there are, nevertheless, differences in power and authority between roles, and certainly there are differences in the community's distribution of honor and prestige (the "great" hunter versus the poor one).

Despite nuances in consumption, prestige, and power, there is in the folk community a homogenization of the population in terms of the distributive system. Simply put, there isn't much in the distributive system to distribute. Food is scarce, and so it is generally shared by all. The role/status system is limited, so there is no wide separation or social distance from the "top" to the "bottom." The stratification system is characteristically flat and horizontalized, with occasional, slight projections of consumption patterns for a few and somewhat more dramatic extensions in power, prestige, and authority.

It was not until the rise of cities that the phenomenon of stratification emerged as a dramatic feature of the local community. Recall that the city developed only when agricultural surpluses made it possible for "nonproductive," agriculturally consuming populations to live in dense, differentiated settlements. Hence, the distributive system had to be greatly enlarged and formalized, for there were now surpluses that had to be allocated in terms of some new normative formula. Furthermore, the simple division of labor characteristic of the folk community had, by this time, elaborated into a relatively complex status/role structure encompassing priests, scribes, farmers, soldiers, judges, scholars, artisans, traders, slaves, and the like. Thus, the existence of surplus, in addition to an expanding division of labor, served as the foundation for newer distributive forms out of which emerged distinctive *strata*—classes or pluralities of men who shared basically the same position in the allocative scheme.

Another dimension to the human condition contributed to the system of social stratification. We have thus far suggested that stratification is somehow a consequence of the division of labor in society and that, with an expanded division of labor, the stratification system (distributive system) grows and elaborates. However, this structural condition is furthered by the distinctive human predisposition to *evaluate*—to give meaning, to bestow value, to make judgments, to discriminate, to equate and balance subjectively (within the norm system). There is probably no act, no relationship, no social form, no social experience, no social event of any sort that does not stand before the cultural-normative bar of judgment.

Almost all human experience is to some degree symbolic (language alone is the vehicle for thought), and the meaning of symbols is the legitimate concern of the culture system. And so it is that acts, codes, behavior, haircuts, colleges, nations, nationalities, religions, noses, skin color, works of art, suits, styles, mannerisms, speech patterns, dialects, regions, villages, etc., etc.—indeed, almost all things in nature, society, and culture—are judged, equated, and evaluated. In short, coupled to the social division of labor with its characteristic differential functions, there is, in addition, *differential evaluation*.

Men perform different functions in different roles, and the community not only evaluates the performance of men in their role capacity but also evaluates the significance and importance of the role itself. We will shortly discuss the major theoretic orientations that sociology has advanced to explain the nature and structure of stratification systems, but first we shall briefly examine a characteristic American attitude toward the phenomenon of stratification.

CLASS AND IDEOLOGY

A stratification system is essentially the distribution of scarcities in a society. Not all good things are free and easily accessible. Fresh air, before this age of air pollution, was literally free to all and hence it did not figure in the allocative system. It is things both valuable and scarce that figure most importantly in the stratification system, and in American society the emphasis has been on the *achievement* of these good things rather than their allocation by ascription into frozen and fixed strata. Indeed, part of the basic ideology of American society is the formal admonition that "all men are born free and equal." But a system of stratification suggests the opposite—that all men are not born in the same and equal social circumstance. There is a characteristically cynical response to the naive assertion of universal freedom and equality in the United States: "Yes, all men are born free and equal, but some are born freer than others."

In the ordering of classes (men who share basically the same position in the allocative scheme), there is always the latent suggestion of privilege. All members of the family share the same class position and hence the family's class circumstances pass on to the children. Thus a rich, powerful, and prestigeful family will pass on to the children wealth, power, and honor. Another child may "inherit" indifference, poverty, disesteem, and powerlessness. Even in the relatively fluid and open class system in the United States, where individuals may be "mobile" in the class structure, there is nonetheless the extant condition of class privilege that violates the ideological tenet of "classlessness" and total freedom.

The folklore of American heroes reveals the ideological viewpoint. Traditionally, the American hero has "made it" from "rags to riches." Since the primary ideology says that all men are basically equal, and since American society is designed to permit full "opportunity" and "freedom" to "all," it then stands to reason that everybody "at the top" got there by "hard work, self-denial, fair play—the American Way." The reality of class and the latent ability of the family to "place" individuals favorably in the class structure is antithetical to the American belief in fundamental equality of everybody. Hence, there has been a predisposition to avoid public recognition of class differences and to avoid class terms. Public officials still disclaim the existence of class in the United States, but worried big-city mayors deplore the loss of "the middle-income groups" from the central cities.

Americans have no ready vocabulary to describe their class memberships or the class structure of their society in general.[1] An American child at seven has acquired some status identity. He probably knows he is a Catholic, Protestant, or Jew—but he isn't really sure what this means.

---

[1]The material in the remaining part of this section originally appeared in the author's, *Class in Suburbia* (Englewood Cliffs, N.J.: Prentice-Hall, Inc., 1963), pp. 33–36. Used with permission of the publisher.

He also knows he is an American, but he may not have much geographic or political insight into what it means. His most meaningful status insights are his age and sex. It is important to know whether you are a boy or a girl, and how old you are. But what parent is willing or, indeed, equipped to tell his child, "You are in the upper-middle class—and don't you forget it!"

In Europe, awareness of class differences is far sharper and more sophisticated than in the United States. The psychological basis for the acceptance and recognition of social class differences in Europe had been established long before the coming of the industrial age. The psychology of social class—the recognition and submission of an inferior social class to the dictates of a superior class—evolved from feudal times. The castelike character of the feudal peasantry and aristocracy, frozen into relatively fixed layers, established the historic tradition for a hierarchic ordering of social classes. As feudalism passed into industrialism, the caste system based on relationship to land gave way to the rise of modern social classes based on production. The financier, the capitalist, and the industrialist scrambled to the uppermost layer of the new social hierarchy, dumping the tottering, dysfunctional nobility along the way. As the wheels of production spun with increasing intensity, the peasants were pulled from the land to form the basis for the new industrial classes—the "wage slaves," the industrial proletariat, the working class.

The United States never knew a feudal period or a significant landed aristocracy. As a consequence, Americans have never been sympathetic to an ideology based upon the principle of inherent privilege. Aristocratic themes may have been popular during the period of the American Revolution, largely focused around Alexander Hamilton and his followers, but they gained little acceptance. The spirit of egalitarianism so prevailed that, by the time of Andrew Jackson, the American class structure was flattened into a wide plateau of social, political, and economic homogeneity. It may possibly have been, as many have called it, "the Age of the Common Man." The country had emerged from an age of vigorous Yankee mercantilism, commerce, and trade to plunge into a period of the most intensive industrialization and city-building that the world had ever known. The recurrent themes of "democracy," "liberty," "equality," and "free society"—the belief that a hard-working man might go as fast and as far as his abilities could take him—made the notions of European classes repugnant to the developing American tradition.

With none of the familiar (European) guideposts to social class and class consciousness, many scholars and laymen alike are prone to discount the usefulness of the concept in the analysis of American social structure. The lines are too blurred, they suggest, and the factors which go into the formation of American social classes are more a matter of the theoretic and methodological caprices of the investigator than the actual social conditions he intends to describe. Yet if Americans, blinded by the ideological blinkers of nineteenth-century classlessness, do not consciously *think* in terms of the historical images of class, do they nevertheless *act* as if class relations were a central and significant part of their lives?

Out of the familiar, everyday conversations of Americans comes the tacit recognition of the patterning of class differences. Often the descriptions of the inequalities in the distribution of power or prestige and wealth are stated in symbolic or the most primitive conceptual devices. Consider the following statements.

(1) On the distribution of social status and prestige:

Well, of course, in this country everybody is equal. That was one of the founding principles of this country. And there really are not any classes here. Of course, there are *people who live differently* than other people and I am not saying who is right or wrong. I just feel that the Italians and Jews have their own way and we have ours. We mind our business in this town and they mind theirs. . . .

Look, if you change the zoning in this community do you know what you'll get? A bunch of builders will throw up a thousand jerry-built shacks on 60 by 100 plots, that's what you'll get! Then you'll get a *working class element* around here and there will be knifing and drinking and a juvenile delinquency problem. You let those kind of people in and Puerto Ricans won't be far behind.

Folks, this is a real nice community here, with people you'll like to have as neighbors. Down the street is a college professor and right across the way is Dr. Parker. He's a retired doctor. Very nice, quiet family. Man next door is an engineer. You can see the *class of people* we have around here.

I was so embarrassed. There were *real swanky people* there. I didn't even understand what they were talking about. I felt so stupid! They just *weren't my kind.* . . .

Now Carter, this girl you've been going around with, do you really know *what kind of background* she has? Don't you think that before it gets really serious you should consider some of the problems: after all, she comes from a Polish family. They are *working people.* She's Catholic, and though I admire the girl for working her way through college, I simply can't see. . . .

(2) On the role of wealth and income:

Now you guys know what this union has done for you. We fought to get you a hospitalization plan, two-week vacations, sick days, and steady pay raises each year. You know who *the owners* are backing for the Senate this year, some Republican bastard who will take it all away from you again! There is only one way you can keep *the working man* represented in Washington and that's to send a Democrat down there to look out for us—you and me! You just vote Democratic all the way and you'll be looking out for *your own interests* and not the *rich man's!*

The whole thing is chaos. Nothing but give-aways. There was a time when a man was willing to put in a good day's work for a good day's wages. But not any more: The unions are squeezing you dry for a *bunch of loafers* who don't want to work! And what's the government doing about it? I'll tell you what they are doing. Nothing! It's Socialism! That's what we are going to get. The government will own everything, tell you what to do, where you can work, what doctor you can go to—everything. All they are interested in is handouts—give-aways. They take it from *those who worked for it and give it to those who want something for nothing.* They call it progress. . . .

Have you heard about Charlie Smith? Got promoted to district manager. He's only been with the company six years and promoted to district manager. That's probably about sixteen thousand a year. Boy, Charlie's *getting up in the world!*

"The owners," "the working man," "getting up in the world," "real swanky people," "working class element," are the commonplace indicators that wide gaps of social distance, wealth, and life style separate millions of people from each other. The recognition of these differences, however, does not come easily and often represents the struggle between social reality and the traditional ideology of classlessness.

FUNCTIONAL VERSUS CONFLICT THEORY

The general theoretic orientation running through this book is usually called by sociologists "functional" theory. Essentially, the core of this viewpoint is concern with the interrelationships of the component parts of the social system. The issue is twofold: (1) the sociological character of a given structure (What is it?) and (2) the relationship of the structure to the other component parts of the system (What does it do?). From a functional point of view, accordingly, we may ask: What is the structure of the stratification system and what is its relationship to the other units of the social (in this case societal) system?

Now this kind of question carries with it the implicit assumption that positive functions (integration-adaptation) arise from the structure of classes. In other words, since stratification systems are almost universal to the generic human social condition (certainly from the time of cities), then stratification must *do something to aid in the integration and adaptation* of the total social system. It must be *functional* to the survival of society itself. And so functionalist sociologists who have inquired into the character of stratification systems have generally sought to link the class structure functionally to the total system of society itself.

However, another school of sociologists (we can identify it as the "conflict school" of stratification) has emphasized and argued almost the direct opposite—it has called attention to the dysfunctional elements of the stratification system. The most massive and influential statement suggesting the negative and dysfunctional features of social stratification can be traced directly to Karl Marx. Although not a sociologist, Marx greatly influenced many sociologists who read his works and who were subsequently inclined to accept certain of the Marxist conclusions—above all, that class systems generate a basic conflict between populations or segments within a society. Such constant and, in a Marxist sense, inevitable conflict between classes is essentially damaging to the social order, and hence the very existence of class structures is inimical to social order.

The Marxist View of Class

We cannot here go into detail regarding the general theory of class advanced by Marx, but some of his principal views deserve at least a brief summation. For Marx, human society is primarily organized around the pursuit of basic needs—food, shelter, clothing. Not only are men "social" in a sort of instinctive sense but the very nature of human association (society) is to facilitate the acquisition of basic needs via the division of labor. In the course of the early history of mankind, according to Marx, a sort of parasitic, exploitative "class" arises which takes for itself the primary modes of production. This class uses and exploits another class (nonowners) for its own greedy and acquisitive purposes. Thus, down through history a class which owns the prevailing modes of production (females and children in folk societies, and capital goods in modern society) dominates the class structure and, through its position of economic strength, gathers for itself political power as well. The state, in short, is simply the vehicle for the maintenance of class dominance and the prevailing economic order.

In the Marxist view, the key structure to the understanding of human history is class. Classes precipitate in the various historical levels (tribal, classical, feudal, and capitalist) in terms of a critical relationship to the prevailing modes of production characteristic of each epoch—essentially ownership and nonownership. There are thus two primary classes in each major historical stage and these are essentially antagonistic to each other. The basis of the antagonism, Marx concluded, is the essential opposition of the "interests" of each polar class to the other. For example, in modern (capitalist) society, the working class, the proletariat, has class interests that are directly opposite to those of the bourgeoisie, the capitalists, the owners of large-scale industry and finance. In order to maximize their profit and increase their wealth (the ultimate guiding necessity of the bourgeoisie), the owners pay their workers as little as possible and force them to work long and grueling hours. On the other hand, the proletariat is interested in fewer working hours, better working conditions, higher pay, and the like. Thus, the two classes are arrayed in a fundamental antagonism. What one wants must be paid for by the other. This is the crux of the conflict issue. For Marx, viewing much of history as class struggle born of this basic structural conflict, the only way out for the oppressed proletariat was violence and revolution.

In the final reckoning, as Marx saw it, the revolution of the working class was a historical necessity. It would be only through such a dramatic remaking of the institutions of society that the profit motive and class interest would be finally removed from human society. Class exploitation could only end if class interest could be eliminated. Thus, the bourgeoisie—the owners—would have to disappear as a class, not physically but socially, since in the final stage of society—a communal society—all men would stand in the same relationship to the prevailing modes of production. Class interest would have come to an end because classes (in the Marxist sense) would no longer exist.

Probably no other figure in the nineteenth century has had so profound an impact on the twentieth as Marx. Not only did the Marxist view of history, class, and society dramatically affect the intellectual climate of the decades that followed, but in the past sixty years many of his primary views have been incorporated into political action and ideology. It is probably true that not one of his major predictions about the circumstances of proletarian revolution has occurred anywhere under the conditions he anticipated. But major nations (the U.S.S.R. and China) have accepted some of the basic views into the official governmental ideology of the nation. The idea of history as essentially class struggle and conflict is central—as is the inevitability of class violence.[2]

In the development of sociology through much of the nineteenth century, almost any interest in the nature of class was based upon the Marxist model. There were simply no conceptual or theoretic alternatives. Indeed, with the possible exception of Max Weber, in Europe, and Thorstein Veblen, in the United States, there was no significant theory and research in the nature of social stratification until the 1920's, with the publication of the Lynds' *Middletown*. This was the first major American community study along class lines. From the 1930's on, however, the analysis of class and stratification grew, and following World War II it has become a major research and conceptual concern in American sociology.

Whereas Marx was the font of inspiration for the conflict school of social stratification, there seems to be no single figure identifiable with the functional approach, although Talcott Parsons and Kingsley Davis are currently the leading advocates.[3] Recall that the conflict approach views stratification essentially from the dysfunctions it produces in society. Class is seen essentially as a negative factor which reduces adaption and the integration of the social system. Certainly if class conflict is the direct result of class interests and the polarization of class hostilities, social integration, solidarity, and cohesiveness of the total system suffer. On the other hand, the functional view stresses the adaptive and integrative functions that accrue from social stratification.

The Functional View

The key to the functional argument is that roles in the societal structure are differentially related to the functional imperatives. Some

[2]On this point, however, the U.S.S.R. and China seem no longer in agreement. It appears that the Soviet Union has adopted a somewhat more pragmatic view of the inevitability of class conflict and seems to feel that the world may achieve the ideal Communist society through emulation rather than revolution and struggle. The Chinese Communists, on the other hand, still cling to a rather orthodox view of Marx—perhaps we should say orthodox views of Marxism, for Marx might well disavow many contentions and views currently ascribed to him. Indeed, at one point Marx publicly stated, "I am not a Marxist" in rebutting some of the extreme positions his followers were taking.

[3]See, for example, Talcott Parsons, "A Revised Analytical Approach to the Theory of Social Stratification," in Reinhard Bendix and S. M. Lipset, *Class, Status and Power: A Reader in Social Stratification* (New York: The Free Press, 1953), pp. 92–128; Kingsley Davis, *Human Society* (New York: The Macmillan Company, 1949) pp. 364–389.

roles are strategic to the maintenance of the basic functional needs and others are not. A mayor, a Congressman, a corporation president, a priest, a general, a banker, a surgeon, a judge, all these roles are close to the critical functional needs: adaptation, integration, tension management, pattern maintenance. Other roles—barber, sales clerk, gas station attendant, housewife, "followers," and the like—though necessary to society are not critically and immediately involved in the integration and stability of the social system.

In addition, the successful performance of some roles calls for long periods of training and for heavy responsibility once the role is assumed. Why should people submit to the ordeal of long training periods and burdensome responsibility? The answer, the functionalists maintain, is that they are *rewarded*. For differential roles there are *differential rewards*. As they say in the Army, "Rank has its privileges." A society rewards performances in the strategic and functionally imperative tasks. And the rewards are not hard to discover—wealth, power, honor. In essence, stratification arises from the differential functional significance of roles, the ability and training required of the occupants of the roles, and the relative scarcity of capable persons to fill the roles.

In the functionalist view of stratification, those at the top of the class pyramid are those closer to the critical functions that must be performed, whereas those toward the bottom, filling the numerous but relatively unimportant roles, constitute the wide base of "common" people who receive relatively modest rewards. Since roles can never be equal in terms of their functional significance to society, stratification and inequality are inevitable.

In addition to the importance of roles, the culture system of each society stresses characteristic values usually arising from the functional imperatives. In short, values, beliefs, ideologies, etc. reflect the structural needs of the societal system. Values reinforce the system needs. But different societies facing the same structural problems may emphasize a *different* ordering of values. Some may stress, for example, religious values (integrative) while others may stress economic values (adaptive). Thus one society may reward persons who place a high premium on religious values; another may reward those who place significance on the governmental or economic spheres. In both societies, the integrative or adaptive needs will be met, but in two different institutional-associational contexts. The stratification system therefore reflects not only the role structure in relation to the functional imperatives but also the unique structuring of values.

The conflict theorists see in the phenomenon of stratification the struggle for scarcities, while the functionalists, viewing society as a social system, regard class structure as not only inevitable but necessary. Conflict theory emphasizes coercion, dominance, control, exploitation, struggle, hostility, and self-interest. Functional theory emphasizes system harmony, integration, solidarity, consensus, balance, and social order. One wonders how such seemingly diametrically opposing theoretical orientations can be subsumed by the same discipline.

One possible answer is that quite possibly both functionalists and conflict advocates are right and that they have singly emphasized both the *functional* and *dysfunctional* elements of the stratification system. No society is perfectly balanced; no social order is all symmetry. No human being is completely integrated into the social structure, and no social structure or system is an ideal fusion of perfectly designed components. Indeed, human society is a crescive, growing, stressful, dynamic ordering of relationships, and it is never in a state of total equilibrium and harmony. The conflict theorists have largely dealt with the dysfunctions—the conflict, the struggle, the disequilibrium generated out of the allocative-distribution system.

Unquestionably there has been "injustice," struggle, and violence down through human history between the "haves" and "have nots." This is what Marx called such dramatic attention to. On the other hand, the functionalists have, with great sociological legitimacy, posed the issue of the inevitability of stratification in human society in regard to system needs and imperatives. Men "in a state of nature" are certainly not equal to each other physically or psychologically. In addition, men in society, while cooperating as they must in order to survive collectively within the system, do not always have mutual and identical ends. Furthermore, when people are faced with issues in which they must decide between their own or their group's interests and the interests of society or others, they almost always choose their own.[4] There is a strong tendency toward self-interest in human affairs. Thus, the functionalists see stratification as a blend between the differential structures and roles of human society, system imperatives which are bound up in these roles coupled to differences in drive, ambition, ability, opportunity, intelligence, and chance circumstances on the level of the individual.

Although the history of sociology is characterized by the polemic between function and conflict theory, there is currently a movement toward the integration of both positions, particularly as viewed by the functional-dysfunctional perspective. Furthermore, even many years ago, such figures as Max Weber were struggling for an eclectic perspective that

[4]Gerhard Lenski, *Power and Privilege* (New York: McGraw-Hill Book Company, 1960) , p. 30.

would successfully accommodate both conflict and functionalist view-points. His classic essay "Class, Status, and Party" is a case in point.

Weber's View of Class, Status, and Power

Unlike Marx's single causal, monistic conception of stratification (economic determinism) Weber's view of the stratification system fused three variables—economic class, honorific status, and power. Formally, he referred to them as "classes," "status groups," and "parties." Class exists when

> ...(1) a number of people have in common a specific causal com-ponent of their life chances, in so far as (2) this component is represented exclusively by economic interests in the possession of goods and opportunities for income, and (3) is represented under the conditions of the commodity or labor markets.[5]

The "class situation" for Weber consists of the "typical chance" for goods, living circumstances, personal life experiences, life chances, all shaped by the "market," the economic order. Property or the lack of property is the basic variable of the class situation. In his clear emphasis on eco-nomic determinants, Weber seems quite similar to Marx. But whereas Marx based his entire scheme of stratification on a single-variable ap-proach, Weber's system of stratification included two other critical con-ceptions.

"In contrast to the purely economically determined 'class situa-tion,'" argues Weber, "we wish to designate as 'status situation' every typical component of the life fate of men that is determined by a specific, positive or negative, social estimation of *honor*."[6]

Now, a point of clarification is in order regarding Weber's use of the term "status" and the manner in which we have been using the concept as an indication of an elementary unit position—the status/role conception. Actually both terms are employed in contemporary sociology with somewhat distinct and separate meanings. Weber's use of "status" dealt largely with the honorific dimension. In this sense, status refers to the subjective world of social honor and prestige—in short, to *differential evaluation*. Actually, status in the role-positional sense also carries with it

---

[5]Max Weber, "Class, Status, Party," in H. H. Gerth and C. Wright Mills, *From Max Weber: Essays in Sociology* (New York: Oxford University Press, 1946), p. 181.
[6]*Ibid.*, pp. 186–187.

the honorific element. As the functionalists have pointed out, roles (status positions) such as "Supreme Court Justice" or "doctor of medicine" claim significantly greater prestige than, say, "garbage man" or "shoe-shine attendant."

Recall our discussion of the role of evaluation and the universal bestowing of differential judgment on all things. For Weber, the world of honor and prestige, of status privilege, of subjective evaluation, is as significant in the stratification order as economic factors. In his view, class precipitates within the social system according to relations linked to *production* and the acquisition of goods. However, merely to be rich is not enough for upper-class placement. The status element must also be present. Riches may provide the possibility for consumption patterns, but the "nouveau riche" may simply consume goods and live by a life style that is not shared by the upper class. A classic case in point would be the Texas truck farmer who inadvertently finds oil on his land. He suddenly becomes a millionaire, but though he may buy a fine house in a "swanky" neighborhood and several Cadillacs in assorted pastel colors with leopard skin upholstery, he will not impress his upper-class neighbors very much. Indeed, they will continue to feel superior because they *consume* according to an upper-class life style, whereas the millionaire farmer consumes by the normative standards of his status group (poor farmers) although he can afford to buy anything. His life style continues to be shaped by his status origins even though his economic class has objectively changed.

In his interest in status groups, Weber emphasized the pursuit of subjective honor and noted that mere property was not enough. Indeed, he points out that the most honorific and esteemed social groups are such that they stand outside of the merely economic. Membership in the First Families of Virginia (F.F.V.) and the Daughters of the American Revolution (D.A.R.), both of which claim high status and usually get it (from status "inferiors"), is simply not purchasable. One has to be "born" into it. Thus, from this perspective, certain elements of status stratification (ancestry, background, religion, neighborhood, family, country clubs, etc.) are not directly achievable. Some are a condition of birth. As Weber points out, stratification by status (the honorific) can ultimately evolve into stratification by caste. That is to say, the same principle of ascribed honor which operates in the realm of status stratification in open-class societies is expressed in its final form in caste societies. Individuals are frozen into castes by the circumstance of birth, and there is no possibility of leaving their caste identification until death. In short, the principle which animates the ladies of the D.A.R., and the honor and prestige they seek through kinship with a long departed ancestor, is essentially the same social force which traditionally bound persons via birth to caste placement in India.

Functional and Conflict Theories

It is at this juncture that we can clearly see the pending integration of the functionalist and conflict approaches to stratification. The functionalists generally consider the *necessity* for class (economic) fluidity in an industrial, urban society. The functional need to place capable people in positions of responsibility, particularly in the political and economic institutional spheres of activity, is obvious. Hence, the view that stratification via differential rewards linked to differential roles is functional. But the conflict theorists, in looking down through human history and out across the current spectrum of human culture, see ancient aristocracies and ineffective elites struggling to maintain their hold on the social structure and their favored relationship to the distributive system. What is functional about an inept and outmoded aristocrat? What is valuable and integrative about an upper class which closes itself to mobile newcomers and persons of talent and achievement?

It is here that the apparent contradictions can be seen. The functionalists are largely concerned with mobility in an industrial society. The conflict theorists focus on the limitations of mobility. They see largely the frozen status structures which are essentially dysfunctional to the total social order. The principle of status relies heavily on exclusivity and denial. Indeed, social honor can exist only if there is also dishonor and disesteem for others.

Furthermore, while the functionalists point out that differential function leads to differential rewards, the conflict school emphasizes those elements of status (denial, exclusivity, life style, manners, rigidity, exploitation, aristocracy, closure, etc.), that are also characteristic of stratification. Even in open-class societies, such as in the West and certainly the United States, the status principle clearly operates (D.A.R., "old" family background, the "right" college). And where it exists, there are barriers to movement and limitations of opportunity. Jews are not hired in certain Wall Street brokerage houses. Italians are denied jobs in some banks, and country clubs are closed to Catholics, or Mexican Americans, or Puerto Ricans, or Negroes, or anyone who is disapproved of in the subjective world of status honor. Indeed, status stratification seems to be the dysfunctional side of the stratification coin that the functional school has largely ignored.

Thus the multidimensional conceptions of Weber, economic class and honorific status, help to fuse and at least partially integrate two apparently contradictory views of social stratification. However, Weber was concerned with a final factor in the stratification system—power. Weber localized the element of power into the phenomenon of parties. Thus, parties may appear out of class interests or status interests. However, the phenomenon of power, the ability to enforce one's will on others, regardless of their own will, has stratification implications far beyond the formal articulation of parties founded on either class or status. Indeed, Gerhard Lenski recently argued that power basically determines the distribution of surplus with a society. And note again that surplus, after the rise of cities, dramatically recast the phenomenon of stratification into far more complex forms than existed in the folk community.

The foundations and sources of power, however, are manifold. Certainly wealth makes it possible to enforce one's will on others. For example, it is generally conceded in the United States that in order to run for political office money is highly desirable. Without the millions of dollars from his personal fortune, would a Nelson Rockefeller or a John Kennedy have gone as far as he did? In addition, status may serve as a foundation of power. The old families, the "right" associations, the "contacts" that emerge from status association can also serve as a backdrop for decision making. Both wealth and status, therefore, can provide the basis for power claims.

Power itself, moreover, may be the basis for additional power. The political precinct captains who do "favors" for their constituents (because they have the power to do so) may eventually ask favors of the people they did favors for. In this fashion, by involving persons in a reciprocal web of favor-giving and favor-asking, the politician advances his ability to move the levers in power in increasingly wider circumstances.

The variable of power in the stratification system of any society is probably not as "independent" as economic and honorific status factors. That is to say, power most likely rests on "something," and it is difficult to regard it as a purely solitary unit of analysis, although some scholars have done so. In short, the roots and foundations of power are complex and difficult to observe. It is clear enough, however, that those who sit at the top of the social hierarchy—those who possess the most wealth and honor—also disproportionately control the actions and behavior of others.

To sum up, the stratification system in a society is essentially the distributive system of that society. Simply put, it is a matter of who gets what in the formal and institutionalized ordering of rewards. When a society evolves to the point of surplus, the distribution becomes more complex because there is simply more to be distributed. Those at the "top" of the stratification system generally receive comparatively greater amounts of wealth, status, and power. Depending on the stratification system, any of these three variables may predominate in a society in time and place. Hence, nineteenth-century India ascribed persons to caste (the status principle) on the basis of birth. In the United States, on the other hand, particularly in the late nineteenth century, during a time of intense industrial and urban growth, stratification proceeded along economic lines. In times of great social change, such as a period of political revolution, sheer power may be the most critical factor within the stratification system. These three, largely in combination, generally serve as the key units of the allocative system.

Conflict theory has emphasized the dysfunctional elements of stratification, calling particular attention to the limitation of opportunities imposed by the status principle. Functional theory, on the other hand, has emphasized the need of a society to place capable persons in role positions of great responsibility. While seemingly in opposition, both theoretic orientations have simply emphasized the functional and dysfunctional elements of stratification within the social order.

THE STRUCTURE OF STRATIFICATION SYSTEMS

Hitherto we have been concerned with the major current theoretic orientations to social stratification and the principal conceptual terms through which stratification is observed—economic class, honorific status, and power. Now we shall briefly present the primary nomenclature of stratification—some of the basic terms used to describe the hierarchic forms in which stratification is characteristically seen.

Open-class Versus Closed Systems

We have already referred to the idea of mobility in social stratification. In some societies, such as the United States and, generally, Western culture, the stratification system is relatively fluid. Hence, it is possible for persons to move from one stratum to another—either "up" or "down" (vertical mobility). Since occupational position (functional role) is a key variable in the stratification scheme, improvement, mobility, and "success" are possible—indeed the "American Way" expects them. In short, an open-class system is characterized by the vertical movement of persons.

Most studies of vertical mobility suggest that the chances are greatest that sons will continue on in the same general occupational stratum as their fathers and that if they do "move up" it will be to the next occupational rung in the stratification ladder. Thus, the upward-mobile son of a blue-collar worker (plumber, semiskilled worker, etc.) will most likely become a white-collar worker in one of the clerical echelons of the "lower-middle class"—salesman, bank clerk, and the like. Spectacular movements from working-class origins to the upper class are rare, in spite of the myths of "rags to riches."

Generally, urbanized and industrialized societies, with their functional needs of placing capable and trained persons in responsible economic, educational, and political institutions, emphasize open-class systems. Nonurbanized, agrarian societies, on the other hand, may have stratification systems in which mobility is hardly present—such as the caste system in India up until fairly recent times. We have already noted that the caste phenomenon emerges from the principle of stratification by ascribed status. In the case of caste, the principle has reached its uttermost extension. Persons are fixed into caste by the conditions of birth, and vertical mobility out of caste is virtually impossible.

Although caste systems can function in slowly changing societies and small villages, it is virtually impossible for dynamic, industrialized, "democratic," urban societies to accommodate to such a condition. The emphasis must be on recruitment through performance and not quality or ascription. Caste flourished in India until recent times and still does function relatively intact in the villages, but it is breaking down in the cities. Like any other fundamental element of social structure, the norms which sustain caste relationships are slow to give way. But the seeming inevitability of intense urbanization and industrialization in the world suggests that caste structures cannot survive much longer.

Ethnicity

Ethnicity refers particularly to an identifiable group carrying on or sustaining a visible subculture within a larger system. In the United States, ethnic groups are usually those immigrant "newcomers" who, for a generation or two, remain visible through the practice of Old World customs, beliefs, and norms. Thus, we may speak of "the Italians," "the Puerto Ricans," "the Jews," "the Mexican-Americans," and the like as ethnic groups.

The stratification system differentially evaluates ethnic groups in terms of some national continuum of honor and prestige. In this fashion, immigrants from England will probably fare better in the status hierarchy than immigrants from Turkey, who, in turn, would "outrank" persons in the colored or nonwhite categories. The general pattern regarding ethnic approval or disapproval seems to award immigrants from the

Northern or Western European areas highest status, followed by new-comers from Southern and Eastern Europe, who in turn rank higher than nonwhite ethnic groups.

Note that ethnicity can be a dimension of a racial group in that the members of the race practice and sustain a normative-ideational sub-culture distinct from that of the majority. One example is the Chinese population of San Francisco (a racial group), some of whom continue to live out a subcultural way of life in a highly visible way. On the other hand, there are those Americans of Chinese origins who have completely assimilated into American society and whose only difference from the American "majority" is the racial factor.

The important point to note in the relationship of ethnicity to the stratification system is that ethnic disapproval (and occasionally, though rarely, approval) derives from the status principle—the subjective world of honor. In the sociological sense, nothing is objectively honorable or dishonorable; only the prevailing mores, the value system, make it so. Thus, the normative order assigns a given ethnic group to a general level on the honorific continuum.

In a sense, American Negroes constitute both a racial group and an ethnic group, in that many millions of Negroes continue to practice and live out a subculture system that originally began in the South and is now expressing itself in some modified form in the Northeastern cities. This subculture (as differentiated from the modal system) has its own speech patterns, expressions, family forms, attitudes, values, and the like—all of which make it visibly different from the national norms. As integration proceeds in American society, as Negroes move increasingly into the national occupational structure, the Negro ethnicity will dis-appear and Negroes will flow along the stratification structure, reflecting the values, the attitudes, the life styles characteristic of their generic class levels.

STRATIFICATION AND COMMUNITY

In a sense, there are at least two stratification systems for each person in the United States: the stratification system in his local community and the stratification system in the national society. Although the two systems are obviously interconnected, they are not always the same, because the prevailing variables of class, status, and power may operate differently at the level of community and at the level of society.

Many researches on stratification, particularly those with strongly descriptive and empirical orientations, were concerned with a specific community and hence may not always apply to the structure of national stratification. A case in point is the pioneering work of W. Lloyd Warner and his associates in the *Yankee City* series. In the 1930's, Warner and his colleagues began the study of stratification in Yankee City, which we know now to be Newburyport, Mass. It was in the context of this research that Warner announced his famous six-level class system: the "upper upper," "lower upper," "upper middle," "lower middle," "upper lower," and "lower lower." Essentially, Warner reported that the widely accepted "upper," "middle," and "lower" class system of the United States was really a six-class structure, with each of the three basic classes divided into two parts.

The point we wish to examine here is whether Warner's class structure of Yankee City was a microcosm of stratification at the national level—whether the six classes of Newburyport appear also at the level of the national society. Warner found that the upper class was really two classes and that the distinction between the upper-uppers and lower-uppers was essentially ancestry, background, "old family" associations, club memberships, and the like. In our terms, the distinctions were essentially status differences. The uper-uppers had lived in Newburyport for several generations, and they claimed and received status emulation and deference from the community. The lower-uppers were simply not part of that ascribed, honorific, prestigeful background, and so they remained lower-uppers.

Now the point of all of this is that the distinctions between "lower" and "upper" in the upper class in Newburyport were founded on a value system shared by the community. The differences between the two "classes" which Warner observed were probably "real" enough, but would they apply throughout the nation? Note that the community recognized classes and recognized who was an upper-upper and who was a lower-upper—at least so Warner reports. But do the citizens of Los Angeles recognize the same distinctions? Are there clear differences (upper-upper and lower-upper) in the topmost class of Chicago, New York, and Miami Beach?

The answer was inadvertently given Warner and his colleagues some years later in their Jonesville study—*Democracy in Jonesville*. In this small, Midwestern community, Warner was not able to find the distinctions between the upper-upper and lower-upper that he noted in Newburyport. In short, the "old families" and the "new people," who constituted separate sections of the upper class in the old New England village all belonged to the same upper class in Midwestern Jonesville. The relatively formal, old, fixed class linkages which separated the upper-class strata in one community did not apply to the other. It is true, of course, that with the exception of the blending of the upper class, the other four distinctions (upper and lower middle and upper and lower lower) were also observed in Jonesville.

The crux of the issue here is that Warner claims to have observed *the* stratification system in America largely by his analysis of status differentials in relatively small communities. But in large cities where people interact mainly through secondary groups and where "backgrounds" and family lineage are relatively unknown and inconsequential (except to intimates), status distinctions are not that important. Urban stratification, therefore, tends to emphasize economic differences, particularly in terms of occupational levels and educational achievement.

Certainly honorific and status distinctions are of significance in metropolitan life, but the chief dimensions of the status principle are ethnicity and race rather than family lineage and ancestry. In the intimate associations of the small town, because people have visibility, stratification can include status elements of background, family "position," and the like. But city life is a mosaic of many worlds—ethnic, racial, class, status, occupational, etc.—all of which are infused with personal anonymity. As a consequence, prestige classes in Warner's sense simply do not apply and have relatively little meaning.

There is probably something of the old upper class in New York City, but very few people know it or see much evidence of it, and, what is more important, very few of its members redeem the status claims of that class. Status, subjective honor, and prestige are "real" only if they are acted on and if there is ideational and normative consensus in the community. The upper-uppers of Newburyport are upper-uppers only if the community largely agrees they are. In the great cities, all infused with mobility and change, there is little status consensus remaining. And so the upper-uppers begin to fade away and only gain some slight satisfaction when a lower-upper recognizes them and, in some fashion or other, as "inferiors" always have, pays out some slight indication, some sign of deference. The mass of city people, however, who plod by the upper-class member with socially sightless eyes, have relatively little regard for high position. The "real" rewards of class in cities are economic position and power, and one's family background remaining relatively meaningless.

OBJECTIVE AND SUBJECTIVE APPROACHES

In the study of social stratification, there are not only the two theoretic orientations—conflict versus functional—but there are also two characteristic empirical research approaches. The "objective" approach essentially leaves the definition of stratification to the researcher. In this way, class may be defined as "life chances in the market" as Weber defined it, or simply by the predominant role of occupation in the American stratification system.

The essential characteristic of such an approach (and latently theoretic view) is that class is viewed "objectively" in terms of some variable that is external to the actor in the structure. He is seen as responding to some massive, objective force which envelops him in the stratification structure. The sociological observer is aware of this force and so places persons in class strata according to their relationship to the objective stratifying force.

In the first major study of class in America, Robert and Helen Lynd's *Middletown*, published in the late 1920's, the structure of Middletown (Muncie, Ind.) was divided into two classes: "business" class and "working" class. This was essentially a primitive occupational division along white- and blue-collar lines. The Lynds felt, however, that occupation alone (the objective class variable) was enough to locate persons meaningfully in the community's class system.

Warner, roughly a decade later, employed an almost entirely different technique. He *asked* persons about the stratification system of Newburyport, and the six-class system that he reports was the product of the *community's* definition of the class structure. The *subjective* approach, thus, leaves the definition of social class to the respondents themselves. And, according to Warner, these six classes are not abstract conceptual entities that he invented but are, rather, "groups recognized by the people of the community. . . ." The six classes are "real" in that they are visible and recognized forces in the community and they critically affect social relationships.

Part of the seeming contradiction between the subjective and objective approaches to social stratification can be resolved by noting again that systems of stratification represent not one but at least three variables—economic class, social honor, and power. The *objective* researchers have always stressed some form of economic class in their study of stratification—occupation, education, wealth, and the like. The *subjective* school, on the other hand, has largely dealt with the variable of honor and prestige, *which must be defined by the community*. (Note again that honorific status is purely subjective, depending upon community definition and community consensus.) Warner and his colleagues were engaged in essentially the study of prestige classes, the dimension of honorific status. The only way to find out how this variable operates within a community is through community research leading to community definition. The objective researchers, however, were convinced that stratification systems are at least partially shaped by objective economic forces (or major differences in power) and consequently proceeded immediately along those lines.

There is one final issue involved in the study of community definitions of stratification such as characterized by the Warner approach. The issue may be posed as a question. Who is in charge of placing persons in stratification systems—the community (respondents) or sociologists? Does the sociologist accept the community's collective definitions of stratification (as Warner apparently did)? Is the community the final determinant of social reality?

Most sociologists would argue otherwise. What people think, the values that underlie their behavior, the content of their ideologies, the nature of the norm systems, and popular definitions of social reality are the *raw data* with which sociologists work. They are not to be regarded, necessarily, as valid descriptions of social reality. If a public-opinion poll reveals that the majority of the members of a community or a society feels there are no classes in the society, is this to be regarded as a statement of social *reality?* No. It is a statement of what people *think* social reality is.

To illustrate from another context, in the thirteenth century most Europeans believed the world was flat. But we know today that the world is spherical. In astronomy and geography, public opinion is in no way related to scientific findings. Similarly, what men think about their social lives, groups, institutions, classes, nations is vital as data to the social scientists, but popular prejudice (or, indeed, truth) cannot be used to validate statements of scientific fact or analysis. Only scientific method can do this.

CLASSES AS IDEAL TYPES

The study of social stratification is currently one of the most active and productive areas in sociology. Almost every year brings forth a significant book devoted to some phase of this field, and the major journals, in almost every issue, report on a current study in which stratification, or some facet of it, receives primary emphasis. Having noted some of the conceptual and theoretic issues, we can now turn to the *structure* of classes in American society. The generalizations and summaries of class forms are essentially ideal types—abstract and conceptually idealized class forms. Although most Americans would probably fall within one of these basic five strata, the strata must nevertheless be viewed as conceptualizations which will neatly summarize the class membership of 200,000,000 persons.

The five class strata that we are about to present have been derived basically from empirical materials found by A. B. Hollingshead and Frederick C. Redlich in their study of social class in New Haven, Conn.[7] Again we confront the problem of stratification within the local community as contrasted with the national structure. However, most sociologists generally employ a five-class conception of national stratification, and there are certainly interrelationships between the local and national structures, particularly on the economic-occupational level.

It is in the realm of subjective status—the honorific and prestige element—that local community-national differences may become manifest. In the East, for example, the "old family" factor, the Ivy League colleges, the summer "cottages" (of about ten rooms) on the Maine coast—in short, life styles—may vary in some fashion from upper class patterns in Texas or on the West Coast. Irrespective of differences in class subcultures, racial and ethnic patterns, or religious differences, which may reflect geographic sections within the national society, there are many elements in the New Haven study which compare accurately with the national picture.

The Upper Class

Hollingshead and his colleagues found that 3.4 per cent of the New Haven population could be classified as upper class. Essentially, they consist of a central core of old families who trace their origins back to the American Revolution and beyond. They are by any standard quite rich, but they have also gathered to themselves prestige, honor, and power. The three critical variables—wealth, status, and power—are concentrated in this stratum. In addition to the pace-setting, honorific old families there are also the *arrivistes*—the upward-mobile, newly rich who have "arrived" at the uppermost level in the stratification system. In Warner's terms, they would be the "lower-uppers," and there are certainly status barriers which separate them from the old families.

Occupationally, the upper class consists of executives, professionals, and major office holders. Some sit on the boards of directors of the large corporations. About 53 per cent of the adults in this class are stable through two or more generations (the old family core group); about 47 per cent are mobiles up from the lower strata—the *arrivistes*.

Among the old families a basic economic characteristic is the careful and prudent care of capital funds. An inherited fortune assures

[7]August B. Hollingshead and Frederick C. Redlich, *Social Class and Mental Illness* (New York: John Wiley & Sons, Inc., 1958) , pp. 69–135, *passim*.

a high level of living and makes possible the upper-class style of life. Although men from the old upper-class families generally work and have a profession, they do not rely heavily on salaries. Income from inherited sources plus earned income (salaries and fees) is the upper-class pattern. However, money is generally overtly minimized by the upper class. The old families simply look upon it as the vehicle necessary to maintain an upper-class style of life. Although the newly rich *arrivistes* have struggled to amass their wealth immediately out of the current economic generation, inherited wealth carries higher status. For the *arrivistes* it will take a generation or two for the rough edges of class mobility to wear off and a "genuine" upper-class life style to set in.

The upper class in New Haven consists largely of the old Americans and there is little ethnicity left, except perhaps for the upward-mobile, newly rich. The honorific old core group ascribes lower status to Jews, Irish, Italians, Greeks, Poles, and persons from southern and eastern Europe. In the status system, wealth comes first, then a family background is "discovered" and wealth, certainly ostentatious consumption, is minimized. Religious affiliation is highly interrelated with the largely Anglo-Saxon ethnic origins (five or six generations removed). Sixty-one per cent of the New Haven upper class is Protestant, 24 per cent Roman Catholic, and 13 per cent Jewish. It is here that regional and urban differences intervene with the national pattern. The relatively high Jewish percentage in the New Haven upper class reflects the New York area with its concentration of Jews—over half of the five million Jews in the United States live in or near the New York metropolitan area.

The upper class is the most highly educated segment of the total New Haven class structure: the median years of school completed by the male heads of families was 17.6. In addition, formal education after the eighth grade is characteristically received in a private school. The core old families send their sons to New England boarding schools, and some four to six years later the majority enter Yale, Harvard, and Princeton or some of the smaller prestige colleges, such as Amherst, Williams, and Dartmouth. The daughters will be sent to Smith, Vassar, Wellesley, Bryn Mawr, Mt. Holyoke, or Radcliffe. Educational differences often critically separate the old families from the newly rich, who are identified by their state university degrees. Their children, however, following the upper-class pattern, are slated for the private boarding school and the Ivy League.

The family structure for the core upper class is almost clanlike in its organization. Each nuclear family is related to a number of other nuclear units by strong family ties. The extended upper-class family controls the marriages of its young people. Since each nuclear family is the recipient of a carefully guarded inherited income, the marriage choices of its young people can be controlled by the threat of being "cut off" from inheritance. Thus, the solidarity of the extended clan is maintained, and children marry down through the generations according to the wishes of the extended kin group and its needs to maintain class position.

The upper class live in houses ranging from the "smaller" ones (8 to 10 rooms) to some as large as 25 to 30 rooms. They are located in the "best" neighborhoods on professionally maintained, spacious grounds up along the ridges and hills of New Haven. In addition, second or third homes are maintained, such as "cottages" in the fashionable summer colonies on Long Island or along the Maine coast.

Characteristic of upper-class life style is the ever-present desire for privacy and the avoidance of scrutiny by the strata below. The club system within the community serves to formalize and maintain class differences. Thus, stratification unfolds through the club organizations to admit some and turn away others. A newly rich of three generations "arrives" when he is finally invited to join one of the two "exclusive" upper-class clubs dominated by the core group of old families.

To summarize, the upper class in New Haven consists of the community's social, business, and professional leaders. They live in the best neighborhoods and in the finest and largest houses. The male heads are fourth- and fifth-generation Ivy League graduates and occupy major positions in leading business concerns. The family income is based on a combination of significant inheritance supplemented by salaries and fees. They are the descendants of the original English settlers of the community. The core upper-class family is stable, cohesive, and secure. The old families, however, are challenged to a degree by the newly rich, upward-mobile *arrivistes* who have the money but lack the family background and some elements of life style to be fully accepted. The New Haven upper class is probably duplicated to a high degree in almost any community with a population over 50,000 and with a history of at least 100 years. They are the social and economic elite of American society, whose way of life subsumes only 3 per cent of the total population.

The Upper-Middle Class

If upper-class membership is almost unattainable for most Americans (even in some respects for the newly rich), the way of life of the upper-middle class represents a practical dream that is within the realm of statistical possibility. Hollingshead placed 9 per cent of the New Haven population in this class. They are a mobile group, 74 per cent having demonstrated vertical mobility in the course of their lives. Forty-nine per cent of the male family heads are business managers, 31 per cent occupy the lesser-ranking professions, such as teaching, engineering, accountancy, pharmacy, and the like.

Hollingshead maintains that upper-middle-class couples (he refers to them as Class II, following Class I) begin their married life in a New Haven apartment but move to the suburbs when their financial situation permits. The home, however, is in the "right" neighborhood with a reputation for an excellent *public* school. Note here the public-school orientation of the upper-middle class. The upper-class pattern of private boarding and secondary schools is an element of a class style that is largely beyond the financial reach of the upper-middle class. So they settle for a strong public school system which, ironically, is probably academically superior to most private schools.

Generally older houses in established upper-middle-class neighborhoods are preferred to houses in the relatively large tract subdivisions. Approximately 80 per cent of the Class II would prefer to leave the city proper to settle into two desirable suburbs, where they often buy houses beyond their means.

Seventy-one per cent of the Class II men are college graduates. In terms of religious affiliation, Protestants account for 45 per cent of the class, Roman Catholics 29 per cent, and Jews 26 per cent. On the ethnic level, Yankee or "old American" stock comprises only 20 per cent, whereas 14 per cent are of English, Scottish, or Welsh ancestry; 12 per cent claim origins from the northern European countries—Germany, Scandinavia, France, Austria, and the Netherlands. An additional 20 per cent have Irish backgrounds. Russian and Polish Jews contribute the largest ethnic concentrations, some 26 per cent, and 8 per cent of the household heads are of Italian background.

The upper-middle class is a stratum of joiners, with memberships ranging throughout the voluntary associations of the community. They serve actively as community leaders and contribute their considerable technical and professional skills to many community enterprises. Here they may brush shoulders with the upper class, whose philanthropy often underwrites many civic and community activities—Y.M.C.A., Boy Scouts, Red Cross, etc.—but whereas the upper class is the financial base of these activities, with the veto power that donors of large sums possess, it is the upper-middle-class members who execute and supervise the policies established from "above."

On the national level, the upper-middle class has led the movement out of cities. In the suburban subdivisions, on the two-acre plot, with the small compact car and station wagon, with a kitchen filled with wondrous appliances, with the color television set and two and a half bathrooms with "simulated" marble-top basins, the upper-middle class epitomizes the American Dream. It is a way of life pictured on the covers of house-and-garden magazines. All of the abundance of American productivity spills into this class and creates a style of life that is heady wine for the strivers below. If the upper class lives subtly behind the veil of expansive greenery which screens their houses and life style from public view, the upper-middle class basks in the limelight of achievement and public consumption. They may not number more than 9 per cent of the national population, but they serve as models for the American Dream, if not the reality.

The Lower-Middle Class

Though Americans dream of the upper-middle class way of life, it is the lower-middle class life that many settle for. Approximately 21 per cent of the New Haven sample belonged to Class III—the lower-middle Class. In this class, three out of four in the labor force would be classified as *employees*. Fifty-one per cent are engaged in a variety of administrative and clerical positions; 9 per cent are semiprofessional or technical workers; 16 per cent are plant supervisors or skilled workers. The administrators in the lower-middle class would typically include section heads in governmental agencies and large business concerns along with managers in shops, services, chain stores, and the like. Clerical workers would characteristically include secretaries, salesmen, bank tellers, bookkeepers, and paperworkers of all descriptions. Furthermore, for the first time, women figure importantly in the work force of a stratum. Twenty-eight per cent of the lower-middle-class wives are employed.

In terms of ethnic characteristics, the immigrations of 1830 through 1870 show up heavily in the New Haven lower-middle class. Thirty-four per cent are Irish and constitute the largest single ethnic group. German and Scandinavian backgrounds constitute another 13 per cent. Nearly half are Roman Catholics, 39 per cent are Protestants, and 14 per cent are Jewish.

The lower-middle-class population in New Haven has heavily suburbanized. The typical family lives in a five- or six-room house located in a "good" residential area in a suburban village. Although men and women of the lower-middle class are less optimistic about their lives and show greater general dissatisfaction with their lot than the upper-middle class, the majority take a positive view. Their lives are physically comfortable in their stable suburban streets. They are looking forward to the day when the mortgages on their houses will be paid off and the children are "on their own."

From the perspective of the lower-middle class, the "big" people are the upper-middles. They have the cars, the acreage, and the formal leadership in the community. They went to college; they fly to the meeting in Kansas City; they are sending their boy to Dartmouth. The lower-middle life style can claim hardly any of these in a patterned way. Lower-middle largely take orders, type the letter, check on the workers, and get a gold watch when they retire. They graduate from high school, they go to church, they pay their bills, they don't cause "trouble," and they pursue their valued goal of respectability. Their lives, in terms of class, are located very much in the comfortable middle of things, and they still live on the positive side in the allocation of wealth, status, and power.

But many workers in the lower-middle class are not "going any-where," and in middle life this becomes painfully and abundantly clear. Their general lack of a college education and the rather routine character of their jobs leads them into peculiar occupational niches. As a con-sequence of frozen occupational perspectives, they cannot build their life and values around organizational or professional themes as do the upper-middle class in the worship of career. So, as Kahl suggests, this stratum pursues the middle of the road in almost all respects. They have no peculiar economic or political axe to grind. They shun the labor unions because of their working-class character. It is perhaps the bland pursuit of respectability and a largely conservative view of the world that shapes the prevailing ethos and the subculture of the lower-middle class.[8]

The Working Class

Close to half of the New Haven population (48.5 per cent) were assigned by the Hollingshead researchers as Class IV—the working class. Thirty-five per cent of the males were skilled manual workers, 52 per cent were semiskilled, 12 per cent were clerical and sales workers. The prevailing occupational character of the working class is that they labor physically; they use their hands and manipulate "things." The term working class, therefore, embraces those of the labor force who do manual labor, who join unions, who earn a "wage" (hourly pay rate) rather than a "salary," and whose characteristic symbol is the blue rather than the white collar of the middle classes.

Because money, at the level of the working class, is a critical factor in providing basic needs for the family, almost all women who are not too ill, too old, or dependent upon a husband, are working. Thirty-

[8] Joseph A. Kahl, *The American Class Structure* (New York: Holt, Rinehart & Winston, Inc., 1957), p. 202.

seven per cent of the wives (without children or with children over 17 years) are employed.

The husbands had completed 9.4 years of school and their wives 10.5 years. However, their children are remaining in school longer. The median number of years of school completed by the adult children of working-class parents was 11 for men and 11.4 for women. However, 47 per cent of the adult daughters and 63 per cent of the sons had not completed their high school education.

Approximately 19 per cent of the working-class households had paid for their homes completely, and 46 per cent had title to the houses they were living in. Seventy-nine per cent of the home-owning working-class families lived in two- or three-family dwellings, most of which were in working-class neighborhoods in New Haven. The single-family working-class houses were generally located in three outlying suburban towns.

About half of the family heads were immigrants from eastern and southern Europe and, according to the researchers, 9 out of 10 of these were still in the process of assimilation into American society. Catholics predominated (63 per cent), Protestants accounted for another 30 per cent, and Jews 7 per cent.

The typical family structure differed from the lower-middle-class pattern in four critical ways: there were more broken homes; more households contained boarders and roomers; the nuclear family unit was larger; and there were more three-generation families living together.

The modal working-class family in New Haven consists of a husband of about 44 years, his wife of 42, both with distinct ethnic characteristics, and four or five children, living in a two-family house. They are Catholics. If the family is Irish, it would be third generation; if Italian, second. The oldest child did not complete high school and would quite possibly be a production worker. The father has been working since his teens and is still a semiskilled production worker.

Kahl has summarized the life goal of the working class as a "getting by." There is enough money to provide the family with adequate living by American standards—there is the TV set, the washing machine, and possibly a new car (on the installment plan) every so often. There are now vacations with pay, which the union finally won in its annual battle with the "company."

But working-class jobs—the great spectrum of semiskilled tasks performed along the assembly line—are very much the same, and there are few differences in pay and responsibility. There just isn't much point in "hard work, initiative, and effort" because "you aren't going anywhere." Too much effort, indeed, might call down negative judgments of one's peers ("eager beaver" or "rate buster"). There is, therefore, a general pattern of alienation from work and, in addition, a general disaffection from and lack of interest in public affairs. The working class read less, participate less, and understand less about the world in which they live when contrasted with the classes "above." Nevertheless, they constitute the largest stratum in American society today and, though the middle-aged generation may have seen The Dream slip away, for their children, who are now finishing high school and entering college in ever greater numbers, the dream is visible, and, for some, within reach.

The Lower Class

The American poor, the alienated, the powerless, and those without honor, are a minority. Hollingshead placed 17 per cent of his sample in Class V—the lower class. Kahl estimates that this class constitutes 10 per cent of American society. Warner located 25 per cent of the Newburyport population and 14 per cent of the Jonesville study in the "lower-lower" class. Whereas the poor and powerless quite possibly constitute the *majority* in many countries, in the United States they seem to account for something between 10 and 20 per cent of the population (20 to 40 million persons), depending on how the class is defined.

Hollingshead found 52 per cent of the Class V adult males in New Haven to be semiskilled and 46 per cent unskilled. Because many of the jobs tend to be intermittent, seasonal, and cyclical, long periods of unemployment and underemployment are characteristic. More wives and mothers are employed outside of the home than in any other class. In view of the fragmentary work patterns, some 87 per cent of the lower-class families in New Haven were listed in the Social Service Index of the Council of Social Agencies. A third of the families were known by several agencies through two or three generations.

Over two-thirds of the New Haven sample lived in slum areas, in crumbling wood and brick tenements built before the turn of the century or in the semirural slums of two suburban towns. Characteristically, the lower class has the lowest educational achievement of any stratum in the community, men having completed about six years of education and women a little less than eight. The class is predominantly Catholic (73 per cent), but less than 10 per cent of the children attend parochial school, although many are located within easy access. Seventy per cent of the lower class in New Haven were made up of immigrant groups from the 1890's on—Italians (48 per cent), Poles, and Slavs. About 4 per cent of lower-class families in New Haven ("Swamp Yankees") trace their ancestry back many generations in the local area. Another 10 per cent are Irish, 9 per cent English, Scottish, and Welsh, and 6 per cent German or Scandinavian.

Hollingshead found about 44 per cent of the New Haven lower-class families to be of the nuclear type—that is, the unit consisting of mother, father, and their children. "Stem" families, consisting of three or four generations living under one roof, constituted 23 per cent of the households. Broken nuclear families of one parent and their minor children accounted for 18 per cent of the lower-class households—almost one in five. Forty-one per cent of the children under seventeen years old come from broken homes. Money is always a problem, and the family regularly lives either in or on the edge of poverty.

The ethos of lower-class subculture is apathy, alienation, indifference, and defeat. Upward mobility is difficult because they lack so many of the elementary requirements for the "race"—certainly formal education, but even basic communication skills, such as simple declarative speech. Since they do not have the manners, the language, the speech, and the appearance required for middle-stratum jobs and occupations, it is difficult for them to get "on the ladder" and begin a climb upward. Furthermore, the subculture of the lower class, with its itinerant job patterns broken up by periods of unemployment, supplemented by the welfare system, makes it difficult for lower-class people to work steadily over a period of time. Even the working-class pattern of remaining on the job for long periods of time is relatively unknown and, consequently, steady work attitudes and practices are hard to maintain. For some lower-class members three or four weeks on a well-paying job is enough to get some money together to go "on a binge" of visceral, genital, and emotional gratification. As a consequence he loses what may have been a good job and the unemployment-welfare pattern begins anew.

RACE RELATIONS AND THE STRATIFICATION SYSTEM

The position of the Negro in American society, in terms of social stratification, has been within the structural unit of caste. Recall that caste is a stratum fixed by the conditions of birth from which there is no patterned or realistic exit. In the American stratification structure, the factor of race—the black man in a society of whites—was the critical force of caste ascription. Recall, too, that the Negro was forcibly introduced into American society in the role of a slave out of social conditions in Africa that were almost universally accepted at that time to be "backward," "primitive," "uncivilized," and "brutish."

Not only was the Negro characterized by "primitive" cultural circumstances in his native Africa, but this was almost always regarded as simply the inevitable social manifestation of a more fundamental force: the Negro was seen at that time by the majority of whites as biologically a truly primitive man, less advanced and closer to the apes. His obvious physical differences from the whites set him off and made him clearly visible in white society.

The Negro wore his differences; they were a physical part of his person and, in consequence of the ideology of white racial superiority, he was assigned his "place" in American society. He was a slave, a valuable piece of plantation stock. Like any other piece of property, he was to be used by his owner. If the owner took care of his property—fences, land, barns, cattle, slaves—he was "well cared for." If the owner neglected his property, he suffered. As a piece of property, the slave was transferable— he could be loaned, borrowed, or sold. As a piece of property, he was something less than a man.

After the Civil War, the formal role of slave was legally abolished and the newer normative design of caste began to take its essential form. While technically "free," the Southern (and to a real extent the Northern) Negro was nevertheless assigned an inferior place in the allocative system. The fact of racial visibility and the normative-ideological-mythical statements of racial inferiority were the essential vehicles through which were forged the primary strictures of the caste system. The principle of caste is essentially the principle of status in its most extended form. The position of the Negro was defined essentially by the subjective world of status definition. He was regarded as simply an inferior man—inferior to white men in all respects—morally, physically, and intellectually. What more convenient a way to recognize such people than by race? Indeed, to many, race was simply "nature's way" of identifying the advanced from the inferior strains of human kind.

By the turn of the century, however, the social sciences were making an appearance in the American university, and eventually the popular "biological" notions of racial behavior came under attack. Essentially the social scientists pointed out that there were few concrete, controlled, definitive data on race differences that would explain the vast gulf in social circumstances between the races. Essentially the sociological (environmental) argument stated that the social differences between the races were due primarily to differential opportunity and the massive restraints imposed upon the Negro by the caste system. In short, the sources of differential behavior between whites and blacks are to be found in social structures and normative systems rather than biological structures and genetic systems. Thus the counterargument was established by social scientists, intellectuals, and "liberals" who could not accept the biological basis as a justification of caste restrictions.

Furthermore, the ideology of "liberty, justice and freedom for all" which is so central to the American creed as to be a part of the Pledge of Allegiance, was utterly inconsistent with the social reality under which most Negroes lived. Despite the biological justifications, in which much of the American public still believed, the national mores were tending toward a more realistic accommodation of the Negro to the American Dream, the American Creed—the essential idea that every man should be given an equal opportunity in the competitive struggle for rewards. There were of course, structural factors in the national society pressing and forcing the ideological and normative changes. Cities were growing and drawing the unskilled, rural laborer off the land and into the factories. The nation was increasingly oriented toward consumership, hence a concentration of unproductive nonconsuming farm laborers in a society of cities and mass markets was dysfunctional to the new economic order. By 1954, the Supreme Court ruled that the "separate but equal" system of racial segregation in the public schools was unconstitutional, and the movement for educational "integration" began.

But this was just one facet of what has become known as the Civil Rights Movement. Not only did Negro groups strive for integration but essentially the entire spectrum of black and "liberal" activity has been directed toward the destruction of the caste system. That is to say, all the indicators, the patterns, the practices that dramatically separated the races (certainly in the public spheres) came under attack. The "white" and "colored" signs over drinking fountains were removed; the "law" that Negroes must sit in the rear of buses was abolished in many Southern cities. Lunch counters were "integrated" after repeated and tense public demonstrations. And, perhaps most importantly, civil-rights groups sought to register Negro voters, so that in the South (where many counties have Negro majorities) there would be Negro representation in local government.

In short, the focal point of the civil rights movement has been to erode the primary public strictures of the caste system and *to move the American Negro into the class structure*. As a caste group, the Negro could never leave his stratum. But as part of the American class structure, he would have the opportunity for upward mobility in terms of the objective variables—job, education, income, etc.—and later, the status variables of honor and prestige.

The greatest gains have generally been in those areas of activity between the races which are less intimate and less sensitive to caste-status relationships. Thus, Negroes have gained spectacularly in voting registration in the South, in addition to the removal of the more humiliating forms of racial evaluation in public places—lunch counters, waiting rooms, public transportation, and the like. In addition, there has been in recent years a comparatively heavy movement of Negroes into higher-paying jobs, both white- and blue-collar.

Lastly, school integration has proceeded faster in the North than the South, but neighborhood residential patterns, reflecting a continuation of the caste principle, have frustrated a significant achievement in this area. As we have seen, as Negroes move into the central city, whites move out. This indicates that, though integration is proceeding at some levels, it is failing at others. In short, caste is rapidly giving way in the political and economic spheres of race relations, but in the intimate world of the school and neighborhood, where status considerations are powerful, the strictures remain.

The plight of many Negroes in American society is that they are essentially *declassed*. In the slave-caste scheme of things, the Negro had a "place." But as caste fades as an operable force in the stratification system, it leaves millions of blacks in a kind of limbo, outside of caste and yet still not structurally a part of the open-class system. Whereas the Irish, the Germans, the Italians, the Poles, and the Russian immigrants could fade and disappear from public view as their ethnicity washed away through cultural assimilation, the Negro is still "visible," and that visibility feeds the status principle—the principle of intrinsic worth, of subjective honor, of differential evaluation.

It is the status identifiability of the Negro that has made open-class possibilities so difficult. If the aspiring, upward-mobile black attempts to affect a life style, a manner of speech, and accomplishment characteristic of whites, he could be damned because he "didn't know his place," was "getting out of line," and "was trying to act like a white man." And he could be sanctioned for it.

An incident illustrates this point. Some time ago, a Negro physician was leaving his hospital in a Southern city. A gang of lower-class whites were loitering around the hospital exit and as the black doctor came through the door, one of the whites shouted, "Hey, boy! What's your name?"

The Negro hesitated for a moment, and as he was surrounded by the leering gang, mumbled, "Doctor Collins."

He was grabbed by the shirt, a fist was shoved under his chin, and again the menacing question, "What's your name, boy?"

Again the muffled reply, hesitantly, "Doctor Collins."

The gang pushed in, the fist tightened under the Negro physician's chin, his head was violently thrust up. He was caught up in terror and personal fear; seven generations found him, and in agony he gasped out, "George. . . ."

Thus, the normative requisites of caste are renewed in the ritual forms of address between status superiors and inferiors. The Negro is a "boy," to be called by his first name. The white superior is "Mr." Smith, indicating deference and recognition of the hierarchic force controlling and defining the relationship. The Polish immigrant or the Italian new-comer might have been "Stanislaus" or "Tony" for a generation or two, but if he were upward-mobile, or his sons or grandsons were, he would eventually be "Mr." But race is visible and status definitions, popular judgments of intrinsic honor, are not easy to change. Thus, the open-class structure into which the American Negro is now entering poses problems of assimilation that the Caucasian immigrants did not encounter.

Although caste forms fade in the United States and the class sys-tem grudgingly yields to the American Negro, there are still many prob-lems of a unique sort that do not repeat the experience of former ethnic groups. The American Negro and his subculture are the product of two to three hundred years of the slave-caste system. And many of the customs, the practices, the attitudes and values, the beliefs, the generic way of life of the American Negro reflect that heritage. For example, the Negro family has a history of instability and breakdown that is unknown in white middle-class society. Permanent familial relationships between adult male and female slaves were not encouraged because of the emotional disruption that would follow when the "family" was broken up by the sale of one or more of its members. Hence, free and easy sexual relations were the pattern, and the pregnant woman and her child were cared for by the paternalistic community of the plantation world.

The Negro male has always been under much more hostile pres-sure from the white world than the female. Females, at least in Western culture, tend to be more compliant and passive, less rebellious, and gen-erally less threatening to a social system dominated by males. As a woman, the Negro female was often assimilated into the white household (the "Mammy" figure) and was generally accommodated into white society —in "her place." Males, on the other hand, were far more frequently treated with suspicion and found it much harder to find permanent work and a role accorded some dignity and approval, in spite of the "Uncle Tom" possibility. As a consequence, the Southern, rural black family developed primarily around the females and their relative permanence within the household. Males were fragmentary, itinerant, disruptive, pass-ing figures, who often threatened rather than supported the structure of family relationships. In essence, the Negro family was comparatively matriarchal and held together largely through the female line rather than the male. Husbands and fathers in the traditional middle-class sense of the role were comparatively rare.

As a consequence of the sexual traditions established in slave times and the peripheral economic and social roles accorded to Negro males following the Civil War, the Negro family has been marginal and unstable. In New York City, for example, in 1960, 25 per cent of the Negro families were headed by women, in contrast to one-tenth of the whites, and the rate of illegitimacy among Negroes is fourteen or fifteen times higher than for whites. Thus the legacy of two hundred years continues to unfold among the Negro population in broken homes, illegitimacy, and instability far beyond the white pattern.

The structure of caste was such that the Negro was not *expected* to follow the white middle-class pattern. Indeed, as we have noted, the black who tried to improve his situation, who attempted upward mobility, could be severely sanctioned for it. Even through the 1930's the lynch mob threatened the Negro who tried to register to vote. He was *expected* to stay in place, to be "immoral," to be "shiftless," and, indeed, to be a thief. ("They all steal, you know, if they get the chance." "You can never trust them out of your sight.") Indeed, the Negro petty thief was often unpunished in the white household *because he was expected to steal*. An "honest" Negro would have threatened the theory of color-caste and the assumption of the intrinsic moral inferiority of the Negro. Hence, a Negro thief would be tolerated in the deep South much more than a Negro who was "trying to act like a white man."

However, there are dynamics to these matters and what was true a decade or even half a decade ago in terms of race relations in the United States may no longer apply today. For example, in 1963, Glazer and Moynihan in their book *Beyond the Melting Pot*,[9] were quite concerned with the lack of Negro owned business in New York. In comparison, they noted that the Puerto Rican migrants to the city had shown a strong interest in business (groceries, cigar stores, shops, repair services etc.), in their ethnic neighborhoods, as did the Italians, the Jews, and the Chinese generations before. They did indicate that West Indian Negroes followed out the old immigrant pattern by showing a significantly greater interest in local businesses than the Southern Negro. However, a recent study indicates that close to 60 per cent of all stores in a 20-block area in the heart of Harlem were owned by Negroes.[10] True, Glazer and Moynihan were talking of New York City *in general*, but the conclusion is obvious—Negroes are entering increasingly into the business and entre-

[9]Nathan Glazer and Daniel Patrick Moynihan, *Beyond the Melting Pot* (Cambridge: The M.I.T. Press, 1963), p. 50.
[10]*The New York Times*, September 16, 1968, Section 1, p. 30.

preneural worlds of American society. The lack of business involvement cited by Glazer and Moynihan just a short time ago, seems no longer to be the case in central Harlem. Indeed, the traditional and often-cited friction between black ghetto residents and Jewish proprietors of local shops no longer fits the Harlem situation. The study found only 30 per cent of the stores in the same 20-block area to be owned by Jews. However, in spite of significant gains made by blacks into business ownership, the problems of recent southern migrants and their subculture of dependency on government agencies persist.

The problem involves more than mere dependency and the inability to act without dependence on government aids and services (welfare, housing agencies, etc.). Many declassed Negro males lack a steady-work ideology, and potential employers are reluctant to hire them. However, as a result of the cumulative impact of the civil rights movement, American industry is finally recognizing some responsibility to the Negro poor and the black ghettos. After the 1967 riots in Detroit, a city more than once wracked with racial violence, automobile manufacturers made jobs available to the "hard core Negro unemployables." The companies went into the ghettos to recruit men who would have been normally ineligible for production-line (largely unskilled) jobs because they would have failed the usual written tests and had jail records, poor employment records, and the like. However, the problem with the hard-core "unemployables" who took the new jobs has been absenteeism and failure to develop the steady work habits of blue-collar workers. Nevertheless, the experiment looks promising. By January 1968, the Ford Motor Company had interviewed 3000 hard-core unemployables in two inner-city employment centers. Of that total, 1600 are on the job.[11] Of the men who were hired, 375 did not "show up" for work; 425 men were rejected because of physical disabilities or because their police records had shown them to be habitually in difficulty with the law. The company had called the retention rate "excellent" and if the experiment is judged successful, tens of thousands of men may enter the labor force into permanent jobs and the promise of better things.

The lack of steady habits, the high rate of absenteeism, the "irresponsibility" often attributed to the declassed Negro is essentially the product of the slave-caste legacy. Part of the traditional criticism of the Negro has been his bizarre life style, judged by white middle-class standards. But the key to this matter is the understanding that the Negro simply has not been part of the open-class system. He had failed to develop working-class or even middle-class aspirations because up until

[11]Gertrude Samuels, "Help Wanted: The Hard-Core Unemployed," *The New York Times Magazine* (January 28, 1968), p. 50.

recent times mobility out of caste for the vast majority of blacks was impossible. It is true, of course, that a small fraction have won national recognition in sports and entertainment, and a handful are in politics and public service. The great bulk of the Negro population, however, continues to languish encapsulated in their caste framework and with little hope for a significant improvement in their basic life chances.

However, with the civil rights movement now having a major impact in American society, and, indeed, with literally a revolution in race relations as the most spectacular change in American society in the past decade, the future for the Negro masses looks much better. Yet part of the human tragedy is that millions of Negroes are still not aware of the new opportunities. Ten of thousands of black children drop out of school each year, failing to realize how much of their occupational and economic future they have thrown away. The racial tradition of anomie and alienation from the national society still persists in spite of the improving opportunities.

Nevertheless, the civil rights movement in itself attests to the rising level of expectations and aspirations of the Negro minority. Although the movement is led primarily by middle-class Negroes, the spirit of discontent has spread throughout the black "community," and this is partly the cause of the summer urban riots. The civil rights movement has made mass demonstrations a legitimate expression of the Negro cause, and the constant public restatement of the condition of the Negro masses has stirred action. But the fact that millions of Negroes are declassed, peripheral, anomic, and alienated makes violence possible. Much of the rioting was simply an anti-society, anti-white, anti-establishment reaction from a peripheral and marginal population.

Getting "Whitey," however, was a response by a relatively small number of blacks whose alienation was such that from both a psychological and a sociological point of view integration is patently impossible. For the majority of the Negro population, who "don't want trouble," who simply want "their share" of the abundance of American society and an opportunity to improve their lives, the urban riots and the militant preaching of separatism and mass violence have basically little appeal. Most Negroes simply want "in," and "in" means being *part of the class structure*, and *having the chance for movement*.

Actually, the number of middle-class Negroes, measured in terms of the *objective* variables—that is, employment in the professions, government, education, and white-collar and supervisory jobs in business—has steadily increased in recent years.

In 1966, according to the *Report of the National Advisory Commission on Civil Disorders*, 28 per cent of all Negro families received incomes of $7,000 or more. This was double the proportion of Negroes earning comparable incomes in 1960, and four times greater than in 1947. In addition, the proportion of blacks working in high status, high skill, and good paying occupations rose faster from 1960 to 1966 than comparable proportions among whites. Furthermore, as Negro incomes have gone up, the size of the lowest income group among blacks (under $3,000 dollars) has decreased, while middle and upper groups have grown larger both relatively and absolutely.[12] As a further indication of rapid improvement in opportunity for better paying jobs, the proportion of non-whites employed in white-collar, technical, and professional jobs has risen from 10.2 per cent in 1950 to 20.8 per cent in 1966.[13]

The key to class mobility, in terms of stratification today, is education. That is why it is imperative for the black child to stay in school; that is why the ghetto schools must be improved and why various means of achieving racial integration at the school level are so critical. The Negro, as a collectivity, cannot become upward-mobile until he has some perception of the life styles, the attitudes, the behavior, the norms, the standards, the practices, the speech, the manners, of the strata above. The middle-class values of "independence," "self-reliance," "initiative," "discipline," "mobility," cannot become a viable force in the Negro community unless declassed blacks are exposed to these values interpersonally, through example, and through the mediation of other persons. If the Negro child remains in the anarchy of the ghetto's classroom, "scholarship" will mean nothing but frustration. If he sees *scholarship* in the classroom with middle-class children (both white and black), if he sees students becoming successful as students, then the possibility of *his own success* has more meaning and reality. In short, the declassed black child cannot aspire to, cannot emulate, cannot internalize the values of the American middle class until he is *exposed* to them. There is little opportunity for the transfer of class values, particularly upward-mobile values, in the all-black classroom of the ghetto.

Some black militants argue that Negroes should not slavishly copy "white" middle-class patterns but should *demand the equality* of "black" values along with "white." Such a position, however, is sociologically impossible and represents a confusion of class with ethnic-racial variables. As we have already suggested, there is now a rising number of *middle-class* Negroes. And these people share the values and life styles of the various levels of the middle class—i.e., family stability, educational ambition, occupational success, etc. In short, class variables have over-

[12]*Report of the National Advisory Commission on Civil Disorders*, New York: Bantam Books, 1968, p. 251.
[13]*Ibid.*, p. 282.

ridden ethnic variables. In New York City, for example, the Negro upper-middle class send their children to private schools for the same reasons as the white upper-middle class. It is not a matter of the "Negro community" losing its "black pride," as the militants charge, but of assimilating into middle-class culture *so as literally to integrate into the mainstream of American society*. It is, after all, upper-middle-class personnel executives who hire college graduates for the "executive training squad," and they look for middle-class symbols in the college diploma, manners, command of the English language, and even haircuts. These are the normative expectations; it is not a question of whether they are "right" or "wrong"; they are class forms, and anyone who wants to "join" is expected to "conform" to class expectations. The Negro or any minority member who wants "in" will generally have to accept the normative framework within which the "majority" stratification system operates. It would be patently impossible to have two nations, one white and one black, within the same societal system, in a state of normative "equality." Particularly if one is only 10 percent of the population. Indeed, the issue has been the inequality of one, the moral and social injustice of the class-caste system, and the need to get rid of racial separatism.

Perhaps the most important lesson that Americans of either race can learn from the present racial circumstances in the United States is the recognition of persons as *carriers* of class life styles. For a long time the black man has been locked by his physical appearance into the rigid circumstances of caste, from which there was no exit. However, the most brutal forms of caste relationships are now passing—the denial of voting rights, public humiliation in all forms, and a limitation of economic opportunity to the lowest-paying and menial jobs.

From this circumstance, the American Negro is now passing into the bottom of the class structure and into somewhat the same position as other "immigrants" before. The fact of race, to be sure, still presents tremendous problems for the upward mobility of Negroes. But there is such mobility and it is increasing. Even now, larger numbers of Negroes are moving into the middle class and are finding homes in some integrated suburbs. These Negro families believe in family stability, believe in normative "responsibility," believe in cleanliness, believe in personal discipline, believe in scholarship, believe in trimmed lawns and painted houses. They are, in short, *middle-class persons who share, along with their white neighbors, the same essential class ethos*. In time, it will be the class ethos that characterizes the Negro population in the United States and not the still lingering remnants of caste of today.

The Report of the National Advisory Commission on Civil Disorders, published in 1968, and subsequent researches that the Commission authorized, all attest to the frustrations of the black American in a society dominated by the white majority. Part of the alienation of many blacks from the "mainstream of American society" can be seen in their atttiudes toward the white and black middle class. Traditionally the lower classes have striven via upward mobility to reach the middle class. However, according to studies reported by the Commission, the young ghetto males who participated in the riots were hostile to the white middle class and did not think much better of Negroes who had reached middle-class status themselves. Indeed, the Commission reported that it was more often than not the black middle class in the ghettos who tried to "cool it" when the riots were taking place.

But the alienation of the rioters is clearly visible in their lack of faith in the system whereby their own personal mobility can be achieved. It appears that increasing numbers of the ghetto residents and black Americans in general are looking to the riots and civil disorder as positive ("revolutionary") actions to advance "the cause." In short, it appears that more blacks are accepting violence as a solution to race relations in the country rather than basing their life chances on upward mobility. Indeed, the assimilation of Negroes into the class structure as indicated here may be a hopeful possibility for only a short time. If enough Negroes are convinced that the only way to redress the abuses of the ghetto and racial discrimination is by taking to the streets, then the time for peaceful assimilation into the class structure via education and changing life styles is over.

As to the element of status and subjective judgment, in the broader perspective, men have always made value judgments of beauty, personal worth, the value of a name, the shape of a nose, the honor of a religon, the "reputation" of a neighborhood, the "name" of a college, and the worth of a minority "out" group. Majorities will simply evaluate minorities in some fashion. And no matter how egalitarian the national ideology, collective judgments, status or otherwise, seem to be generic to the social condition and will presumably last as long as organized society does. Some men, by some subjective norm or standard, will simply be judged inferior or superior to others. In short, differential evaluation founded upon some shared consensus of honor seems to be endemic to human society.

Perhaps the critical point to all of this is that by the national standard of "life, liberty, and the pursuit of happiness," of "freedom for all," there is still (in terms of social stratification) the invidious role of privilege and inherent advantage for some in the "competitive" system. By the public standard, by the popular and oft repeated American Creed, a man should be judged by what he does as an individual in his lifetime.

Yet this is the normative-ideological ideal rather than hard judgment of reality. So while children sing the verses of "freedom for all" in their ritual expressions of patriotic solidarity, their parents go about their "real" lives surrounded by class and caste, privilege and status, prejudice and inherent advantage. Yet there is no society without it, and probably today we have gone as far as any historic society to liberate each child from the limitations imposed by class and caste. However, in view of what we saw in the New Haven materials and our discussion of race relations, the equalitarian ideal seems far away and out of reach.

Yet the mores strain to reach it, and in time the gross inconsistencies between ideology and reality (*freedom for all* in a caste-class society) militate for change toward the ideological goal. Finally, in a society that has never been, and will probably never be, the ultimate norm toward which all "democratic" men strive is a social design that will permit each human being to produce and create to the relative full of his abilities. And to achieve this intention, nothing should frustrate the effort but the inner resources of the man himself—his own limitations.

SOCIETY

We have almost completed our presentation of the basic concepts of sociology, but one more major unit of analysis must be discussed—the idea of society. We have left the concept of society to the very end of our discussion because it is the broadest and most inclusive social system of all.

Society is similar to community in that it, too, is a "survival" system and the totality of relationships which it subsumes can theoretically go on forever. However, society is more inclusive than community in that specific localities, rural or urban, may be a part of a larger system of functional interdependence. That is to say, whereas community is a population living in permanent and self-contained interdependence within a limited locality, society consists of a more inclusive system of relationships, the final structure of functional interrelationships. Thus, society may fuse all kinds of communities (folk, rural, urban, metropolitan) into its larger framework and spread over a vast territory binding millions of persons together in increasing specialization and interdependence. Society is the final design—the most abstract and complex concept in the literature of sociology—and yet it began with the most elementary social relationship.

A society is a group, and hence social-system perspectives can apply to it. Thus, at the societal level, the functional prerequisites of adaptation, integration, goal attainment, tension management, and pattern maintenance must also be satisfied. It is at this analytic level that the spectacular social anatomy of the major functional institutions of modern societies can be viewed as structural responses to system needs.

Recall that institutions were seen as role combinations oriented toward some strategic function characteristic of a complex group. Institutions, in essence, are formalized, definite, established ways of doing things. Through the normative system, roles are given definition and content, invested with meaning, and charged with positive or negative obligations to harmonize relationships and interaction with others. Institutions, however, should not be confused with groups—concrete system entities—but are rather the normative forms through which complex groups function. Whereas mores and folkways are the primary normative devices sustained by relatively informal and unorganized social groups, institutions appear in specific and formally organized secondary groups or associations. Thus, we may note that customary law, mores, and folkways are *noninstitutionalized* normative forms, whereas institutions always require formal associations to support them.

Within the societal system, we should be clear on the distinction between institutions and associations. Institutions are the normative procedures characteristic of associations. In turn, associations are complex groups whose major internal forms and procedures are defined by institutions. Laws, for example, are institutionalized norms which appear under "a" government (an association) at a certain point in social development. Governance may be regarded as an institutional complex; "the" government of the United States, on the other hand, is an association—a specific group. Hence, we may identify "business," "war," "religion," "government," and "entertainment" as institutional complexes characteristic of associational societies. "A" church (United Church of Christ), "a" corporation (U. S. Steel), "an" army (the United States Army), "a" government (the United States of America), are the associational groups which sustain and support the institutional forms of *religion, business, war,* and *government* respectively.

However, the major associations of contemporary society and their supporting panoply of institutions do not emerge from social caprice or spontaneity; they have a direct relationship to the functional imperatives. Government most closely responds to the societal needs for adaptation (the external environment) and also integration (relationships between the structural units) within the society. Furthermore, the economy has significant adaptive functions in that its institutional forms directly involve the external environment and the society's relationship to it via subsistence activities and the production of food, shelter, clothing—the basic economic needs. Furthermore, the family system provides the society with an orderly arrangement for the reproduction and socialization of new persons. In addition, the family is the most immediate institutional agency for tension management and pattern maintenance, although these necessities may also pass on to government (formal controls, laws, sanctioning, etc.).

In this fashion, the massive institutional-associational complexes of great societies—government, religion, economy, family (the primary anatomy of societal structures)—can be seen as system responses to the functional imperatives at the final level of interdependence. As we noted before, all systems must solve these problems, "a" family, "a" corporation, "a" religion as specific, concrete entities. And within their internal arrangements, their substructures, we can find units addressed to these functional problems. It is, however, at the level of community and society that these needs can be seen as the initiating force behind the major social forms (family, government, economy, religion).

This is perhaps one of the most compelling ideas that the student will encounter in his first exposure to sociology. We all have an idea of "system" as somehow an interrelated "whole" with each part contributing to the survival of the total. We can appreciate this, certainly, from the biological idea that each organ or "subsystem" enables the total entity to survive. We can also appreciate the idea of system in psychology—the personality as a system, with each component and dimension of the personality (in Freud's view, id, ego, superego) all functionally related to the other. But human society, on the popular level of everyday experience and ideology, is not seen as an interdependent structure in which *system needs* create and fashion substructures. And although we may be caught up in the study of the specific institutions (government, economy, family, education, military, religion, etc.) only sociology can point out that these substructural units of society all play a role in the final structure of relationships—the massive entity of society itself. It is in analysis of this kind, at this level, that the reality of society can be seen.

Neither space, time, nor intention permits a detailed inquiry into the primary societal institutions, but many introductory texts devote at least a chapter to the family, the polity, the economy, and religion. Our purpose here has been simply to explicate the functional role that these institutions play in the structural arrangements of society. Furthermore, as we close the substantive content of this presentation, we can also suggest that the view of society and its constituent elements which we have presented has been essentially a static one. That is to say, our primary interest has been the analysis of the *logical* linkages between units of the social system from primary group to society. Our interest has been the principal and necessary concepts that will bring the student to the final assessment of society itself. However, we have not dealt inclusively with the entire subject matter of sociology; this is almost impossible today, given the growth of the discipline and the explosion of its substantive content. Hence, while presenting the predominant structural units, we have not considered what are perhaps equally vital and necessary elements in the assessment of reality, social, physical, biological, or other: the elements of process and dynamics.

There is a relationship between structures and time; over time, structures change and alter their forms. And certainly, as one looks back over the years from the beginning of this century, there have been fantastic changes in the structural characteristic of American society. Why societies, why groups are volatile in the course of time is a subject that we cannot here deal with, but the student should be well aware of the summary and quite elementary character of our introduction, and that we have touched upon only some of the basic and fundamental concerns of sociology.

Actually, the sequence of concepts that we have introduced has proceeded from the most elemental to the most complex of sociological concepts, in which the factors of time, of process, of dynamics, were not seriously considered. Each concept was in turn subsumed, as an element, into a more complex idea that led us finally to the consideration of society. It might be well to review briefly the formal sequence of concepts by considering the diagram in Figure 6.

We can assume that man, with his unique ability to think symbolically and abstractly (language), produces a culture system characterized by technology, values, and norms. Our analysis begins with man (1), the actor—the socialized dimension of the total man. And man, as actor, responds particularly to (2) norms—the ideal expectations, the rules, the guides, that shape the content of interaction and social relationships. Norms (mores, folkways, laws, etc.), however, do not exist in a fragmented and unconnected fashion. Some characteristically relate to each other and, together, form a complex of interrelated expectations, and it is this fusion and combination of normative forms that serves to give (3) the role/status unit its distinctive set of potentials and expectations. That is to say, the actor, by occupying a role and actualizing its potentials in concert with other actors occupying other roles, forms primary linkages in which the elementary (4) social relationship occurs.

Social relationships are primary linkages between pluralities of actors who orient to the definition of the social situation established by the norm, role, status complex. This definition of the situation makes it possible for the actors to possess a high degree of predictability in the situation and orient to the expectations of the others in the relational

FIGURE 6

The Primary Concepts in Order of the Inclusiveness of the Relationships

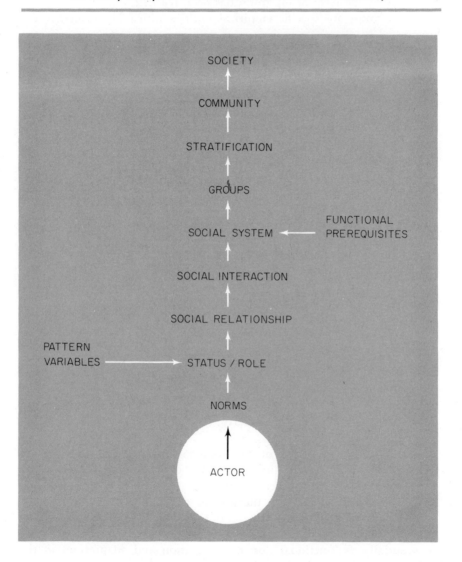

pattern. When social relationships unfold in certain recurrent generic
forms, the phenomenon of (5) social interaction occurs. Social interaction
is the term given to the basic, reciprocal, recurrent forms in which rela-

tionships occur again and again, such as cooperation, competition, and conflict. When the conceptual units of norms, roles, relationships, and interaction occur within a recurrent, concrete empirical situation and where the actors share a psychic sense of identity with each other as participants, the level of (6) group has been reached.

Groups are specific empirical entities which are primarily distinguished by the characteristic relationships and interactive forms sustained by the actors within the system. Two broad group forms have been observed by sociologists in the primary versus secondary (*Gemeinschaft-Gesellschaft*) dichotomy. Essentially, primary groups are small, durable systems whose role definitions are characterized by affect, quality, particularism, diffuseness, and collectivity-orientation. Larger, formal, associational groups (secondary—*Gesellschaft*) are characterized by roles and linkages marked by affect neutrality, performance, universalism, specificity, and self-orientation. Furthermore, groups may be seen as *social systems*—that is, the collectivity, the relational system, can be viewed as an emergent reality independent of the particular persons who comprise its membership.

As social systems, all enduring groups must solve four functional problems if they are to endure: the problem of adaptation to the external environment, the problem of the integration, cohesion, and solidarity of the sub-units within the system, the problem of goal achievement within the system, and the problem of tension management and pattern maintenance within the system. The last focuses particularly on the condition of *the actors* within the system, whereas the integrative function deals with the relationship of the sub-units to each other within the total system.

In the concept of community (7) we encounter a survival system for the first time. That is to say, community consists of a population, inhabiting a specific locality, sustained by a system of relationships which not only satisfies the functional prerequisites but also provides (through the family system) for the orderly and responsible replacement of population.

With the emergence of the urban community social stratification (8), the hierarchic distribution of status honor, economic possessions, and power, is elaborated because of the new economic surpluses and social complexity created by the greater social efficiency of the city— increased division of labor, differentiation, and interdependence. The structure of stratification systems has been viewed by some sociologists as essentially dysfunctional (loss of integration and adaptation) to the collective whole largely through the status variable and the restrictive, closure principle inherent in it. Others, however, have seen stratification as essentially the expression of a functional need of the society to institutionalize rewards (wealth, honor, power) in order to induce those relatively scarce and talented persons to occupy the critical roles characterized by heavy responsibility and training. In essence, the two views have simply emphasized the dysfunctional and functional aspects of the stratification system respectively.

Finally (9), the level of society is reached, which consists of essentially the ultimate system of functional interdependence and interrelatedness. Within the massive institutional-association forms of the societal system, the functional imperatives may be seen in the structural units of polity, family, religion, and economy. Each singly or in combination represents a substructural response to a functional imperative at the ultimate level of a group form—society itself.

The entity of society could not exist were it not for the vital part played by each of the preceding concepts. Society cannot exist without community or stratification. Groups cannot exist without social interaction, and social interaction cannot exist without elementary social relationships, and these cannot exist without role, and role, in turn, is shaped by norms. There is much more to sociology than these nine critical ideas, but if the linkages between them are clear and the pattern variables and the functional imperatives are understood then the introductory student has gone far in this brief intellectual encounter with the sociological perspective.

SUGGESTED READINGS

BALTZELL, E. DIGBY, *Philadelphia Gentleman*. New York: The Free Press, 1958.
    One of the few and excellent studies of the American upper class.

BARBER, BERNARD, *Social Stratification*. New York: Harcourt, Brace & World, Inc., 1957.
    An excellent general review of social stratification with strong historical interests. Written from the functional perspective.

BENDIX, REINHARD, and SEYMOUR M. LIPSET, *Class, Status and Power*. New York: The Free Press, 1966.
    Now in its second edition, this anthology continues to be the definitive source of the basic literature in social stratification.

BENDIX, REINHARD, and SEYMOUR M. LIPSET, *Social Mobility in Industrial Society*. Berkeley: University of California Press, 1959.
    Basically an analysis of class mobility in the industrial countries.

DJILAS, MILOVAN, *The New Class*. New York: Frederick A. Praeger, Inc., 1957.
    A former political prisoner in Yugoslavia, the author maintains that the Communist leaders have become a new ruling class within the bloc countries.

GLAZER, NATHAN, and DANIEL PATRICK MOYNIHAN, *Beyond the Melting Pot*. Cambridge: The M.I.T. Press, 1963.
    An excellent discussion of the Negroes, Puerto Ricans, Jews, Italians, and Irish in New York City. Although the principal unit of analysis is ethnicity, class themes are also involved.

HOLLINGSHEAD, AUGUST B., and FREDERICK C. REDLICH, *Social Class and Mental Illness*. New York: John Wiley & Sons, Inc., 1958.
    A major research study dealing with the linkages between social class and mental health. Set in New Haven, the study demonstrated significant differences between the strata in mental illness.

KAHL, JOSEPH A., *The American Class Structure*. New York: Holt, Rinehart & Winston, Inc., 1964.

> *A solid textbook presentation of the principal sociological concerns with social stratification in the United States.*

LENSKI, GERHARD, *Power and Privilege*. New York: McGraw-Hill Book Company, 1966.

> *Analyzes stratification as a facet of the distributive system. Strong historical and cross-cultural materials.*

MILLS, C. WRIGHT, *White Collar*. New York: Oxford University Press, 1951.

> *Quite possibly on its way to being a classic, this book deals with the historical development of the American middle class and its current social, economic, and political characteristics.*

INDEX